# The Politics
# of Accounting
# Regulation

Organizing Transnational Standard Setting in
Financial Reporting

Sebastian Botzem

*Social Science Research Center Berlin, Germany*

**Edward Elgar**
Cheltenham, UK • Northampton, MA, USA

Published by
Edward Elgar Publishing Limited
The Lypiatts
15 Lansdown Road
Cheltenham
Glos GL50 2JA
UK

Edward Elgar Publishing, Inc.
William Pratt House
9 Dewey Court
Northampton
Massachusetts 01060
USA

Paperback edition 2014

A catalogue record for this book
is available from the British Library

Library of Congress Control Number: 2011932889

ISBN 978 1 84980 177 5 (cased)
      978 1 78347 584 1 (paperback)

Typeset by Servis Filmsetting Ltd, Stockport, Cheshire

Printed and bound by CPI Group (UK) Ltd, Croydon, CR0 4YY

# Contents

| | | |
|---|---|---|
| *List of figures* | | vi |
| *List of tables* | | vii |
| *Abbreviations* | | viii |
| *Acknowledgments* | | x |
| | | |
| 1 | Introduction: the globalization of accounting | 1 |
| 2 | Research on transnational accounting standardization | 17 |
| 3 | Historical background: competing regulatory initiatives | 32 |
| 4 | Defining the content of international accounting standards | 61 |
| 5 | Organizational characteristics of the International Accounting Standards Board | 94 |
| 6 | The role of individuals and organizations in transnational standard setting | 126 |
| 7 | The politics of transnational accounting regulation | 165 |
| | | |
| *Appendix:* | *Network data* | 181 |
| *References* | | 196 |
| *Index* | | 215 |

# Figures

| | | |
|---|---|---|
| 4.1 | IASB standards production, 1973–2009 | 63 |
| 4.2 | Valuation hierarchy for fair value measurement | 71 |
| 5.1 | IASB organizational structure, 2009 | 99 |
| 5.2 | Steps in the constitutional amendment process, 2003–05 | 102 |
| 6.1 | Number of Board members for the IASC and the IASB, 1973–2009 | 128 |
| 6.2 | IASB organizational network, 2001 | 146 |
| 6.3 | IASB organizational network, 2006 | 148 |
| 6.4 | IASB organizational network, 2009 | 149 |

# Tables

| | | |
|---|---|---|
| 3.1 | Overview of the various initiatives for cross-border harmonization in accounting | 57 |
| 4.1 | Addressees and their information needs according to the conceptual framework of 1989 | 85 |
| 5.1 | Organizational structure of transnational standard setting | 105 |
| 5.2 | IASB revenue, 2000–2009 | 113 |
| 5.3 | IASB expenditure, 2000–2009 | 114 |
| 5.4 | The six stages of the consultation procedure | 118 |
| 6.1 | Board membership as of June 30, 2009 | 131 |
| 6.2 | Length of service on the Board of the IASB, 2001–09 | 137 |
| 6.3 | Appointment rules and responsibilities of the IASB bodies | 141 |
| 6.4 | Number of representatives on the three IASB bodies, 2001–09 | 143 |
| 6.5 | Organizational core of the transnational standard-setting network | 151 |
| 6.6 | Individuals represented by interest group affiliation, 2001–09 | 156 |
| 6.7 | IASB membership by interest group affiliation, per year, 2001–09 | 158 |
| 6.8 | Users of financial statements by type of organization, 2001–09 | 159 |

# Abbreviations

| | |
|---|---|
| AASB | Accounting Standards Board, Australia/New Zealand |
| AcSB | Accounting Standards Board, Canada |
| AICPA | American Institute of Certified Public Accountants |
| AISG | Accountants International Study Group |
| AMF | Autorité des Marchés Financiers, France |
| ARC | Accounting Regulatory Committee, EC |
| ARG | Analyst Representative Group |
| ASB | Accounting Standards Board, UK |
| ASCG | Accounting Standards Committe of Germany (see DRSC) |
| CEA | European Insurance Association |
| CFA | Chartered Financial Analyst Institute |
| CICA | Canadian Institute of Chartered Accountants |
| CNC | Conseil National de la Comptabilité, France |
| DCF | discounted cash flow |
| CSRC | China Securities Regulatory Commission |
| DRSC | Deutsches Rechnungslegungs Standards Committee |
| DTT | Deloitte Touche Tohmatsu |
| E+Y | Ernst and Young |
| EACB | European Association of Co-operative Banks |
| EC | European Commission |
| ECB | European Central Bank |
| ECOFIN | European Council of Economic and Finance Ministers |
| ECOSOC | Economic and Social Council |
| EFAA | European Federation of Accountants and Auditors |
| EFFAS | European Federation of Financial Analysts Societies |
| EFRAG | European Financial Reporting Advisory Group |
| ERT | European Round Table |
| ESBG | European Savings Banks Group |
| EU | European Union |
| FASB | Financial Accounting Standards Board, USA |
| FBE | European Banking Federation |
| FEE | Fédération des Experts Comptables Européens |
| FEI | Financial Executives International |
| FESE | Federation of European Securities Exchanges |

| | |
|---|---|
| FSA | Financial Services Authority, UK |
| FSB | Financial Stability Board |
| FVA | fair value accounting |
| IAFEI | International Association of Financial Executives Institutes |
| IAS | International Accounting Standards |
| IASB | International Accounting Standards Board |
| IASC | International Accounting Standards Committee |
| IASCF | International Accounting Standards Committee Foundation |
| ICAEW | Institute of Chartered Accountants in England and Wales |
| ICFTU | International Confederation of Free Trade Unions |
| IFAC | International Federation of Accountants |
| IFRIC | International Financial Reporting Standards Interpretations Committee |
| IFRS | International Financial Reporting Standards |
| IOSCO | International Organization of Securities Commissions |
| ISA | International Standards on Auditing |
| ISAR | International Standards in Accounting and Reporting |
| ISO | International Organization for Standardization |
| KPMG | KPMG (Klynveld, Peat, Marwick and Goerdeler) |
| MPIfG | Max Planck Institute for the Study of Societies |
| OECD | Organisation for Economic Co-operation and Development |
| PAAinE | Pro-active Accounting Activities in Europe |
| PwC | PricewaterhouseCoopers |
| P&L | profit and loss account |
| SAC | Standards Advisory Council |
| SEC | Securities and Exchange Commission, USA |
| SIC | Standing Interpretations Committee |
| SME | small and medium-sized enterprises |
| SWP | Strategy Working Party |
| UEAPME | European Association of Craft, Small- and Medium-sized Enterprises |
| UEC | Union Européenne des Experts Comptables, Economiques et Financiers |
| UNCTAD | UN Conference on Trade and Development |
| UNICE | Union of Industrial and Employers' Confederations of Europe |
| US GAAP | United States generally accepted accounting principles |

# Acknowledgments

Like most books, this one would not have been written without the contributions of many colleagues and friends who helped and encouraged me along the way. I would like to thank them for making this publication possible. Most of the conceptual ideas originated during my time at the doctoral program "Research on Organizational Paths" at the Free University of Berlin. I would like to explicitly thank Sigrid Quack for many comments and suggestions, as well as Jörg Sydow and Leonhard Dobusch. My colleagues at the Social Science Research Center, Berlin were always willing to listen, discuss, and provide helpful observations to improve my argument. Most of all, I would like to thank Arndt Sorge, Dieter Plehwe, Jeanette Hofmann, and Holger Straßheim. While doing field research, I particularly profited from exchanges with members of the LSE Department of Accounting, as well as encouraging and insightful discussions with Anthony Hopwood. My interview partners were very kind in answering many questions and sharing with me their reflections on, insight into, and knowledge about the IASB's development. Thomas Frank, Katja Walther, and Robert Müller provided great help in putting together much of this book. Special thanks go to Sylvia Pichorner, who meticulously went through many pages numerous times to correct spelling and check citations. In writing this book, Stephan Elkins provided invaluable help with translating many text passages and language-editing the entire manuscript. I am also indebted to the Social Science Research Center for its financial support in making this publication possible. Most importantly, I would like to thank Maren and Jakob for their support during many long days, and for reminding me of the truly valuable things in life.

# 1. Introduction: the globalization of accounting

The financial crisis of 2007–09 is frequently referred to as the most drastic and consequential episode in more than two generations. Housing prices plummeted, banks were taken over or went bankrupt, and production declined in many countries. Many people lost their jobs and sweeping austerity measures are likely to affect public spending for years to come. The financial sector was hit particularly hard. Some institutions took excessive risks and experimented with complex and opaque products they were ill-equipped to handle. The interbank market dried up, and even bank runs made front-page news. Vibrant discussions of the reasons soon emerged and brought to prominence an aspect of financial market regulation that had previously been discussed only among experts: Accounting rules now became the object of heated debate. Off-balance sheet accounting and the procyclical characteristics of fair value accounting were quickly identified as one important cause of the financial crisis. Moreover, more than just accounting rules were criticized. The G20 questioned the governance structures for standard setting in international accounting and called for immediate actions. In particular, it asked the standardization body to review its membership, to enhance transparency, and to ensure appropriate relationships with public authorities (G20, 2008, p. 6). Political reactions to the financial crisis moved accounting standards and transnational standardization bodies into a spotlight that they had successfully avoided for decades.

For most of the time, accounting regulation had been the business of practitioners and experts. Once a federation of national associations, today's International Accounting Standards Board (IASB) is a private standard-setting body with more than 100 employees and an annual budget exceeding £12 million sterling. Since 1973 it has been in charge of producing a coherent set of international standards. Over the years, the IASB has been asked by many jurisdictions to develop standards for listed companies filing financial statements. Even before the financial crisis, criticism had mounted and the IASB's private governance structure was challenged despite increasing diffusion of its standards. However, the heated debate over IASB and its standards can also be taken as a sign of the organization's relevance in regulating cross-border capitalism. It is this core position and the economic and political implications of private standardization that make the IASB a worthwhile object of study. As will become clear, there are no simple explanations for the rise and dominance of the IASB and its standards today. Instead, I present a comprehensive and historically informed approach to understanding organizational developments, rule setting procedures, and dominant actor coalitions.

IASB's uniqueness among international standard setters is widely acknowledged. Out of the 12 key standards identified by the Financial Stability Board (FSB) as ensuring a stable and well-functioning financial system, only those relating to accounting and auditing are set by private bodies (FSB, 2011). Other rules are drafted by intergovernmental organizations, such as the International Monetary Fund (IMF) or IOSCO, the International Organization of Securities Commissions. In accounting and auditing, however, professional actors dominate. Auditing standards are set by the International Federation of Accountants (IFAC), the accountancy profession's global organization. In accounting, the IASB is the center of a regulatory network orchestrating a multitude of actors.

The distinct features of international accounting standardization have increasingly become an object of academic interest. Different interpretations are placed on the emergence of the IASB and the contribution of this private standard-setting body to the harmonization of rules for financial reporting. A more detailed discussion of different approaches follows in Chapter 2, but a number of strands stand out. First and foremost, there are functionalist accounts that argue in favor of a coherent set of standards as a necessary condition for cross-border capital mobility. These perspectives are prominent among accounting studies where much of the debate centers around accounting standards as a means of facilitating (or impeding) information flows between firms and providers of capital. Frequently, the IASB and its standards are considered to be a good, under current conditions perhaps even optimal, solution to overcoming information asymmetries. The organization's capital-market orientation and its close liaison with business are praised as a lean and responsive way of practical problem-solving. Catering to the information needs of capital market actors and allowing them to engage with a private regulatory body are frequently interpreted as functionally adequate means of providing corporate information (cf. Nobes and Parker, 1985, 2004; Sunder, 2002). Political approaches have placed accounting standardization in the wider ambit of regulating global capitalism. The IASB and its success are interpreted as a function of US American financial market dominance (Simmons, 2001) or as a compromise of transatlantic bargaining processes (Posner, 2010). Complementary works on private authority have outlined how professional actors and business interests have concurred in the establishment of a private self-regulatory regime, drawing on specialized expertise and catering largely to the interests of globally active businesses (Porter, 2005; Nölke and Perry, 2007).

All of these perspectives have some merit and contribute to understanding the IASB's role in global financial market regulation. However, they only touch upon selected aspects of private global accounting regulation and often fail to give a coherent and discrete explanation of the IASB's emergence and the diffusion of its rules. What is missing so far is a broad analysis of historical developments and organizational characteristics bringing together the approaches mentioned above. This book intends to give such a comprehensive account linking different theoretical perspectives and discussing the sociological underpinnings. It presents a reconstruction of the developments in private accounting regulation at the transnational level. In particular, the book focuses on organizational characteristics to capture the complexity of this process. Furthermore, the case of international accounting regulation permits us to derive lessons about processes of transnational institution building in general. The long-term perspective applied here reveals mechanisms of institution building beyond the nation state, which is characterized by private and public actors from numerous jurisdictions struggling over rules and procedures.

The IASB and its transformation over more than three decades are at the heart of this book. It considers the actors' motives and the conditions they face in establishing and shaping rule setting beyond the nation state. In particular, I answer the following questions in this book: How can the emergence of a private regulator be characterized and explained? What are the mechanisms underlying transnational standardization in accounting? Who are the core actors, and how did they influence developments? Finally, what more general conclusions can be drawn to inform future research into financial market regulation, with particular regard to transnational institution building?

In the remainder of this chapter, I will give a brief introduction to the IASB and its normative foundations, outline the content of the book, provide some relevant background information on the societal relevance of accounting standardization, and discuss the global diffusion of standards.

## 1.1 CONTENT OF THE BOOK

Attempts at standardizing accounting rules started decades ago. In most cases, professionals and their associations played a crucial role. Today's

IASB is built on these efforts, making it a unique case of a private rule-setting organization that develops quasi-binding standards for the world's capital markets. Over recent decades, the IASB has developed a broad set of standards to foster the global harmonization of financial market information. Its standards, known as International Accounting Standards (IAS) and International Financial Reporting Standards (IFRS), are used by thousands of corporations in more than 100 countries when preparing financial reports. What is now the IASB was founded in the early 1970s and the organization has been an object of controversy ever since.[1] In addition to the organizational design, the content of standards has also been disputed even though market logic has always played a prominent role. Today, a clear-cut orientation toward market values, in particular fair value accounting, dominates. In practice, market prices are inter-preted as 'fair values,' triggering prompt adjustments in financial reports, thus introducing an element of procyclicality into corporate statements.

The IASB and its embeddedness in a wider, transnational regula-tory network are at the heart of this book. Not only has the content of rules been contested, the organizational structure and composition of its decision-making bodies have also been the object of bargaining and inter-est group politics. As a result of these interactions, the IASB is more than a transnational arena for standard setting. Over time, it has acquired the properties of an actor in its own right and has turned into a core player in regulating accounting at the transnational level. In this analysis, I will take up earlier work, which has pointed out the importance of interests in standard setting, and go one step further to not only provide a detailed characterization of the organization's current configuration but also shed light on the political character of organizational structures and standard setting procedures and elucidate the contested nature of accounting regu-lation. Demonstrating the political nature of the standard setting endeavor and its organizational representation is the main goal of the book.

Studying how actors shape rule setting beyond the nation state is central to this longitudinal analysis. A process perspective allows us to grasp the dynamics of transnational institution building and also take into account unintended consequences, paradoxical effects, and power struggles. In the final chapter, I will propose an institutionalist interpretation of the empiri-cal findings, arguing that a transnational regulatory path has emerged that is dominated by the IASB and certain actor constellations. Hence, a precise characterization of these constellations is one key aspect of the study. Some of the positions within the wider regulatory network are predefined by the IASB's constitution, which puts particular emphasis on the expertise shared by accounting practitioners. Professional competence and practical experience are key qualifications expected of the members of the organization's board who are engaged in standard setting, as well as of the foundation's trustees tasked with overseeing standardization activities.

Accounting standards are predominantly concerned with offering a framework that allows corporate information to be translated into numbers. Measurable and calculable constructs give an indication of a company's economic performance. At the firm level, the availability of comparable, reliable, and meaningful financial information is a key requisite to attract external investment. Multinational corporations use financial reports to frame performance according to numerical logics and to address the information needs of third parties. Publishing annual reports, however, is more than a legal requirement. It also permits the presenting of financial and other information to specifically address the needs of shareholders and other capital providers. In addition, the needs of other stakeholders, tax authorities, and other interested parties are addressed. Listed corporations therefore use financial reporting to paint a picture of the organization's activities, channeling specific information about past and present affairs as well as giving an indication of future objectives. Numbers play a crucial part in defining an organization's image. This makes financial statements a contested terrain and points to the political nature of standards, which are at the heart of financial reporting and auditing.

Although discussions about nonfinancial and future-oriented reporting are on the rise (cf. Chahed, 2011), most attention is still given to the numerical composition of the financial reporting framework. At the national level, the rules for drafting, presenting, and auditing annual reports were once commonly shaped in an interplay of professional actors, academics, accounting practitioners, lawmakers, and business interest groups. Financial statements used to reflect historical traditions, cultural backgrounds, socioeconomic conditions, and the balance of political power. Today, the increasing role of the IASB contributes to detaching accounting standardization from existing national traditions. While implementation and enforcement largely remain local affairs, the development of quasi-binding standards is orchestrated transnationally by the IASB. To a considerable degree, the *locus* of rule making has shifted, and standardization has become disembedded and detached from long-standing national contexts.

Much of today's interest in the IASB is rooted in this unique setup of accounting standardization. Its effective consultation procedures, the assemblage of renowned individuals and organizations, and a self-confident display of professional expertise make the organization a "successful" case of private cross-border rule-making. As will be shown in Chapter 3, a historical perspective reveals that for more than 25 years the

IASB's prospects were unclear. Developments were blocked by opposing interests and a lack of recognition by third parties impeded significant progress. For years, the absence of public authority was an impediment to effective transnational regulation. A closer look suggests that, for a considerable time, the emergence of a private rule-setting arrangement seemed unlikely. Consequently, the fact that the IASB has emerged as the dominant standard setter not only calls for empirical explanation but also provides a vantage point for theoretical considerations. Understanding how IASB became a "strategic networker, seeking to entrench its standards in the operations of other key actors" (Braithwaite and Drahos, 2000, p. 121) will contribute to getting a better picture of transnational self-regulation and explaining institution building beyond the nation state. The book explicitly links norms, organizational structures, and actor constellations to reconstruct how a coalition of actors established, reformed, and solidified a private standard-setting organization that today sets the tone in the field of accounting regulation. Conceptually, the book provides generalizable findings with regard to the mechanisms of transnational institution building.

The book is structured as follows: Chapter 1 provides an introductory overview of the globalization of accounting. It also points out the societal dimensions of accounting rules and discusses the global spread of IAS/IFRS. Chapter 2 gives an outline of central theoretical approaches to explain transnational accounting standardization and presents the research design and methodology. Chapter 3 gives a condensed account of the IASB's origins and early history, underlining that contest over the means and goals of the organization has been prevalent from the beginning. By putting the private regulatory arrangements into historical context, I indicate how the IASB managed to outcompete public endeavors to make international rules by drawing on anti-statist professionalism. Chapter 4 analyzes changes in the normative content of accounting standards, in particular the increasing capital-market orientation embodied in fair value accounting. It becomes clear that accounting standards are both a result of and a further force driving financialized global capitalism. Chapter 5 reconstructs the organizational developments of the IASB and uncovers how the privately run standard setter established procedures to consult with interested parties without handing over too much influence to outsiders. The analysis shows how democratic accountability was subordinated to the effectiveness of expertise-based standardization largely driven by—private and public—Anglo-American actors. Chapter 6 complements the organizational dimension with an analysis of the dominant individuals and the most influential organizations in the wider international standardization network. Accountants and globally active auditing firms accompanied by national regulators and selected international organizations dominate standard setting. Surprisingly, users of financial statements, by many considered to be the prime addressees of those statements, do not play a significant role. Finally, Chapter 7 sums up the empirical findings and relates them to the theoretical debates on transnational institution building, interpreting the developments as the emergence of a transnational regulatory path.

In a nutshell, the book argues that standardization is much more than a "technical" affair orchestrated by a few dedicated individuals striving to find the one best solution in international standardization. Instead, the politics of accounting regulation shows that economic globalization is constructed by many actors and succeeds when carefully linking the normative content of standards to organizational structures, consultation procedures, and stable actor coalitions. This explains how, even in times of financial crisis, the IASB displays remarkable institutional stability and continues to shape financial reporting practices worldwide.

## 1.2 THE SOCIETAL RELEVANCE OF FINANCIAL REPORTING: THE POLITICS OF ACCOUNTING REGULATION

The objective of publishing financial statements is to give an account of an entity's financial and economic activities. States, nonprofit foundations, cooperatives, and profit-making organizations all issue financial and nonfinancial information to inform shareholders, stakeholders, and other third parties. Organizations use formal annual reports to comply with legal requirements but also to conform to more general norms of accountability, reliability, and validity. For corporations, proper book keeping and transparent reporting are key elements in any strategy to disseminate information regarding their current state and future prospects. Financial statements serve to inform market actors and public authorities and assist them in making decisions, such as buying or selling shares, granting loans or purchasing products. Individuals might base their job search on the information published while tax authorities draw on accounts to levy taxes. The information function of financial statements, however, is contextualized in time and space and subject to change.

Depending on the national context and the particular legal status of a corporation, the groups to which financial reporting information is addressed will vary: In Anglo-American countries, shareholders and investors are considered the most relevant target group for the financial statements issued by listed companies. In continental Europe, annual reports

also serve tax authorities, which have traditionally used them to determine the taxes of profit and nonprofit entities. Over time, the orientation toward anonymous outsiders, namely the providers of capital, has
increased in many jurisdictions. This is symbolized by a shift in vocabulary
from "accounting" to "financial reporting." While the former stresses
the recording, classifying, and summarizing of financial transactions and
events, reporting puts more emphasis on formally presenting corporate
affairs to investors. The preparation of financial statements encompasses
both accounting for past periods and depicting reasonable expectations
for the future. As well as practitioners, many accounting scholars suggest
or at least imply that the information disclosed in financial statements is
an "objective" representation of a company's economic situation. Such a
positivist understanding dominates institutional economics, particularly
transaction cost and positive accounting theory. Interpretative accounting
theory, institutionalist research, and radical accounting theory, on the other
hand, have challenged this view. Most of the literature on accounting in the
fields of sociology and political economy is in line with the latter approaches
and rejects assumptions that economic reality can be objectifiable, or easily
transposed into numbers. Instead, drafting a financial report is a constructive act in which numerical and other data are assembled by both following
and interpreting existing accounting standards. This latter view is the basis
of this book, which shares the assumptions of post-positivist theories.

More critical approaches also allow consideration of the distributive
effects induced by accounting standards. Today, the most pertinent aspect
of financial statements is to determine a corporation's profit or loss, which
in turn serves as the basis for determining dividends and management
remuneration. Corporate results are also processed by financial market
actors and influence credit lines, ratings, and the stock market valuation of
the reporting entity. These distributive effects make accounting standards
a worthwhile target of different interest groups: Whenever national or
international standard-setting bodies

> formulate accounting rules, governmental and quasi-governmental agencies,
> companies preparing financial statements, financial analysts and investment
> advisors, auditors and tax advisors, employees' representatives, accounting
> professors, lawyers, and other affected parties all make their influence felt. They
> propose changes or defend the status quo, comment on suggestions of others,
> wield knowledge, money, and other instruments of power—all this to promote
> accounting rules that are as favourable to them as possible. (Ordelheide, 2004,
> pp. 271ff.)

Both at the national and international level, lobbying activities have been
analyzed as part of an overt conflict over the precise wording of particular

standards (Cooper and Robson, 2006, pp. 426ff.). This political dimension remains one important aspect of standardization that is more than the "technical" quest for the one best solution. This is why, in this book, I extend the view beyond the first dimension of power (cf. Lukes, 1974) and investigate the institutional rules of the game, which determine how and by whom international accounting standards are set. The analysis follows a research tradition that regards organizational and institutional practices as core features of financial accounting (cf. Hopwood and Miller, 1994; Chapman et al., 2009).

Harmonization is a central element of profit distribution because it gives preference to one paradigm. The vast differences between previously coexisting accounting approaches become clear when considering the variation in corporate results as a consequence of applying the respective standards. The most prominent example of large discrepancies between German and US accounting standards is Daimler-Benz's financial statement of 1993. Being listed on the New York Stock Exchange, the carmaker is required to produce earnings figures according to US generally accepted accounting principles (US GAAP). In 1993, those figures showed a loss of DM1.8 billion. For the same year, group accounts prepared in line with the German Commercial Code disclosed a profit of DM615 million (Glaum, 2000, p. 37). First and foremost, the discrepancies irritated analysts and investors, and practitioners frequently used them to underline the need for globally harmonized standards in financial accounting. As will be shown in Chapter 3, accounting's embeddedness in wider socioeconomic relations, expressing specific national and historical conditions, is to be reckoned with when trying to harmonize standards.

Daimler-Benz and its 1993 financial report was an exceptional case. As a rule, German corporate accounts used to be tightly coupled to the legal and tax system. In general, this favored income smoothing and setting up liability reserves. In financial market-oriented countries (or outsider systems), the presentation of favorable economic results tends to positively influence the share price. Whereas in Germany displaying high profits potentially leads to higher taxes, the US system favors claiming higher profits and dividends, and thus contributes to short-termism and outsider control (cf. Hall and Soskice, 2001). In this regard, changes in Germany are only one example of a more profound shift in socioeconomic configurations. Some ten years after the Daimler-Benz example quoted above, the transformation from the "old" accounting regime defined by the German Commercial Code to a "new" arrangement in accordance with European and international standards resulted in a substantial overall increase in profits merely by applying different standards. A study by the investment bank Sal. Oppenheim shows that the introduction of IAS/IFRS in Germany led to a substantial rise in corporate profits. The shift to international standards in 2004 and 2005 boosted net profits declared by the 30 biggest listed companies in Germany by between 10 and 15 percent. Goodwill accounting and the financial reporting of pensions have significantly contributed to the increase; the trend toward allowing discretion in recognition and measurement as well as the move toward fair value accounting were particularly important. The study also points to the procyclical nature of market-oriented valuation: "In the event of an upswing, the new accounting principles mean significantly higher earning with increasing momentum and volatility" (Sal. Oppenheim, 2007). In the financial crisis this volatility became evident.

Another incompatibility between "old" German and "new" international standards became evident in distinguishing between debt and equity. Amendments to IAS 32 *Financial Instruments* (puttable instruments) were criticized as being insufficient to cover the practical requirements of German partnerships (DRSC, 2005, p. 8). In effect, adopting the international definition of "equity" would have meant that substantially more capital would need to be attracted than under the previous arrangement, which was more favorable to insiders and owners. Consequently, a German interpretation of IAS 32 was issued to address specific circumstances related to German company law, which are particularly important for partnerships and cooperatives (DRSC, 2008, p. 62). As the latter constitute one of the core pillars of the German banking system, what may seem to be a minor detail on first glance has huge implications for the economy as a whole. This led to the diffusion of IAS/IFRS in Germany being interpreted as the introduction of formerly alien norms that have the potential to "Americanize" German corporate law through strengthening capital market logics (Lütz and Eberle, 2008). Even though apparently technical in nature, IAS/IFRS are far more than mere classifications or neutral rules for financial reporting. They spur an orientation toward financial indicators and drive the marketization of corporate relationships, including the strengthening of outsider control and short-termism (Deeg, 2001, 2010; Volmer et al., 2007). This paves the way for an increase in management pay since executive compensation is increasingly tied to corporate performance and the stock market value of the firm (Lazonick and O'Sullivan, 2000; Boyer, 2007); a trend some German actors welcomed even though—or perhaps because—it implied a rupture with previous traditions.

More fundamentally, the relevance of standardizing financial reporting extends beyond the presentation of corporate results. Accounting rules are constitutive for the current economic system as a whole:

Accounting is a societal institution. [. . .] Accounting is concerned with nothing less than the conceptualization of capital, its concrete expression in numbers, as well as budgeting and monitoring, and thus with a societal institution that is so central to our economic system that it has given it its name. Even though we speak of the "market economy," it is evident that the rules by which capital or income are determined are among the central institutions of our economic system. These rules are politico-economic because they are means by which societal groups can alter or improve their economic situation. (Ordelheide, 2004, p. 269)

Changes in accounting standards also reflect more profound developments in modern society. The audit explosion has affected all spheres of individual and organizational life (Power, 1994, 1997; Porter, 1995). Against the background of numerical abstraction as a means of "governing at a distance" (Rose and Miller, 1992), the societal impact of international accounting standards is increasingly becoming an area of investigation. The introduction of IAS/IFRS leads to significant changes in the socioeconomic "calculation regime" (Biondi and Suzuki, 2007, p. 590). In particular, the introduction of market values through fair value accounting (FVA) encourages capital providers to adjust their decisions based on values expressed in prices or models (cf. Power, 2010). Even though FVA's precise effects are not yet sufficiently understood, general trends are visible: Short-termism gains weight, the bargaining position of labor is weakened, and capital markets become core institutions for economic coordination and exchange (Perry and Nölke, 2006, p. 574). In this context, international accounting standards are a product as well as a driver of financialization (cf. Froud et al., 2000; Epstein, 2005; Krippner, 2005). Building on the above-mentioned perspective of a "politics of accounting," the dynamics and struggles of establishing a regulatory arrangement to set globally accepted standards point to a need for a new analytical dimension: The institutional setting in which IAS/IFRS are defined. This book sheds light on this particular aspect of transnational standardization by analyzing the politics of accounting regulation.

## 1.3   THE GLOBAL DIFFUSION OF INTERNATIONAL ACCOUNTING NORMS

The dissemination of harmonized standards is a foundation of the global mobility of capital and the growing importance of organized capital markets, that is, stock exchanges. This renders the relatively late diffusion of the IASB's standards in the first decade of the twenty-first century particularly noteworthy. For three decades, the IASB and its predecessor have produced rules that had only very limited impact. Despite this, many functionalist perspectives attribute the IASB's emergence and success to the usefulness of its standards. While, today, the dissemination of IAS/IFRS is impressive, far-reaching implementation of the standards does not explain how this historical development came about. Instead, explaining the IASB's genesis requires an organizational perspective. Current success is not the result of the diffusion of the standards; rather, the diffusion of the standards is the product of organizational and political decisions, which laid the foundations for their success.

Harmonized standards allow a comparison of corporate performance and are said to be used for investment decisions worldwide. A closer look at the origins of IAS diffusion patterns, however, shows that initially private actors did not play a central role in adopting the standards. Instead, formal adoption of IAS first occurred outside the developed world in countries such as Guatemala (2002), Jamaica (2002), and Tadzhikistan (2002) under pressure from international organizations (Cooper and Robson, 2006, p. 421). Some countries, such as Tanzania (2004), even introduced IAS for both listed and nonlisted companies, effectively replacing the local standards with internationally drafted rules. The breakthrough for IAS/IFRS came when the European Union issued a regulation requiring the adoption of IASB's standards from 2005 onwards. As early as 1995, the European Commission argued for the adoption of IAS to impede European multinationals from submitting to US accounting standards (EC, 1995). For a long time, private corporations were reluctant to voluntarily adopt IAS. When they did do so, corporations based in France, Germany, and Switzerland mostly issued IAS-based reports in addition to those required by national legal provisions.

Early diffusion of IAS/IFRS was characterized by bringing nonAnglo-American jurisdictions in line with capital market logic. Peripheral countries, such as developing nations or post-Soviet states, were the first to adopt IAS/IFRS to modernize their national standards, under pressure from the IMF, the World Bank, or the World Trade Organization (WTO). These organizations succeeded in calling for more transparent accounting standards after economic crises, such as the Asian financial crisis of 1997–98. Weak accounting and reporting standards, and poor auditing practices, were considered core problems, and government officials of the G7, representing industrialized countries, gave the IASB's predecessor "an official mandate from national governments and protected the Committee [the IASB's predecessor] against competition from existing and potential rivals" (Martinez-Diaz, 2005, p. 13). Furthermore, leading international financial institutions, such as the IMF and the World Bank, took advantage of the Asian crisis to incorporate IAS/IFRS into their political goals and policies. The World Bank was particularly engaged and demanded that IAS be integrated into the disclosure requirements of borrowers (cf. Neu and Ocampo, 2007). "Also, the Bank increased the number of accountants on its staff to 125 by the mid-1990s to help borrowing states produce financial reports compliant with IASC standards" (Martinez-Diaz, 2005, p. 14).

Another reason for introducing IAS is related to the extension of accountancy services, which was discussed in the General Agreement on Trade in Services (GATS) and the WTO. Already in the 1990s, European representatives of the accounting industry (Fédération des Experts Comptables Européens, FEE) proposed expanding trade in accountancy services:

> The US government subsequently submitted two proposals for an accountancy annex that included many of the ideas put forward by the FEE and the US accounting industry, including requests for (1) procedures and guidelines to promote mutual recognition of professional qualifications, (2) recognition of the role of the International Accounting Standards Committee (IASC) in developing international financial reporting standards, and (3) recognition of the International Federation of Accountants' (IFAC) role in developing international standards and guidelines. (Arnold, 2005, pp. 310ff.)

The accountancy profession has discussed the advantages and drawbacks of cross-border comparability of national accounting standards for more than 100 years. From the beginning, easing transatlantic capital flows was an important dimension in this endeavor, which US and British accountants developed into a profitable business (cf. Samuels and Piper, 1985; Daniels et al., 1989). Early on, professional associations were particularly active and used international congresses to discuss accounting issues. The 1st World Congress of Accountants took place in St. Louis in 1904 and was dominated by Anglo-American professionals, who traditionally have taken a critical stance toward the role of public authorities in setting standards in accounting and auditing (Willmott et al., 2000).

In 1973, the establishment of the IASB's predecessor, the IASC, marked the initiation of a formalized standard-setting process. Chapter 3 shows that the organization immediately commenced its standard setting activities. While the formal adoption of IAS/IFRS took almost three decades, even voluntary application by some multinational corporations from continental Europe took at least 15 years. Research indicates that nonlocal standards were seldom applied in Europe. Cuijpers and Buijink (2005, p. 494) find that in 1999 out of over 1600 European firms (excluding the UK and Ireland) less than 7 percent opted for nonlocal standards, that is US GAAP or IAS. All in all, they conclude:

We find that the rate of adoption of non-local GAAP by non-financial firms domiciled and listed in the EU in 1999 is relatively low. Apparently, voluntary adoption of IAS or US GAAP brings no net economic benefits for a large majority of firms. However, we find that adopters of non-local GAAP have some common characteristics that discriminate them from non-adopters. Firms that use non-local GAAP are more likely to be listed on a US exchange or the EASDAQ exchange, have more geographically dispersed operations, and are larger on average than firms using local GAAP. (Cuijpers and Buijink, 2005, p. 518)

The later indications underline the importance of using IAS/IFRS, particularly for big corporations aiming to achieve crossborder listing and improve their reputation with international investors. Interestingly, Cuijpers and Buijink do not find evidence of a lower cost of capital for these adopters (2005, p. 518). Instead, the use of IAS might primarily aim to generate legitimacy for internationally active corporations wanting to demonstrate their fondness for the Anglo-American rules. In France, the proportion of the largest 100 companies using nonlocal standards at no time between 1985 and 2000 exceeded 40 percent. Concluding their study, Stolowy and Ding (2003) observe that French firms were eager to address the information needs of international actors but also considered political developments. They "observed the existence of a certain degree of oppor-tunism by these groups, and a constant cost–benefit trade-off, determined not only by developments in French accounting regulations, but also by the changing power balance between the IASC and the SEC-FASB" (Stolowy and Ding, 2003, p. 196).

In sum, initial diffusion of IAS/IFRS in the early 2000s was pre-dominantly secured by public actors and was not driven by corporations actively applying the rules. Consequently, in their own documents of the late 1990s, IASB referred to a number of—mostly public—actors when discussing the introduction of IAS around the world. At the time, private corporations played only a minor role:

International Accounting Standards have done a great deal both to improve and to harmonise financial reporting around the world. They are used: (a) as a basis for national accounting requirements in many countries; (b) as an inter-national benchmark by some countries that develop their own requirements (including certain major industrialised countries, regional organisations such as the European Union, and an increasing number of emerging markets such as China and many other countries in Asia, Central Europe and the countries of the former Soviet Union); (c) by stock exchanges and regulatory authorities that allow foreign or domestic companies to present financial statements in accordance with International Accounting Standards; (d) by supra-national bodies that rely on IASC to produce accounting standards that improve the quality of financial reporting and the comparability of financial statements, instead of developing their own requirements; (e) by the World Bank Group and other development agencies that require borrowers and recipients of other forms of aid to follow high standards of financial reporting and accountability; and (f) by a growing number of individual companies. (SWP, 1998, pp. 3ff.)

A more detailed characterization of the genesis of the IASB's standards is given in the later sections of this book, specifically in Chapter 4. At this point, it is important to stress the more general trends in the IAS/IFRS success story: The diffusion of standards happened only after a coherent, capital market-oriented set of rules had been developed and—as will be shown in Chapter 5—after the IASB modeled its organizational structure after the US standard setter. The global dissemination of IAS/IFRS therefore does not explain the IASB's development to become the sole transnational standard setter in accounting. Today, however, the IASB's influence extends far beyond listed companies in industrialized countries. The standard setter is eager to expand the reach of its norms to small and medium-sized companies (SMEs) and even nonprofit organizations. Remarkably, some IASB members consider it common sense that the basic assumption of decision usefulness of IAS/IFRS is even applicable to organizations that are not publicly listed and have no intention to go public. The normative foundations embodied in IASB's standards nevertheless cater almost exclusively to the information needs of capital market actors. Fair value accounting is as much a rationale for the preparation of corporate financial statements as it is characterized by the "self-generated, even missionary nature of pressures to reform" (Power, 2010, p. 208). As such, FVA is closely related to the rise of the IASB, the dominance of professionals and experts, and to the formation of identity for those working in standardization (Power, 2010, p. 206).

Equally remarkable is how international accounting standards, despite open criticism, have weathered the storm brought about by the global financial crisis of 2008. While crises have always been an important catalyst for redrafting financial market regulations (cf. Kindleberger, 2000), recent legal reforms in the USA have primarily aimed at introducing stricter controls on the application of accounting rules and auditing requirements. The rule setting procedures, however, have remained largely untouched. Neither the Sarbanes–Oxley Act of 2002 nor the Dodd–Frank Act of 2010 put accounting standards into the limelight. The emphasis is on misuse of existing rules instead of the problematic nature of the rules as such (cf. Froud et al., 2004). The reaction to the financial crisis is covered in more detail in Chapter 4, but at this stage it can be said that, at large, the IASB's success remains unchallenged. More than 100 jurisdictions permit or require IAS/IFRS for domestically listed companies, among

them the European Community, Australia, and Brazil. About 90 coun-
tries have fully conformed to the standards; others, including Canada and
Korea, are expected to complete transition to IAS/IFRS in 2011. Mexico
and Argentina will require IAS/IFRS for all listed companies in 2012, and
Japan has introduced a roadmap for adoption for 2015 or 2016. Pending
the SEC's decision to adopt IAS/IFRS in 2011, listed companies in the
USA could be required to use the international standards starting 2015 (cf.
AICPA, 2011; IASplus, 2011a).

Despite IASB's dominance today, the relatively late diffusion of IAS/
IFRS points to an underexposed aspect of transnational standardization:
The standard setting organization emerged over many years, but the diffusion of its standards happened at a relatively late stage in the process.
What therefore needs to be explained is how a standardization arrangement developed and stabilized over a period of more than three decades
while its regulatory output has only recently found acceptance. To answer
that question, this book discusses in detail how a private rule-setting
arrangement has successfully managed its transition from a nonbind-
ing professional project to a quasi-global standard setter. To be able to
understand the development, I draw on theoretical concepts focusing on
transnational standardization in accounting studies, political economy,
and sociology, which are discussed in the next chapter.

## NOTE

1.  IASB changed its name in 2001 when the International Accounting Standards Committee
    (IASC) was restructured and renamed. The organizational changes are treated in depth
    in Chapters 3 and 4. In this introduction, the abbreviation IASB is used for ease of
    reading even when covering the period before 2000.

# 2. Research on transnational accounting standardization

The standardization of accounting, especially in the transnational sphere, has been an object of research across a variety of disciplines. In principle, the broad attention that it has received is a quite fortunate circumstance since a comprehensive approach is needed to understand the subject matter as well as the organizational and political dimensions of standard setting. Nevertheless, many of these streams of research coexist side by side and only rarely take account of related contributions in the neighboring disciplines. In this book, I will attempt to remedy this situation by drawing on different contributions from the fields of accounting, sociology, and political economy to explain transnational accounting standardization. The intention here is to offer a more comprehensive account of transnational institution building by drawing on a variety of approaches with the aim of improving our understanding through empirical and theoretical cross-fertilization.

In recent years, standardization issues have enjoyed increasing attention in social scientific research. In the transnational realm, special interest is devoted to the ordering capacity of standards. Particular attention is given to the private character of many standard setting arrangements, which are often considered to be self-regulatory in nature. The seemingly voluntary character of standards changes when they become de facto binding rules that have an impact on a wide array of third parties, which may be private but also public actors. More generally speaking, transnational accounting standards can be considered as design standards in the realm of international business (Timmermanns and Epstein, 2010). As such, they are intended to ease cross-border coordination by improving communication flows and, subsequently, by lowering transaction costs. This functional understanding is at the core of many contributions of institutional economics (Williamson, 1985; North, 1990) but offers only limited insights into the origin of standardization processes and the emergence of standard setting organizations. At the heart of many functional considerations is the assumption of increasing global "collective welfare by coordinating and constraining individual behaviour" (Abbott and Snidal, 2001, p. 345). While there is no doubt a trade-off between individual and collective wellbeing, it is precisely the acceptance of this fact that suggests the need to go beyond a simplified diffusion perspective in order to learn more about the distributive effects of transnational standards. A more elaborate understanding of the process dynamics of standardization recognizes practices and procedures of standardization as well as organizational and political conditions for transnational rule making.

In accounting, the development of specific standards began in the 1970s. However, proliferation of IAS/IFRS proved to be a slow and cumbersome process which, until the early years of this century, was only marginally successful. Much of the mainstream standardization literature fails to recognize the difficulties in disseminating standards for most of the last three decades. Instead of merely focusing on transaction cost reductions, comprehensive approaches to standardization point to the interrelatedness of different phases, such as the formation, diffusion, adoption, and reformation of standards, as analytically distinct, yet empirically related sequences (cf. Brunsson and Jacobsson, 2000). In addition, they are aware of the multiplicity of actors involved and of dispersed agency (Quack, 2007).

Therefore, instead of applying a linear perspective of accounting standardization, the approach proposed here considers the interrelation between the diffusion and formation of standards to be a recursive process (cf. Halliday and Carruthers, 2007; Quack, 2007). Organizational and procedural aspects of transnational standard setting are not only of empirical but also of conceptual relevance, as they shape the recursivity of transnational rule making. Considering the dynamics of transnational standardization, I propose a wide definition of the term *standard*, which is generally considered to be something between an unwritten social norm and a mandatory directive, characterized by defining specifications:

> They [standards] define the properties and features of tools and products. Such standards are explicit and more or less detailed specifications of individual components of social and/or technical systems, ensuring their uniformity and their mutual compatibility. (Timmermans and Epstein, 2010, p. 72)

For the purpose of this book, financial statements are considered to be social and technical systems, which are *ex post* reconstructions of a corporation's performance during a specific period compiled in financial reports. International standards can be viewed as having harmonizing effects at two levels: "[F]ollowing a rule implies doing similar things on similar occasions, thus producing uniformity *across time*. When rules apply to many actors, as standards do, these actors will tend to behave in a similar way, producing uniformity *across space*" (Brunsson and Jacobsson, 2000, p. 14, emphasis added). By definition, but perhaps contrary to a more suggestive notion prominent in institutional economics, standards are not a neutral method for coordination. They entail distributive effects because the social order they establish "requires the submission of diverse actors" (Timmermans and Epstein, 2010, p. 84).

In the case of accounting, the aim of global homogeneity inherent in today's IAS/IFRS strengthens the global diffusion of market-oriented values. Furthermore, the establishment of the IASB, as an intricate element of accounting standardization, fosters a private, self-regulatory, and expertise-based mode of rule making, which is largely detached from societal or political demands at the national level. Under such conditions, standardization is administered by a small coalition of "accounting policy bureaucrats" (Power, 2009, p. 329) biased in favor of distributive logics—or scripts—that benefit capital markets: "Standardization consists of building a society around a standard with an implied script that brings people and things together in a world already full of competing conventions and standards" (Timmermans and Epstein, 2010, p. 84).

Consequently, I understand accounting standardization to be a process of formalizing and codifying norms in such a way as to predominantly reflect the needs and preferences of capital market actors. That is not to imply that international standards are applied consistently, however, or even interpreted similarly around the world. In fact, learning and local adaptation result in standards being used in a variety of ways (Storz, 2007; for a more general account see Czarniawska and Sevón, 1996). There is considerable scope for local adaptation to accommodate the ambiguities of global harmonization—and such flexibility is in fact a prerequisite for effective diffusion. In international politics, standards often exhibit properties of "soft law," filling a regulatory void (Cutler et al., 1999; Mattli, 2003; Kerwer, 2005; Pattberg, 2005). In this regard, they are "pervasive mechanisms of international governance" (Abbott and Snidal, 2001, p. 345).

The considerable volume of literature on standards in general stands in contrast to a relatively small amount of work on standard setting organizations themselves. While some studies focus on actor constellations within standard setters or discuss the need for institutional fit between national and international levels of standardization (Büthe and Mattli, 2011), standard setting organizations often remain black boxes (David and Greenstein, 1990). Notable exceptions are found in organizational studies (cf. Schmidt and Werle, 1998; Tamm Hallström, 2004; Djelic and Sahlin-Andersson, 2006); but more often than not, a thorough analysis of the organizational environment is lacking. To overcome these deficiencies, I apply an interdisciplinary perspective drawing on work from the fields of accounting, sociology, and political economy to explain the emergence of effective, private rule making in accountancy.

## 2.1　CONCEPTUAL APPROACHES TO ACCOUNTING STANDARDIZATION

### 2.1.1　Accounting Studies

In much of the accounting literature, the reduction of transaction and agency costs is at the heart of considerations (cf. Cooper and Robson, 2006, p. 429). Transaction cost-oriented accounting theory predominantly interprets accounting standards as an instrument to reduce costs related to economic transactions, particularly reducing "information impactedness" (Williamson, 1975). In a similar vein, positive accounting theory interprets harmonized standards as instruments for reducing agency costs. In this line of thinking, standards are instruments for measuring performance and behavior with the objective of guiding the behavior of the users of corporate reports. Both approaches, however, contribute little to an understanding of the specific institutional frameworks in which standards are set.

Like much of the textbook literature on accounting standards, the approaches of institutional economics usually take the procedural and organizational aspects of standard setting as a given and focus predominantly on the authoritative rules themselves (for a comprehensive overview of research on the international harmonization of financial accounting standards, see Baker and Barbu, 2007). The discussion then revolves around individual standards and related technicalities of bookkeeping and accounting. Treatments of the IASB often focus on formal procedures and configurations (see for example Nobes and Parker, 2004; Wüstemann and Kierzek, 2007a; for a more comprehensive overview see Kirsch, 2007; Zimmermann et al., 2008). While there is ample debate about the content of individual standards and interpretations, in-depth research on the institutional framework of rule setting remains scarce.

In much research into financial reporting, international standards are considered as constituting an additional layer of rules beyond the national level that are no more than a mere extension of pre-existing national arrangements. This goes hand in hand with a comparative perspective focusing on national jurisdictions, which are interpreted as systemically distinct. While the general heuristic value of these classifications is largely undisputed—and will be discussed in more depth in Chapter 3—overemphasizing and simplifying particularities attributed to national systems has been criticized as a somewhat artificial construction of national accounting systems, suggesting relative stability and underestimating change (for a critical perspective see Hopwood, 1987).

Adequately considering the contextual and social dimensions of accounting, and understanding accounting as practice (see for example Hopwood, 1983; Burchell et al., 1985; Hopwood and Miller, 1994; Hopwood, 1996; Vollmer, 2007; Chapman et al., 2009) does not just lead to a more nuanced understanding of accounting's role in organizations and society. Such constructivist approaches also allow us to bridge the gap between accounting studies and works on transnational institution building, even though international standard setting, so far, has not been a particularly strong focus of constructivist work.

Nevertheless, the increasing relevance of IAS/IFRS has also brought more attention to the IASB's organizational configuration. The most comprehensive contribution to understanding the organization's early history has been made by accounting historians. Camfferman and Zeff (2007) have presented a rich account of the first 30 years of international standard setting, covering the period up to the IASB's organizational reform in 2001. Their extensive documentation for the first time recounts the IASB's development in detail (Camfferman and Zeff, 2007). Unfortunately, an Anglo-American bias in their view of global endeavors toward standardization leads them to miss some of the diversity characteristic of early activities in this area and underestimate the political nature of events (for a critical review see Botzem and Quack, 2009). That notwithstanding, Camfferman and Zeff (2007) present a variety of valuable details on normative discussions as well as on the genesis of organizational characteristics. In doing so they also shed light on some of the bargaining and horse-trading that has gone on in the IASB and its environment. However, the book fails to give sufficient account of how expertise is used to control access to the processes of standard setting and underestimates the role of professional auditing firms. Nevertheless, it complements and adds to the evidence provided by earlier studies that have come to a critical assessment of the influence of interest group politics in national standard setting (see for example York et al., 1993; MacArthur, 1996; Larson, 1997; McLeay et al., 2000). Despite the limitations inherent in a pluralistic understanding of power (Dahl, 1957), these works demonstrate how interest groups target and shape standard setting.

Since the 1970s, accounting studies have increasingly given weight to societal and organizational phenomena and put the role of accounting in society into the spotlight. In short, the "discipline became more reflective" (Miller, 2002, p. 1779). Societal and organizational approaches were also among the first to take an interest in international standard setting. Here, again, it was Anthony Hopwood who early on saw a need to remedy conceptual myopia by linking empirical developments with conceptual considerations:

> While accounting in action is now embedded in multi-national enterprises and multi-national audit firms, and subject to emerging forms of supranational regulation, accounting research still tends to focus on national contexts and thereby remains largely influenced by national traditions and national schools of thought. (Hopwood, 1997, p. iii)

Such approaches, even though often situated in the field of management accounting (for instance Burchell et al., 1985; Young 1994, 2006), have reflected the need to capture the overall political nature of standardization: "[F]ocussing on standard setting and the negotiations and politics associated with specific accounting rules can lead to a serious neglect of more systematic, institutional similarities in the structure, form and assumed purposes of accounting and audit rules" (Cooper and Robson, 2006, p. 426). Recently, such approaches have taken increasing interest in the IASB and recognized the organization's growing impact on accountancy issues (Hopwood, 1994; Gallhofer and Haslam, 2006, 2007; Cooper and Robson, 2006; Suddaby et al., 2007). Much of the literature takes a critical view of the implications of international standardization for socioeconomic conditions in general and accounting practices in particular (Hopwood and Miller, 1994; Willmott and Sikka, 1997; Power, 1997; Biondi and Suzuki, 2007). Moreover, while there are voices expressing discomfort with the IASB and its procedures, we still largely lack systematic analyses of the organization and those procedures (for notable exceptions see Gallhofer and Haslam, 2007, pp. 636ff.; Suddaby et al., 2007, pp. 353ff.).

Nevertheless, the emergence, codification, and interpretation of rules in a broader sense have preoccupied critical accounting scholars for many years. One of the first conceptualizations dates back to 1985, when Burchell et al. put emphasis on the particular characteristics of the social space in which decisions are made.[1] They coined the term "accounting constellation," which "is seen to be comprised of a very particular field of relations which existed between certain institutions, economic and administrative processes, bodies of knowledge, systems of norms and measurement, and classification techniques" (Burchell at al., 1985, p. 400). Originally conceptualized at the national level, the accounting constellation can be adapted to the transnational sphere. A related suggestion for capturing transnational standardization activities has been put forward by Suddaby et al. (2007), who suggest an organizational field perspective (following DiMaggio and Powell, 1983 and Hoffman, 1999). In particular, the authors point to the complexity of fields and the relevance of boundaries: "Fields are demarcated by boundaries of space, meaning, identity and power. The spatial elements of field boundaries are reflected in patterns of interaction" (Suddaby et al., 2007, p. 355). In conceptual terms, transnational institution-building is considered to be a process constituting an emergent field or an accounting constellation, which allows analysis to incorporate "unintended interdependencies between the processes and the practices in the separate arenas" (Burchell et al., 1985, p. 403). This includes interorganizational relations that consider "the complex of alliances, agreements and accords that now exists between [national and international regulatory] agencies on various accounting and auditing matters" (Cooper and Robson, 2006, p. 431).

### 2.1.2 Sociology of Professions and Organization Studies

The relevance of numbers in ordering social activities is a recurrent theme in sociology (see for example Rose and Miller, 1992; Vollmer, 2007). Research on accounting also plays a role in sociology, particularly by debating the harmonizing effects of standards in both auditing and accounting. While the general interest in accounting as a technique of rationalized governance (Drori et al., 2004) provides a point of entry, insights into standard setting procedures can most fruitfully be derived from the sociology of professions and organization studies.

The objects of interest for the sociology of professions are professional associations, individuals, and firms. Particular attention is given to the self-organizing capacity of professions in such fields as law, engineering, medicine, and accounting (cf. Abbott, 1988). The development and maintenance of a distinct system of knowledge is one of the backbones of professional influence, making the framing of expertise one of the central activities. To a large extent developments in professions are fueled by disputes over professional work (Covaleski et al., 2003). Such controversies can arise between professions—for example between law and accounting (Sugarman, 1995)—but also between different organizational types as *loci* of expertise: Greenwood et al. (2002), for instance, have shown how, in Canada, globally operating professional services firms are dominating national professional associations engaged in a rivalry for hegemony in the "arenas of social construction" (Greenwood et al., 2002, p. 74). At the national level, education and training has been one of the core activities pursued by the accounting professions in order to hold on to their central role in applying and interpreting standards for accounting and auditing (cf. Ramirez, 2001, 2010).

Self-regulation is a feature at the heart of how the professions conceive of themselves and represents one of their core strategic objectives. Especially in Anglo-American countries, the accounting professions enjoy a high degree of independence, often aggressively invoke anti-statist rhetoric, and engage in spreading self-regulatory beliefs and *laissez faire* attitudes toward regulation and oversight (cf. Macdonald, 1995; Willmott, 2000). Self-regulation is considered to have the advantage of leading to solutions based on practical experience, which—if applied by individuals with a sufficient degree of judgment—is believed to allow for a problem-oriented, "technical" development of rules. The effectiveness of self-regulation, however, comes with a considerable degree of social closure by leaving the education, training, and certification of its members to the professions. The transnationalization of standard setting has spurred these dynamics further and led to a weakening of national professions, substantially altering the determinants of social closure. Today, generating and upholding the power to interpret standards and the organizational *modi operandi* of standard setting are new elements of closure apparent in transnational standard setting.

In organization studies, the role of expertise is also considered a key aspect in analyzing the standardization of accounting. The IASB and its predecessor have attracted considerable attention as cases of self-regulation beyond the nation state. Tamm Hallström's (2004) seminal book shows how the organization and its dominant actors managed to become recognized by the relevant players in the field, in particular by cooperating with "reference organizations" (Tamm Hallström, 2004, pp. 152ff.), such as the international organization of securities regulators (IOSCO) and the European Union. Internally, IASB's work was characterized by different conceptions of how the participating individuals are to perform their role. The work of an expert is by no means self-evident: "Experts could be ascribed with several different roles" depending on the national and organizational background (Tamm Hallström, 2004, p. 94). The more recent formalization of the IASB's consultation procedures and processes of organizational reconfiguration has led to a specification of the individuals' tasks in their roles as standard setters, advisers, or trustees, covered in more detail in Chapter 5. In more general terms, organizational theory has pointed to the rise of multistakeholder organizations in which membership and participation are open to various stakeholders from different jurisdictions and with wide-ranging views (Fransen and Kolk, 2007, p. 675). With its organizational reform in 2001, the IASB changed from a multistakeholder organization to a nonprofit foundation without membership (cf. Tamm Hallström and Boström, 2010).

The particular role played by auditing firms has also been a central theme in organization studies. Their organization as partnerships is an aspect considered to provide superior incentives to professionals. Partnerships operate more secretively than public corporations and rely more on personal, trust-based relationships (Greenwood and Empson, 2003; Greenwood et al., 2007). A number of mergers and acquisitions, and

Arthur Andersen's demise in 2002, have led to a considerable concentration of the global auditing market, divided up between only four big firms. The oligopoly not only dominates the market for auditing services (Oxera, 2006) but also significantly influences international standard setting due to the considerable resources and expertise they control (Walton, 2004a, p. 121; Cooper and Robson, 2006, pp. 431ff.). In addition to the services offered, the reputation that globally active auditing firms may possess makes them boundary spanners both for their customers and for standard setting activities. With national and sectoral boundaries becoming increasingly porous and contested, spanning boundaries is a vital activity in globalized markets. "[Boundary spanners] aim at modulating, regulating, and sometimes controlling what kinds of resources, signals, information, and ideas pass in and pass out of the semipermeable membranes that are the boundaries of the organization" (Ansell and Weber, 1999, pp. 81ff.).

Sociologists have often applied institutional approaches in explaining the harmonization of international accounting and the emergence and development of international standards, and the IASB in particular. Anglo-American actors were particularly influential in positioning the IASB as the hub of a transnational network of standard setting, linking international organizations, national standard setters, professional associations, and corporations (Braithwaite and Drahos, 2000, p. 121). While the emergence of the IASB is clearly a case of building an institution beyond the nation state, the transformative effects of transnational standardization emerge out of multilevel interactions (Djelic and Quack, 2003). Much of the conflictual nature of cross-border standardization has been defused by following detailed procedures in standard setting. In fact, "contest and conflict, usually seen as an impediment to successful standardization, can become a driving force of international standardization if organized within a commonly accepted procedural framework" (Botzem and Quack, 2006, p. 268). In addition to the organizational prerequisites, effective conflict mediation depends on the existence of an accounting community both capable of exercising influence and willing to do so (cf. Power, 2009; Ramirez, 2010).

### 2.1.3 International Political Economy

Accounting standardization is attracting increasing attention in the field of international political economy because it epitomizes a particularly far-reaching private regulatory arrangement. Depending on theoretical standpoints, the case of the IASB is interpreted as an object of or a challenge to national rule-making authority. In international relations, for example, the field of accounting standardization is depicted as one in which the USA has the potential to affect global markets and foreign regulators alike (Simmons, 2001). During the late twentieth century, owing to incentives for smaller jurisdictions to emulate US rules and only insignificant negative externalities for the hegemonic power, Simmons suggests that accounting harmonization was likely to proceed in a decentralized fashion: "There is little reason to create an international institution in this case" (Simmons, 2001, p. 600). Only a few years later, however, a dozen jurisdictions introduced the IASB's rules, making them de facto mandatory for thousands of firms. The high degree of autonomy enjoyed by the IASB poses a particular challenge to statist approaches, which give particular emphasis to the influential role of national regulators, such as the US Securities and Exchange Commission (cf. Eaton, 2005; De Lange and Howieson, 2006; Posner, 2009). More nuanced approaches point to the interrelation of national and international standard setting. They analyze the role of interest groups (Mattli and Büthe, 2003, 2005) and discuss the conditions of institutional fit (Mattli, 2003; Büthe and Mattli, 2011). Despite the internationalization of rule making, these approaches still predominantly assign most power to public authorities, often at the national level, neglecting much of the self-regulatory practice in accountancy in Anglo-America and beyond.

Other traditions of international political economy attribute much greater relevance to economic pressures for harmonization. Martinez-Diaz (2005), for example, describes the impact of national deregulation and privatization during the 1980s and 1990s as a catalyst for globalized investment in general and an incentive for the cross-border listing of big corporations in particular. Both trends fostered the perceived need for a globally harmonized accounting framework. Comparative political economy approaches have pointed to overall changes in the configuration of capitalist systems, which, today, display a higher degree of capital-market orientation (cf. Lütz and Eberle, 2008; Deeg, 2010) and a subsequent orientation toward investor information. This makes accounting standards a core instrument in broadening and deepening the impact of globalized finance (Nölke, 2009). More precisely, accounting standards play a constitutive role in the "financialization" of the global economy, in particular the spread of fair value accounting (Perry and Nölke, 2006; Boyer, 2007).

Approaches focusing on private authority discuss different sources of power than statist conceptions. Porter (2005), for instance, argues that practical and professional expertise provides an independent source of technical authority and attributes a superior problem-solving capacity to expertise-based standardization—interestingly, much in line with functional approaches in accounting studies. Others are more critical and highlight the influence exercised by private companies engaged in standard setting, above all the small number of globally active auditing firms (Perry and Nölke, 2005; Botzem, 2008).

More recent work has suggested alternative explanations for the IASB's successful development in becoming the sole transnational standard setter. Leblond (2011) argues for a principal–agent framework to explain the IASB's high degree of autonomy. He attributes the organization's leeway to the existence of multiple principals—essentially in the USA and the EU—along with different interests and only limited means of controlling the agent (Leblond, 2011, p. 458). An additional explanation is given by Posner (2010), who ascribes changes in the international politics of accounting standards to a sequence of effects that took place in the transatlantic political arena. Despite taking a more nuanced view than much of the more classical international relations literature, both authors regard the influence of public authority highly while failing to adequately account for the content of international accounting standards and for normative changes over time. Instead of giving priority to large jurisdictions, as is still the case in many political economy approaches, my contribution in this book aims to bring together various strands of the literature, and explain the emergence and development of the IASB, as well as its persistence during the financial crisis.

## 2.2    TRANSNATIONAL INSTITUTION BUILDING IN ACCOUNTANCY

Existing research devoted to international accounting standardization provides an ample basis for explaining the IASB's development into the core standard-setting organization. However, the theoretical overview revealed that debates are more often than not confined to (sub)disciplinary considerations, often impeding cross-fertilization and subsequent conceptual progress. The book seeks to overcome scholarly myopia by recognizing a multiplicity of different arguments in order to explain the developments at the transnational level. A prime focus will be on identifying mechanisms of transnational institution building and tracing them back to changing actor constellations. In addition to the contributions mentioned above, I also draw on institutionalist concepts, therefore, to account for the emergence of regulatory arrangements beyond the nation state. As in other cases of transnational standardization, accounting is a field in which change is omnipresent, driven largely by private actors (cf. Djelic and Sahlin-Andersson, 2006). However, public and private regulation are not considered opposites but are thought to be related, indeed interdependent, elements of global private politics (Büthe, 2010, p. 20). For the genesis of such institutional arrangements, "processes and mechanisms that connect ideas, interests and institutions" are specifically significant (Orenstein and Schmitz, 2006, pp. 23ff.) and will be discussed here; they will also be considered with regard to issues of power and legitimacy.

Changing actor constellations and power struggles are of particular importance in transnational institution building. In my understanding, power extends beyond asymmetrical social relationships (Dahl, 1957) to also include the institutional rules of the game (Bachrach and Baratz, 1970) and ideological power (Lukes, 1974, pp. 21ff.). The latter not only includes the mechanisms for controlling conflict but also helps to account for the structural dimensions of power. Consequently, influence and domination in transnational standardization are not characterized just as *power over* someone but also as *power to do* something.

Considerations of power are always related to issues of legitimacy as another indispensable attribute of effective institution building. As a core element, legitimacy is necessary not only to achieve "day-to-day compliance, but [also] long-term stability" (Mayntz, 2010). It is itself a scarce resource that needs to be continuously constructed if actors are to be effective in transnational rule setting. Thus, legitimacy is not stable; instead it "must be repeatedly created, recreated, and conquered" (Tamm Hallström and Boström, 2010, p. 160).

As it has emerged, transnational accounting standardization comprises formal rules, rule-setting procedures, and the actors involved. These dimensions are analytically distinct but empirically linked. Institutional theory is particularly suited to account for the relations between these dimensions because it explicitly considers the density and complementarity of institutions. However, we still lack a precise understanding of what is meant by institutional complementarity. Crouch (2005, pp. 359ff.), for instance, refers to three different meanings of complementarity: 1) various components of a whole compensating for each other's deficiencies; 2) in the economic sphere, the price dependency of related goods; and 3) complementarity as similarity. For the purpose of this book, the first dimension is the most interesting as it also alludes to the "functional performance" of an institutional setting, which is another important aspect when trying to explain the emergence of a private regulator (cf. Höpner, 2005).

For the purposes of this analysis, institutional complementarity is therefore understood in terms of institutional elements standing in a complementary as well as a compensatory relation to one another. Instead of assuming rationally designed institutions in transnational standardization, we can instead expect to find that rules, procedures, and dominant actor groups complement one another, having emerged incrementally over many years and proven to be highly consequential (Djelic and Quack, 2003; Streeck and Thelen, 2005). The empirical investigation therefore also sets out to explain the fit between standards, standard setting procedures, and standard setters. Therefore, at the transnational level, the emergence of "institutional density" (Pierson, 2000) can be observed which—once established—hampers change:

> In contexts of complex social interdependence, new institutions and policies are costly to create and often generate learning effects, coordination effects, and adaptive expectations. Institutions and policies may encourage individuals and organizations to invest in specialized skills, deepen relationships with other individuals and organizations, and develop particular political and social identities. (Pierson, 2000, p. 529)

Such reinforcing dynamics are particularly well explored in path dependence research. Originating in historical economics (David, 1985) and econometrics (Arthur, 1989, 1994), mainstream path-dependence literature is concerned with lack of change and excessive stability (at the macro level, see for example Mahoney, 2000; Deeg, 2001; Pierson, 2004; Schneiberg, 2007). Organizational accounts provide a more nuanced explanation (Sydow et al., 2009), pointing to the need to identify mechanisms in order to understand and explain reinforcing dynamics. In this book, I draw on these concepts but also go beyond them. In order to illuminate how reinforcing properties help to establish order at levels beyond the nation state, the focus needs to shift more toward explaining how actors shape these dynamics. Therefore, emphasis rests on the properties of path creation and path shaping (cf. Garud and Karnøe, 2001, 2003; Crouch and Farrell, 2004) instead of on the properties of subsequent path dependence. In line with more agency-centered approaches (Djelic and Quack, 2007), reflexive behavior of actors, understood as "flexible responses to dynamic situations" (Llewellyn, 2007, p. 138), is acknowledged. Consequently, my conceptual contribution is directed at extending path research by bringing in agency. I propose an actor-centered approach to analyze how individuals and organizations shape reinforcing dynamics and bring about the transnational regulatory path of accounting standardization.

## 2.3 METHODOLOGY

To investigate the IASB's development empirically, I apply a research strategy of "causal reconstruction," which links initial conditions to observable outcomes (cf. Mayntz, 2004). To explain the organization's genesis and its establishment as the private transnational regulator, the analysis focuses on the identification of mechanisms for building institutions (cf. David, 1985; Arthur, 1989; Mahoney, 2000; Pierson, 2004; Campbell, 2005). The literature on such mechanisms has grown substantially in recent years (see for instance Braithwaite and Drahos, 2000; Mahoney, 2001; Davis and Marquis, 2005; Falleti and Lynch, 2009), yet conceptualization of them varies widely. In this study, I limit myself to an *ex post* reconstruction in which the mechanisms identified are my analytical constructions (cf. Mahoney, 2001; Mayntz, 2004). In this way, I avoid the often rather crude functionalist conceptions that tend to view such mechanisms as externally triggered, law-like, cause-and-effect relationships (see Braithwaite and Drahos, 2000, pp. 15ff. for a critical assessment).

A mechanism-based research strategy provides an alternative to correlational analysis (Mahoney, 2001) and allows me to generalize from investigations of a critical case, such as the IASB, to further work on theoretical conceptualizations (Yin, 2009, pp. 47ff.). These generalizations aim at capturing the factors that explain the emergence and persistence of institutions by applying an explicit process perspective (cf. Pierson, 2004; Posner, 2010). "In process theories, time is of the essence, in particular, the time ordering of the contributory events" (Scott, 2001, p. 93). Selected methodology gives particular attention to iterative processes linking the normative content of standards, organizational procedures, and dominant actor constellations. Covering more than four decades of accounting standardization, the empirical findings seek to enrich the debates on transnational institution building by providing a better understanding of institutional complementarity, reinforcing dynamics, and organizational adaptability to external shocks, such as the financial crisis and its aftermath.

The development of the International Accounting Standards Board, as analyzed here, covers a period of roughly 40 years from the founding of the organization in the early 1970s until today. The focus of my research is on the last 12 years, spanning from 1997 until 2009. Particular attention is devoted to the IASB's organizational reconfiguration in 2001 and the years thereafter. Both the collection and the analyses of data relied on different methods aimed at triangulating analytical techniques. Sources were primary and secondary material from the IASB and academic literature on the organization. In addition, seven high-profile individuals with experience in international standard setting were interviewed in the summer of 2007; the interviews were taped and transcribed (on file with the author). A number of leading researchers were also consulted to verify the empirical results throughout the process.

Data analysis was both quantitative and qualitative. Data on the IASB and its standards were further analyzed using descriptive statistics and network tools, as shown in Chapter 6. Content analysis of written documents and interview transcripts followed a frame analysis approach to capture contests over beliefs and over the interpretation of events and institutional configurations (cf. Gamson, 1992; Ferree et al., 2002). "On most policy issues, there are competing packages available. [. . .] One can view policy issues as, in part, a symbolic contest over which interpretation will prevail" (Gamson and Modigliani, 1989, p. 2). The four chapters following this one illustrate the struggles over issues in transnational accounting standardization. I will start with a historical account covering the period from the early 1970s to the late 1990s.

## NOTE

1. The concept of the *accounting constellation* is similar to the notion of an *accounting complex,* in which accounting becomes part of broader discourses in other bodies of knowledge (Miller, 1986).

# 3. Historical background: competing regulatory initiatives

Transnational standardization by the IASB was one of three initiatives launched to achieve a uniform set of international accounting standards. The other two major attempts at harmonizing financial accounting originated in the European Community and the United Nations. On one hand, they were competing initiatives since all three vied for a dominant position in cross-border regulation; on the other hand, they were linked to one another through the relationships among the various actors.

The following account of the international standardization of financial accounting provided in this chapter intends to demonstrate that both the European Community's initiative and the efforts of the United Nations pursued the goal of establishing a more demanding and mandatory form of regulation early on. It will also show that the IASB's success had its root in the facts that the Board sought compulsory regulations to a lesser extent than the competing initiatives, and that the decisions defining those standards were initially made by an exclusive circle of accounting practitioners from firms and professional associations. This chapter underlines the significance of the actors involved in the various endeavors and how, in some cases, they played the projects off against each other. The rise of IASB was closely tied to the difficulties of the rival initiatives, which eventually were no longer in a position to successfully compete with the IASB. The following account traces the most significant events from the 1960s to the 1990s.[1] The subsequent chapters focus on the years from 1997 to 2009.

Today, the IASB is a private, not-for-profit, standard-setting organization issuing standards (IAS/IFRS) which are primarily geared toward the information needs of actors in financial markets. However, a look back in history reveals that the close alignment with those particular information needs was contested for a long time. Only since the mid-1990s has the IASB gradually managed to gain recognition as the legitimate standard-setting institution. As European and international initiatives failed, the IASB was able to present itself as the single most relevant standard setter in accounting.

The differences between the three cross-border initiatives relate to characteristic national features of financial accounting. In every country, financial accounting is embedded in a specific set of socioeconomic arrangements that are strongly influenced by the legislation defining the requirements for reporting and taxation for companies operating within these jurisdictions. Comparative accounting research discusses national differences mainly with an eye to their significance for capital markets. Other characteristics, such as legal traditions, the make-up of professional associations, and the situation in the markets for auditing services, are often underestimated. Another problematic aspect is that much of the academic literature focuses almost exclusively on industrialized countries (by contrast, see the development of accounting in China described by Suzuki et al., 2007).

## 3.1 VARYING NATIONAL TRADITIONS IN ACCOUNTING REGULATION

Different national accounting practices and principles are the starting point for international harmonization. The objective of all such initiatives is to establish common standards across the variety of the national accounting systems. At the same time, the characteristic national features also represent a source for transnational standardization to draw on. They provide a basis for standardization in three ways.

1. National accounting traditions affect the ways in which actors operate outside of their national jurisdiction. Apart from the material resources at their disposal, these also include immaterial resources such as cultural background and the ideas they subscribe to. For instance, we can expect it to be easier for actors from Anglo-American countries to participate actively in international standard setting because of similarities between international rule setting procedures and the ones in their countries. In contrast, individuals and organizations from other national backgrounds must first learn to use procedures marked by their Anglo-American origin effectively.
2. International standardization is inconceivable without connections to national jurisdictions. Regulatory endeavors extending beyond state boundaries are linked to action at the national level. There exists a tandem structure between national and international standardization, which is of particular significance for the specification and dissemination of standards. This interpenetration of various levels is an essential condition for transnational standards to be effective (see Mattli, 2003).
3. The application of international norms also depends on the degree of discrepancy between national traditions and transnational rules and

norms. Although the various ways in which continental Europe has dealt with standards do not add up to a single, clear picture, studies indicate that where state regulation was once dominant there was an early application of IAS/IFRS (Stolowy and Ding, 2003). For companies based in continental Europe, it was of particular importance to demonstrate that they were following common, internationally accepted practices. As far as legislation for the introduction of international standards is concerned, the European Union clearly stands out. IAS/IFRS have been in force there since 2005. With some simplification, we might say that those countries whose national norms had little resemblance to IAS/IFRS were among the first to introduce them. This underscores the legitimating function international standards have: Companies use them to signal their willingness to address the information needs of capital market actors.

National requirements and practices in financial accounting reflect socioeconomic features characteristic of a country. Such distinctive features of social and economic institutions are among the issues discussed in economic sociology and comparative economics. The "varieties of capitalism" approach distinguishes between liberal and coordinated economic systems (Hall and Soskice, 2001). In liberal economies (USA and UK), market exchange based on private agreements under common law is predominant. Coordinated economies (Germany and Sweden) are characterized by relationships of economic exchange that rely more strongly on trust and institutional complementarities.

Similar distinctions can also be found in comparative research on international accounting. In that context, a dichotomy has developed between Anglo-American and continental European countries based on inductive theorizing (Nobes, 1985). The proposed classification distinguishes between commercially driven, market-oriented (Anglo-American) accounting systems, on one hand, and uniform, tax-dominated (continental European) accounting systems, on the other (Nobes, 2004a, p. 66). In the Anglo-American countries and the Netherlands, practical business considerations and a system of associations which is of British origin and shows high regard for self-regulation by experts are said to dominate. The other group is comprised of countries with accounting systems based on abstract principles from which more precise rules are derived. This category includes countries with "plan-based" accounting systems (France, Belgium, Spain), or "statute-based" accounting systems (Germany, Japan), and also countries (such as Sweden) that rely on macroeconomic systems for economic control. In this second group, the relation between company and tax law also plays an important role. This distinguishes these countries from the Anglo-American countries and the USA in particular. In the USA, federal regulatory power derives from federal responsibility for regulating and overseeing securities trading. For this reason, US-American accounting standards apply to listed companies only.

The increases he observed in the cross-border movement of capital caused Nobes to put forward a modified classification system that builds on the greater significance of available capital. He places the Anglo-American countries and the Netherlands (along with the IASB accounting standards) in the first group. In those accounting systems, the availability of investment capital is crucial ("strong equity"). In contrast, he perceives investment capital to be of lesser significance ("weak equity") in the remaining continental European countries and Japan (Nobes, 2004a, p. 69).[2] The focus on capital markets, however, is inadequate to explain the persistence of national differences. Nobes's classification obscures both sectoral differences and the influence exerted by certain groups of actors: First and foremost, the accounting practitioners, their associations and firms.

A comprehensive analysis thus requires additional criteria in order to get a better grasp on national distinctions, which also play a role in international harmonization. In the following, three additional constitutive features of accounting will be taken into account: The legal system, the organization of professional associations in the field of accounting, and the market for auditing services. They characterize some national differences that continue to persist even in the light of increasing pressure for adaptation emanating from transnational standardization. Peculiarities of the legal system, the organizational landscape of professional associations, and auditing markets will be briefly addressed in what follows.

Comparison of different legal systems shows the significance of institutional arrangements and the connections to issues concerning tax law. In countries with an Anglo-Saxon legal tradition, the concept of *common law* is predominant and affords greater scope for contractual agreements between individuals. In those countries, accounting provisions mainly derive from the stipulations of stock exchange law (Bush, 2005). For listed companies, there exists no tight linkage between accounting and tax law. By contrast, in continental European countries and Japan, which subscribe to the *civil law* approach, collectively binding, abstract norms from which individual provisions are derived are the rule.

In the German case, for instance, the requirements for financial accounting and reporting originate in commercial and tax law (authoritative principle), which long ago defined the basic principles of accounting (Glaum, 2000, p. 31). Although company accounting has always served the purpose of financial reporting, today's primary focus on the information needs of capital market actors is hard to reconcile with the authoritative principle. Changed information needs (Volmer et al., 2007) can lead to conflicts between reporting the highest possible profits (as a signal to investors), on one hand, and reporting the lowest possible profits (to minimize the tax base), on the other. This points to conflicting objectives that will be elaborated in detail in Chapter 5 in the discussion of how the most relevant addressees for financial reporting were defined.

A second distinction between national traditions arises from differences in how professional accounting associations are endowed with authority and interpret their mandate. Even though they all focus on issues related to preparing, auditing, and certifying financial statements, the associations differ in how they are organized, fulfill their own, and represent member interests. In pluralistic Anglo-American societies, the landscape of professional associations is mostly of a competitive type. Associations compete for members and political influence (Abbott, 1988; Macdonald, 1995, pp. 100ff.). In Great Britain, in particular, professional associations interpret their social role in terms of a strong emphasis on autonomy and are mindful of maintaining a distance from state influence (Sugarman, 1995; Willmott, 2000). In continental Europe, the relationship between the state and such associations is much closer. There, the state vests associations with wide-ranging authority to make decisions, which frequently leads to monopolistic dominance in a given body's field of interest representation (cf. Büthe and Mattli, 2011). This occurs especially in those continental European countries with strong corporatist traditions where state-granted regulatory authority is subject to a high degree of formalization (Streeck, 1994). A chamber system based on mandatory membership serves as an additional means of coordination.

Professional associations play a prominent role in defining the body of knowledge deemed relevant, evaluating forms of professional association, and exercising interpretative power when setting standards (see Reed, 1996). This points to the social nature of expertise, emphasized in critical accounting research (cf. Hopwood and Miller, 1994; Cooper and Robson, 2006). Such expertise does not represent a universal nor, indeed, an objective stock of knowledge to be turned to as ultimate grounds for deciding matters of fact, but rather a body of knowledge that an expert community has determined relevant (Covaleski et al., 2003; Young, 2006).

The role of professional associations in organizing social closure is well researched at the national level. By controlling education and training programs and issuing certificates, professional bodies are able to exert huge influence (Ramirez, 2001). In addition, professional ethics and general codes of conduct are other important instruments by which associations and their members maintain power (Macdonald, 2000).

However, the national professional associations are increasingly faced with challenges arising from globalization and international standardization. This is evidenced, for instance, by developments tilting the balance in favor of large accounting firms in the course of economic internationalization (Greenwood et al., 2002). Referring to the implementation of European law in Germany as an example, Evans and Honold (2007) show how national elites attempt to take advantage of European provisions to consolidate their elite status.

The structure of national markets for auditing services is a third element, although one that is losing significance in the wake of increasing market concentration and internationalization. Initially, there was a considerable discrepancy between large Anglo-American auditing firms and those in continental Europe, which were often organized as small partnerships. While the former mainly provided services that greatly relied on company reputation, the latter primarily operated at the regional level and had strong roots in personal networks (Ramirez, 2007). The auditors employed in globally operating accounting firms were actively involved in international standardization from the outset and were instrumental in pushing standards that were in tune with the practical necessities of internationally oriented corporations. Currently, only the big accounting firms or those organized as international networks appear to be in a position to provide the services needed to handle the complex accounting requirements of multinational corporations—requirements in the development of which they were strongly involved (see Morgan and Quack, 2005).

At present, national standard setters are frequently either active employees of big accounting companies or have been seconded by those employers to participate in standard setting projects. This development can be observed in continental Europe today, where once academics and centralized professional bodies had a much greater influence on financial accounting. Although practitioners were also involved in standard setting on the Continent, prior to the concentration of the market in the 1980s, those involved had either been partners or employees of small firms in which banks and the German states had played an important role for a long time (see Camfferman and Zeff, 2007; on the history of auditing in Germany, see Markus, 1996; von Eitzen, 1996).

In the past 20 years, a strong concentration in the international market for accounting services can be observed (Suddaby et al., 2007). A global oligopoly consisting of four companies (or company networks), the "Big Four", has come to dominate the market: PricewaterhouseCoopers (PwC), Deloitte Touche Tohmatsu (DTT), KPMG, and Ernst and Young (E+Y). They are the product of a series of national and international mergers, which have occurred at an increasing pace since the late 1970s.

Although the companies each have more than 100,000 employees world-wide, they are mainly rooted in the USA and Great Britain. KPMG is the only company among the Big Four whose corporate culture has significant roots in (continental) Europe, in the Netherlands and Germany specifically.

The Big Four almost completely dominate the audit market for big listed corporations. Only one out of the 100 largest companies in the UK is not among their clients. The figures are similar for other industrialized countries. The Big Four audit 99 percent of the large companies in Italy, 97 percent in the USA, and 96 percent in Canada. They are also dominant in Russia with a market share of 90 percent, in Japan with 84 percent, and in Germany with 83 percent. In France, they provide their services to 61 percent of the largest listed companies.[3] In some sectors, due to specialization, there is not even a choice between four service providers. According to a study commissioned by the British Financial Services Authority (FSA), this oligopoly represents a threat to any independent financial oversight and leads to inflated auditing fees (Oxera, 2006).

Effective sanctions can hardly be imposed any longer without running the risk of fueling further concentration of the audit market. The demise of another big audit firm like Arthur Andersen is hardly conceivable. Each of the Big Four is too big to fail.[4] For this reason, there has been a recurrent suggestion of applying antitrust laws to break up the oligopoly (see Cooper and Robson, 2006, p. 425). The market dominance of the big auditing firms is not problematic just from an economic point of view. It also affects transnational standardization, since the Big Four command vast resources and expertise that can be brought to bear in international standard setting (Walton, 2004a, p. 121; Cooper and Robson, 2006, pp. 431ff.). A comparison of the three standardization initiatives shows that the Big Four are among the most prominent actors involved in international harmonization. Their influence played a crucial role in establishing the IASB.

## 3.2 HARMONIZATION INITIATIVES ACROSS BORDERS

The IASB's role has been dominant only since the mid-1990s. For a long time, there were questions as to what would be codified in the IAS/IFRS while the organization's structure was also a subject of dispute. In fact, we may speak of a nonlinear process of organizational development. Instead of smoothly progressing from one stage to the next, as the IASB protagonists would have us believe (Thorell and Whittington, 1994), there is ample evidence suggesting that organizational development involved considerable conflict and struggle over the content of codification, the structure of the organization, and the actors involved (see Botzem and Quack, 2006; Cooper and Robson, 2006; Gallhofer and Haslam, 2007). The rivalry between the initiatives for cross-border standardization supports this interpretation. In the following, the development of the single European market, of the UN initiatives, and of the IASB will be described, compared, and assessed.

### 3.2.1 The European Community's Single European Market Project

In the mid-1960s, initial attempts were made to draw up accounting rules within the framework of the European Community. In creating a single market, rules were devised that were supposed to take into consideration economic freedom both at the company and the individual level: "In general, the harmonization of company law should promote freedom of establishment for companies and firms providing an equivalent level of protection for members (shareholders and employees) and other persons (mainly creditors) in all member states" (van Hulle, 2004, p. 350).

The embodiment of accounting issues in European company law had given the European Commission the authority to regulate accounting early on. From the outset, the harmonization of accounting was thus attuned to freedom of enterprise and mobility of capital.

Directives were the traditional means by which harmonization of accounting was to be achieved. They were subject to negotiation between the Commission, the Council of Ministers, and the EU Parliament and implemented into national law once the final decision had been adopted. Directives have a binding effect on national legislators and oblige them to implement European provisions within their jurisdictions. Drafting directives frequently involved cumbersome negotiations and decision-making processes drawn out over several years. At the same time, the directives defined options allowing for discretion and thus enabled national differences to be taken into account. They initially achieved a superficial harmonization at the formal level by requiring that accounting and the preparation of financial statements accord with European requirements. The Fourth EC Directive of 1978 and Seventh EC Directive of 1983 are the most important provisions for the regulation of accounting in company law.

The Fourth EC Directive (78/660/EEC on the annual accounts of certain types of company) defines the types of company that are required to prepare annual accounts and the format the accounts must conform to. It further requires that annual accounts must give a "true and fair view" of the company's economic situation.[5] The Seventh EC Directive (83/349/EEC on consolidated accounts of companies with share capital) codifies the legal provisions concerning the consolidated accounts of corporations.[6] The purpose of the directive was to create transparency concerning the various national traditions and accounting practices and to ensure that these did not conflict with the development of the Single Market. In the course of creating the Single Market and establishing the Single European Act of 1987, a more active strategy was adopted, geared toward abolishing barriers to the mobility of capital and companies (Hopwood, 1990, p. 61).

The initial starting point for the harmonization efforts in the 1960s was comparability of national rules. The immediate goal was to make sure that the various financial statements conform to comparable standards: "Equivalence" was the overall political objective of the EC Commission (see van Hulle, 2004, p. 350). However, the aims of increasing capital mobility and creating conditions for competition on equal terms by ensuring comparability of company information while respecting national differences proved infeasible. The divergent implementation of the directives in the individual member states led to only limited comparability of national provisions (Haller, 2002, p. 157; for an overview of the use of options by the member states, see p. 158). Some member states even perceived these efforts as going too far. In Germany, for instance, the implementation of the directive met serious resistance since small and medium-sized companies opposed the provisions requiring disclosure of financial information. Opposition also came from the UK where the directive was perceived as an obstacle to establishing local accounting standards in line with particular international developments in the Anglo-American world (van Hulle, 2004, p. 352).

Noteworthy is the embodiment in law of the requirement that annual company accounts must give a true and fair view of the assets, liabilities, financial position, and profit or loss. This provision was introduced in both directives at the request of the Danish, Dutch, and UK governments (Nobes, 1985, p. 348), which sought to establish fair value accounting in all of Europe. In addition, the aim was to orient the Fourth EC Directive along those lines instead of attuning it more to the continental European precautionary principle as initially planned. This decision opened up scope for accounting and auditing practitioners to exercise discretion and further advanced capital market orientation in continental Europe as well even though—or probably for just that reason—there was no commonly agreed perception of what exactly was meant by "true and fair view." Even in the UK, where the principle originated, there was no authoritative definition that would have allowed precise criteria for truth and fairness to be determined (Haller, 2002, p. 157).

The emerging system of European associations also played a key role in aligning the directives with the principles of fair value accounting. The European accounting associations took a critical stand against the first draft of the Fourth Directive, which was initially based on the German Stock Corporation Act of 1965 (Nobes, 1985, p. 348). Their interests were coordinated by the Groupe d'Etudes des Experts Comptables de la CEE (Groupe d'Etudes), established in 1966, which cooperated with the European Commission in the harmonization of accounting. The associations from the countries wishing to join the EC at that time (Denmark, Ireland, and the UK) were invited and the European accountants' federation became the voice of Anglo-Saxon interests: "The *Groupe* has been largely won round to many Anglo-Saxon concepts like the predominance of the 'true and fair view' and all that that entails for secret reserves, tax-based depreciation, inflation adjustments, and so on" (Nobes, 1985, p. 346, author's emphasis).

With the increasing significance of the European Community as a forum for the regulation of accounting, the landscape of European associations championing free-market interests evolved as well. In 1987, there was a merger between the Groupe d'Etudes, membership of which was confined to the national associations of the EC member states, and the Union Européenne des Experts Comptables, Economiques et Financiers (UEC), which was entrusted with representing the interests of the accounting profession at the European level (Samuels and Piper, 1985, p. 115). The merger resulted in the creation of FEE (Fédération des Experts Comptables Européens) as the sole European federation of the national accountants' associations, which has a strong capital-market orientation. FEE currently represents more than 500,000 individuals organized in 44 national associations from 32 countries and plays an active role in European organizations and bodies. Today, FEE is a major promoter of the application of IAS/IFRS in Europe.

The Seventh Directive proved to be a significant factor in the European harmonization of accounting standards since it required separate annual and consolidated accounts in all countries. This paved the way for the separation of financial reporting and tax assessment, which has always been a requirement for listed companies in Anglo-American countries.

Only consolidated accounts must be prepared in accordance with IAS. The annual accounts of listed companies can continue to be governed by national law derived from Accounting Directives. This situation was unavoidable because of the close link that exists between accounting and taxation in many member states. To the extent that there is such a link, it would be difficult for a company to prepare its annual accounts in accordance with IAS, because doing so would significantly affect the taxation required to pay. (van Hulle, 2004, p. 364)

European harmonization via directives proved a cumbersome road due to the inability to achieve sufficient common ground to overcome conflicting interests. Most notably, massive resistance came from the UK. British associations had regarded European harmonization with great skepticism prior to the UK's accession to the EC in 1973. Reservations traditionally had been directed against statist intervention of the continental European type: "British accountancy bodies were worried by the potential consequences of what they saw as the imposition of continental European statutory and state control on the much more discretionary relationship between corporate management and auditor in the UK" (Hopwood, 1994, p. 243). Moreover, in the UK, the European directives were perceived as an obstacle to the development of international accounting standards. Instead, the UK favored collaborating with other Anglo-American standard setters and cofounded the Group of Four aimed at developing standards under private leadership:

> Instead, the United Kingdom sought to keep as much freedom as possible to continue the harmonization process internationally through the cooperation with "leading" standard-setters within the so-called Group of 4 (comprising the United Kingdom, Canada, the United States, and Australia/New Zealand), and with organizations such as the International Accounting Standards Committee (IASC). (van Hulle, 2004, pp. 352ff.)

From the late 1980s on, it became clear that the European harmonization strategy was inadequate and that the European nation states were reluctant to implement the directives into law. At the same time, the growing importance of international capital markets heightened the pressure to provide relevant financial information for preparing accounts (Hopwood, 1990, p. 59). The European Commission responded to this by establishing an informal advisory body in 1990: The Accounting Advisory Forum. It was comprised of representatives of the national standard-setting agencies, the users of financial statements (analysts and investors), and the companies preparing accounts (van Hulle, 2004, p. 354). The forum provided a platform for deliberation but lacked the authority to make binding decisions. Although a series of discussion papers contributed to resolving some of the open questions concerning the directive, the forum activities were not adequate to make substantial progress toward a common European regulatory framework. The forum remained an advisory body and did not become the nucleus for a genuine European standard setter that would have enabled independent concerted action at the European level (see Camfferman and Zeff, 2007, p. 423). In 1995, the European Commission opted for a change in strategy and supported the IASB instead of continuing to pursue an independent harmonization process of its own (European Commission, 1995; also Flower, 1997).

The decision was preceded by a number of listings of large European firms in the USA. In 1993, Daimler-Benz AG was the first German company to have shares listed on a US stock exchange. Other companies also seized the opportunity to gain access to the US capital market by preparing financial statements in accordance with US standards in addition to accounts following domestic requirements. The increasingly widespread application of the United States General Accepted Accounting Principles (US GAAP) alarmed the European Commission since the Commission had no say in the development, interpretation, or application of US GAAP. The decision to support the IASB was motivated by the opportunity IAS offered to establish a set of standards alternative to US GAAP outside of the USA (see European Commission, 1995). The decision in favor of the IASB strengthened private, transnational standard setting at a time when its position was still far from consolidated. With this decision, the Commission at the same time opted against creating a European standard-setting body, which would, however, have entailed sizable costs and have required voluntary cooperation by private actors (Hopwood, 1990, p. 73), thus rendering it a less promising endeavor.

During the British EU presidency in 1998, steps were taken to prepare for the final recognition of IAS/IFRS in Europe. The booming stock market triggered by the New Economy and the financial crisis in Asia in 1997/1998 were taken as an opportunity to argue for greater transparency in company accounting via IAS (Martinez-Diaz, 2005). In their pursuit of a single European financial market, the heads of state and government reached a decision at the Lisbon Summit in 2000 on the mandatory introduction of IAS for the consolidated annual accounts of all listed companies in Europe. With the adoption of EU Regulation (EC) No. 1606/2002, IASB standards became directly applicable law in the member states after being adopted by the EU. The regulation has been in force since January 2005 and explicitly allows member states to adopt provisions regulating corporate accounting that extend the requirements to bodies other than listed companies.

The 2002 regulation marks the farewell to any independent European attempt to harmonize accounting. However, the European Commission (EC) did make adoption of the international standards conditional upon their compliance with existing directives and reserved the right to subject each standard to a formal process of approval before it is put into force throughout Europe (see Wüstemann and Kierzek, 2007a). For consultation purposes, the EC has appointed various advisory committees on which private and state actors are represented (for the comitology procedure as regards accounting, see van Hulle, 2004, p. 366). The European Financial Reporting Advisory Group (EFRAG) provides the setting for deliberation with representatives of industry, investors, and accountants. Cooperation with the member states is organized in the Contact Committee, which was instituted by the Fourth EC Directive (Hopwood, 1990, p. 84). In reality, association and company representatives strongly dominate the decision-making process for the approval of individual IAS/IFRS; yet, with this construct, the EU has nevertheless reserved the formal right of making the final decision. Nonetheless, the EU's ultimate decision-making authority in these matters must not obscure the fact that European interests do not play a prominent role in the development of IAS/IFRS (for a critical assessment, see Chiapello and Medjad, 2007). The dominance of representatives from associations, accounting firms, and business typically results in the straightforward adoption of both IAS/IFRS and IASB decisions regarding the interpretation of standards, which then apply without further modification. The fragility of this division of labor, however, becomes apparent in instances of open political conflict between the EU and the IASB. European exceptions from IAS 39 (financial instruments) are a case in point, which will be addressed in more detail in Chapter 4.

Summing up, we may say that the harmonization of accounting in the course of creating a single European market was the first concrete step toward establishing legally binding rules across Europe. Initially, the directives proved to be a viable instrument to ensure comparability. As the European Community grew larger, state-coordinated standardization reached its limits since the wide range of interests made it increasingly difficult and time-consuming to find common ground. Apart from the representatives of large European companies, accountants from the UK were the most pronounced supporters of privatizing the standardization of accounting and preferably cooperated with Anglo-Saxon associations and standard setting authorities. They established close cooperation with Canadian, US, Australian, and New Zealand organizations (the Group of Four), which to some degree have a common historical background and share a similar legal philosophy and appreciation for professional self-regulation. The increasingly widespread application of US standards among European companies caused the European Commission to speed up its decision to abandon the pursuit of an independent, statist, harmonization process. From 1995 on, the Commission switched to supporting the IASB instead.

The section which follows describes a similar development with regard to the harmonization initiative launched by the United Nations, which initially started out with demands for mandatory disclosure requirements for multinational corporations while today the UN is mainly involved in the worldwide implementation of IASB standards.

### 3.2.2 Regulating Multinational Corporations under the UN Regime

In the 1970s, the United Nations became a place of increasing debate about economic cooperation and development issues. In particular, developing countries (forming The Group of 77) sought to improve their negotiating position *vis-à-vis* the industrialized countries and called for a more wide-ranging disclosure of the activities of multinational corporations operating within their jurisdictions. These issues were primarily debated in the Economic and Social Council (ECOSOC) and the UN Conference on Trade and Development (UNCTAD). At two international conferences, the UNCTAD conference in 1972 and the UN General Assembly in 1974, developing countries raised demands for a "new international economic order" that was to restructure economic relations between the industrialized and the developing world.

The exploitation of raw materials was one of the most pressing issues. This sparked an international debate about the need for controlling the activities of foreign multinational corporations in developing countries. ECOSOC had been discussing this since 1972 and set up an expert committee to consider both general and taxation disclosure requirements for multinational corporations. The committee's composition was based on quotas reflecting the representation of the member states in ECOSOC. However, the experts were directly appointed by the UN General Secretary so that the appointees were not delegates of their national governments (for details on the members of the expert Group of Eminent Persons, see Rahman, 1998, pp. 595ff.). The consultations resulted in an agreement calling for stricter disclosure requirements. The final report spoke of serious shortcomings in the disclosure of both financial and nonfinancial information (Rahman, 1998, p. 599). Thereafter, obstruction of efforts aimed at international regulation began, mainly at the instigation of the industrialized countries.

As Rahman (1998) describes, the majority of the delegations from the industrialized world advocated the interests of multinational corporations; as a result of their partisanship, the critical positions that ECOSOC had adopted were successively weakened and neutralized. They managed to secure influence over the composition of future expert committees, thus ensuring that instead of formulating concrete accounting requirements the targets for corporate financial reporting would remain vague. Most notably, however, the delegations representing the industrialized countries enforced a ruling that decisions be made unanimously, thus giving them the power to veto unwelcome decisions (see Rahman, 1998). This allowed calls for extensive nonfinancial disclosure to be warded off and voices critical of market liberalism in the United Nations to be sidelined (Samuels and Piper, 1985, p. 86). From then on, demands related in particular to the information needs of analysts and investors were considered legitimate: "Appropriate disclosures be made to meet the needs of users who have a *'legitimate' interests in the affairs of the entity*" (Rahman, 1998, p. 609, author's emphasis).

The influence of multinational corporations and their representatives, especially the International Chamber of Commerce in Paris and the International Organization of Employers, was the main factor in preventing stricter rules requiring comprehensive disclosure of company information (Rahman, 1998, p. 605). This strategy involved the search for alternative bodies of regulation before which the interests of companies, accounting firms, and industry representatives could expect greater consideration (for details about so-called "forum shifting", see Braithwaite and Drahos, 2000, pp. 564ff.). In the process, the IASB and the Organisation for Economic Co-operation and Development (OECD) were positioned against the UN:

> The IASC (International Accounting Standards Committee) was established in June 1973 as a caucus of professional accounting bodies and it started challenging the UN's authority with the rapid production of international accounting standards [. . .]. The United Nations' position was further undermined by the OECD, which reflected the official political position of the industrially developed OECD nations participating in the UN debates. (Rahman, 1998, p. 605)

At the same time, the OECD cooperated with the UN. Since the 1950s, they had collaborated in developing criteria for national statistical surveys (Samuels and Piper, 1985, p. 56), mainly for the purpose of standardizing economic data for tax assessment. In the postwar era, this cooperation for the most part had been predicated on ideas of macroeconomic planning and control (Suzuki, 2003; Cooper and Robson, 2006, p. 431).

The massive influence the interest groups representing multinational corporations exerted over UNCTAD prevented the UN from adopting mandatory rules for the disclosure of company information. An alliance of government delegations from industrialized countries and representatives of international business organizations brought the negotiations to a deadlock and, above all, prevented provisions requiring nonfinancial disclosure. Today, the Economic and Social Council no longer constitutes a relevant arena for the harmonization of accounting standards. Instead, the UN is chiefly preoccupied with disseminating and implementing IAS/IFRS and, in so doing, contributes to assimilating the national accounting systems of developing countries to IASB standards. Coordination takes place within the framework of the International Standards on Accounting and Reporting (ISAR) working group, founded by UNCTAD in 1982:

> ISAR assists developing countries and economies in transition to implement best practices in accounting and corporate transparency in order to facilitate investment flows and economic development. ISAR achieves this through an integrated process of research, intergovernmental consensus building, information dissemination and technical cooperation. (UNCTAD, 1982)

Today, ISAR supports the introduction of IAS/IFRS and promotes the dissemination of market-oriented accounting standards in developing countries. ISAR's shift in strategy occurred in 1988 when it accepted the IASC's conceptual framework (then still in draft form) as a guideline. The proposition was introduced by a Nigerian representative who was a member of both bodies and, with this proposal, paved the way for the UNCTAD working group's decision to recognize the IASC (Cairns, 2001, pp. 17ff.). UNCTAD is supported by other international organizations, such as the World Bank, which has made the availability of loans conditional upon countries adopting IAS/IFRS (see Hegarty et al., 2005).

Regulatory efforts within the framework of the UN have undergone a fundamental change since the late 1980s. While stricter regulation was initially at the center of attention, today UNCTAD directs its efforts to supporting developing countries in establishing institutional and technical capacities and pushing for the introduction of IAS/IFRS (UNCTAD, 2006, p. 6). For this, the assistance of national professional associations plays an important role:

> Successful implementation of IFRS needs extensive and ongoing support from professional accountancy associations. Therefore, an IFRS implementation programme needs to adequately assess the state of readiness of relevant professional accountancy organizations so that the necessary resources are available to ensure competent and continuous support from such organizations. (UNCTAD, 2006, p. 15)

In conclusion, we may state that attempts within the framework of the United Nations aimed at establishing mandatory rules for the comprehensive disclosure of financial and nonfinancial information were limited to a short period beginning in the mid-1970s. The industrialized countries quickly succeeded in channeling developing countries' strong criticism of the dominant international economic order. Upon the industrialized countries' interventions, far-reaching calls for nonfinancial disclosure were no longer a subject for negotiation. The representatives of multinational corporations played a crucial role in this respect by watering down

UN decisions and bringing alternative forums into play, the IASB in particular.

However, there was also a change in the mission of the UN, now limiting UNCTAD to pursuing the introduction of IAS/IFRS in developing countries. The representatives of multinational corporations and the accounting profession were successful in assigning the task of defining disclosure requirements for companies to the IASB and thus to a private initiative that had been dominated by the interests of the industrialized world from the very beginning. At the same time, the IASB sought to include representatives of developing countries. As early as 1978, representatives of national professional associations from South Africa and Nigeria were appointed to the IASB decision-making body. In their main occupation, however, these representatives were on the payroll of some of the major accounting companies (Touche Ross and Peat Marwick, and Peat Marwick and Cooper Brothers respectively) and were seconded to work on the IASB (Camfferman and Zeff, 2007, p. 510).

### 3.2.3  Professional Self-regulation within the IASB Framework

A small circle of Anglo-American accountants formed the nucleus of the actors involved in the development of the International Accounting Standards (IAS). The formation of the Accountants International Study Group (AISG)—the precursor to the early IASC—goes back to the activities of Sir Henry Benson, the former chairman of the Institute of Chartered Accountants in England and Wales (ICAEW). In 1966, he invited representatives of the Canadian and US associations to join him in establishing a study group to promote exchange among practitioners of those three countries. Consultations took place in joint working and discussion groups and in conducting comparative studies (Thomas, 1970). First contacts at institutional level had long since been established at international conferences. The first World Congress of Accountants was held in 1904 during the World's Fair in St. Louis, USA. Disclosure requirements, the quality and auditing of accounts, and the possible bases for comparison of company information were already issues at the time (Samuels and Piper, 1985). British and American practitioners employed by accounting firms, some of which maintained a network of international offices, dominated the early debates (Daniels et al., 1989). Few continental Europeans participated in these exchanges. On the Continent, the nature of debates was more strongly shaped by academics, who were preoccupied with abstract and systematic accounting issues (Forrester, 1984).

The exclusive cooperation among accountants from English, Canadian, and US organizations, who were also partners of international auditing firms, provided the starting point for transnational standard setting in the accounting field. "I think the Accountants International Study Group is an acorn from which, properly handled not only a mighty oak tree grows, but a thoroughly good forest of sound timber" (Thomas, 1970, p. 63). In 1973, AISG participants established the International Accounting Standards Committee (IASC). The study group existed until 1977 and published a total of 20 studies on various topics, some of which laid the groundwork for the early IASC standards.

At the 10th World Congress of Accountants in 1972, Sir Henry Benson invited professional accountancy bodies from six other countries, Australia, Mexico, Japan, the Netherlands, France, and Germany, to join the organizations from the UK, Canada, and the USA in establishing the IASC. In 1973, the IASC commenced operations in London, and Benson, who was a senior partner of Coopers & Lybrand at the time, became its first chairman.[7] Up until 2001, the vast majority of IASC officials were seconded to work for the standard setting organization (Camfferman and Zeff, 2007, pp. 504ff.). This delegation of personnel by companies and universities ensured a continuous exchange of staff and at the same time constituted a form of sponsorship since salaries were typically paid by the seconding organizations.

In the 1970s and 1980s, the main focus of IASC activities was on the production of standards. In the first ten years, 22 standards were developed and adopted (see Chapter 4). The early IAS, however, were not precisely defined rules that could be expected to bring greater clarity to financial accounting. Instead of formulating concrete requirements, the IASC was initially preoccupied with identifying a range of accounting matters and organizing the rules and norms applied in various countries according to a coherent system. Over a period of 15 years, standards were developed by selecting national rules, compiling, and editing them, which led to little more than a set of normative principles aimed at achieving some degree of international comparability (Thorell and Whittington, 1994). Various, sometimes contradictory, accounting options existed in parallel within a single standard.

The alternative options codified in the standards were responsible for the lack of precision in terms of normative content, which was a characteristic feature of IAS well into the 1990s (Haller, 2002). After a first effort at reducing the options given in the standards in 1982 (Camfferman and Zeff, 2007, p. 264), five years later another attempt at revising the standards was taken under pressure from stock market oversight authorities to eliminate some of the alternative accounting requirements. The revision proceeded in two work packages, which went back to recommendations issued by the international representation of national securities commissions, the International Organization of Securities Commissions (IOSCO). This was to bring IAS in line with capital market requirements and to promote their global dissemination. Ten standards were selected and revised in joint projects with the IOSCO (first was the Comparability Project, 1987–90 and later the Improvements Project 1990–93).

> The main changes, of course, were the elimination of options, or the designation of some options as allowed alternative treatments, in line with the positions in the Statement of Intent, as modified by the board's decisions of October 1992. Another significant change, called for by IOSCO, was an expansion of the disclosure requirements included in the standards. (Camfferman and Zeff, 2007, p. 285)

The stepwise specification of requirements was part of the rivalry between the IASC and the European and UN-sponsored initiatives. The initially voluntary nature of IAS gave the IASC an opportunity to prove its relevance in practice since companies were free to apply the standards voluntarily. In contrast, current IAS/IFRS include fewer options and are clearly geared toward the information needs of actors in global financial markets.

Next to developing standards, the IASC has continuously worked on building links with public and private organizations and, over the years, has emerged as the hub of an international standardization network in the field of accounting (Braithwaite and Drahos, 2000, p. 121). Over the years, the IASC has established a vast number of relationships with national accounting associations and standard setters, involving, for instance, national organizations from Belgium, India, New Zealand, Pakistan, and Zimbabwe, which became associated members as early as 1974. In 1981, the IASC launched a joint project with standard setters from the UK, the Netherlands, and the USA on accounting for income taxes. Since 1984, there have been formal meetings with the Securities and Exchange Commission (SEC). Cooperation with the central bank governors of a number of industrialized countries in matters concerning the financial statements of banks has been ongoing since 1976. Meetings have been held with the OECD since 1979, and since 1989 the IASC has been cooperating with the FEE.

In addition, the IASC has amended its statutes several times to enable cooperation with various other interest groups. In 1977, two national delegations (South Africa and Nigeria) were admitted for the first time, increasing the number of professional associations from the nine founding members to eleven. In the same year, formal oversight of IASC was assigned to the global organization of the national accountancy associations, the International Federation of Accountants (IFAC), which was under the dominant influence of North American associations (Samuels and Piper, 1985, p. 79). IFAC had been a weak organization that exercised little control over the IASC and whose oversight function had mainly been symbolic. Later, IFAC focused on the development of international auditing standards (known as International Standards on Auditing, ISA; for details see Camfferman and Zeff, 2007) that were to ensure the consistent and proper application of IAS/IFRS and thus to secure common standards in auditing.

A second amendment of the statutes in 1982 enabled the appointment of four additional delegations that were not sent by national professional accountancy associations but were to represent selected interest groups. For this purpose, the IASC Board was authorized to coopt representatives of those constituencies onto the board as members with full voting rights. The goal was to include groups other than the professional accountancy associations "to achieve the worldwide adoption, application, and enforcement of the IASC's standards, matters which the accountancy profession was largely powerless to influence" (Camfferman and Zeff, 2007, p. 88).

In the course of the 1980s and 1990s, the IASC refined its cooperation strategy. Additional bodies were installed to broaden cooperation with a selected group of organizations. In 1981, the Consultative Group was formed, which included, among others, representatives of various securities commissions, the International Chamber of Commerce, the World Bank, and of international organizations of financial analysts and financial executives. As well as investors, governments, and the general public, unions were also among the recognized interest groups involved in international standardization in the 1980s. Accordingly, the International Confederation of Free Trade Unions (ICFTU) and the Christian World Confederation of Labour were represented in the Consultative Group. However, their membership of the IASC ended with the organizational reform in 2000. In principle, they supported the efforts aimed at developing common standards since they require reliable and comparable information for their own work in representing labor interests at company level, and also in European works councils. Nonetheless, their support of the IASC was not tantamount to general approval of the specific content of regulations: "As a result, union accounting experts played a constructive role in IAS development and helped pave the way for IAS acceptance all across Europe. This, however, does not mean that all IAS rules enjoyed full approval" (Müller, 2001—translated from German).

One of the Consultative Group's tasks was to integrate important actors and to familiarize them with the IASC Board where all the important decisions were made:

The Group was viewed as a kind of *training ground* for future board delegations, and, indeed the three non-auditor delegations that eventually joined the
board (the financial analysts' delegations, the delegation from IAFEI [the
International Association of Financial Executives Institutes], and the delegation of the Federation of Swiss Industrial Holding Companies) all had
their origins in the Consultative Group. (Camfferman and Zeff, 2007, p. 87,
emphasis in original)

The integration of organizations and decision makers at the national and
international levels has been a defining feature of the course of IASC
history and a key factor in organizational development. Due to the lack
of formal rule-setting authority, third-party recognition has always been
at the heart of the matter (Tamm Hallström, 2004). As well as temporary
working groups in which practitioners from companies, associations, and
universities came together to develop specific standards, the IASC established permanent cooperation with IOSCO (a member of the Consultative
Group since 1987), the Financial Accounting Standards Board (FASB; US
standard setter; membership since 1988), and the European Commission
(membership since 1990).

Moreover, the IASC Board, as the main decision-making body, con-
tinually increased the number of its members. In the 1980s, representatives of two national professional accountancy associations were added
(Italy in 1983, Taiwan in 1984) but later had to give up their seats, when
they were replaced by representatives of other national associations. As
mentioned above, the board was further expanded by including parties
with vested interests in financial markets, such as the International
Coordinating Committee of Financial Analysts Associations (1986), the
Financial Executives Institute, IAFEI (1996), and the Federation of Swiss
Industrial Holding Companies (1995). This amounted to strengthening
the representation of such interest groups, most notably analysts, investors, and representatives of large multinational corporations. Moreover,
observers were admitted to the IASC Board (FASB 1988, European
Commission 1990, People's Republic of China 1997); those granted
observer status were not entitled to vote but were allowed to participate
in debates.

Although opening up the IASC, these expansions never posed
a challenge to Anglo-American dominance of the organization.
The involvement of capital market actors, especially, enhanced the
information orientation of the standards and reinforced the IASC's
anti-statist inclination. Moreover, a group of national standard setters
from the Anglo-American countries formed a joint working group
(Group of Four) to which the IASC was also invited (+1). From 1994
on, the Group of 4+1 issued a series of discussion papers aiming to

influence international standard setting early on. The group was composed of representatives of the respective standard setters from the USA (FASB), the UK (the Accounting Standards Board, ASB), Canada (the Accounting Standards Board, AcSB), and Australia/New Zealand (the Accounting Standards Board, AASB). The working group was not an official body of the IASC but nevertheless had great influence since it debated important issues and was involved in the preparation of decisions.

In the 1990s, the four national standard setters took a leading role in cross-border standard setting. Late in that decade, there was even a threat to establish the G4+1 as the official standard-setting body in the four countries represented in the group should the European Commission gain too much influence over the IASC (Street, 2006; Camfferman and Zeff, 2007, p. 14). This development testifies to the culminating conflict between Washington and Brussels over political influence on events involving the IASC (see Martinez-Diaz, 2005). Even though the IASC's expansion and integration strategy can be considered a success in terms of disseminating its standards, the organization reached the limits of its capacity for standard setting (Walton, 2003; Tamm Hallström, 2004). The decision making became a protracted and cumbersome process. In 1997 began a process of organizational restructuring, which will be described in detail in Chapter 5.

Summing up, we may characterize the IASC's development over its first 25 years as a process largely shaped by the cooperation of British, Canadian, and US accounting practitioners and their associations. From the outset, the dominant approach was a pragmatic one initially based on voluntary commitment and allowing for a wide range of options. Although few conclusions can be drawn about financial statements based on IAS during the early stages, they were limited to financial disclosure. On one hand, the lack of precise regulations worked to the benefit of Anglo-American accounting firms, which now offer their services worldwide. On the other hand, multinational corporations of continental European origin also exploited IAS to emphasize the international profile of their operations and to address global capital markets. The mode by which standards were developed facilitated an incremental and issue-specific approach. Instead of formulating general norms from which specific accounting requirements are then derived, as was common practice in continental Europe, IAS are more geared toward defining solutions for concrete problems. In addition, IAS are continuously revised and, since 1997, officially interpreted and specified through an IASC body set up specifically for this purpose.

The attention given to external relations is evidence of the fact that the

IASC recognized early on the significance of the subsequent adoption, application, and implementation of its standards to ensure the global dissemination of its norms. This insight was acknowledged by employing a strategy of involving a number of state and nonstate organizations. There is reason to suspect that the ambiguity and openness characteristic of the IAS facilitated the process of establishing the IASC, because standardization as compilation and editing allowed precise specification to be avoided and enabled a wide range of divergent interests to be integrated. For instance, continental European companies could apply IAS as proof of their capital market orientation without coming into conflict with national company and tax laws. The early close cooperation with private actors operating in capital markets is a feature that clearly distinguishes the IASC from initiatives at the European level or within the framework of the UN.

Actors from the Anglo-American world had the most influence on the IASC. Apart from professional associations, which were capable of defending their autonomy against state intervention in the international arena as well as locally, other main actors involved in the IASC were companies, national standard setters, and supervisory authorities. Globally operating accounting firms were employers of the majority of the IASC delegates and also provided expertise. Reflecting the increased significance of stock exchanges in the global allocation of financial capital, the stock markets and their oversight bodies played an important role in the harmonization of accounting rules.

The initiative to eliminate the options in the IAS mainly emerged from national securities commissions whose international umbrella organization (IOSCO) had long since been under the dominant influence of the US SEC (Simmons, 2001). However, the alignment of IAS with the needs of capital market actors was also supported by international organizations, such as the OECD and the World Bank. In contrast, there was little cooperation between representatives of national governments and the IASC. With the exception of European Commission representatives and members of the Chinese government, no permanent institutional contacts with governments were maintained. Once it became apparent that IAS were not being applied just as voluntary guidelines but were also being used to complement and, in some cases, even replace national regulations, attempts at directly exerting political influence upon the IASC mounted. A conflict arose between Washington and Brussels over the structure of the IASC successor organization in which the Anglo-American protagonists prevailed. Comparison of the three cross-border initiatives shows how the IASC emerged from the rivalry as the major transnational standard-setting entity.

## 3.3 COMPARING RIVAL INITIATIVES FOR HARMONIZING ACCOUNTING RULES

So far, this overview has shown the differences between the three regulatory endeavors. They varied in terms of prerequisites, regulatory ambition, and the cast of actors they relied on. From the very start, both the regulatory efforts of the European Community and the efforts in the context of the UN to define a set of uniform requirements for the disclosure of company information committed themselves to prescribing mandatory accounting requirements. The IASB took a different route by initially issuing unspecific standards for voluntary application. The competing schemes gave the various actors the opportunity to seek an appropriate setting for the pursuit of their specific regulatory interests. To close this chapter, the main features of those regulatory endeavors will be summarized.

The aim of the European endeavor was to establish the comparability of national standards in the process of creating a single European market. For this purpose, the European Commission developed directives and regulations governing conditions for the mutual recognition of the various principles of financial accounting. Initially, this further increased the diversity of accounting systems in Europe yet facilitated the spread of the "true and fair view" approach on the Continent. Especially in the early years, continental Europe played a very influential role, which, from the first, triggered resistance by British practitioners and professional accountancy associations. European harmonization, however, proved cumbersome. Statist regulation by directives and the difficulties of balancing conflicting national interests were major obstacles to mandatory European regulation. The growing mobility of capital fueled by the international liberalization of financial markets resulted in US standards becoming a threat to the European Community in the 1990s owing to the fact that European companies had begun to apply US GAAP in drafting financial statements. The EC responded to these developments by extending political support to the IASC.

Efforts within the United Nations to establish rules requiring the disclosure of company information can only be adequately understood against the backdrop of demands in the 1970s for effective control of the operations of multinational corporations in developing countries. Representatives of developing countries aimed for provisions requiring companies to provide extensive disclosure of financial and nonfinancial information. This was to hold companies liable for taxation and to (re)gain political control. Decision making and consultations within the United Nations were dominated by government representatives of the industrialized countries, who successfully protected the interests of multinational corporations in the negotiations. Corporate interests also found effective support from the ranks of association representatives in their pursuit of the establishment of the IASC as an alternative standard setter. Today, the UN's focus is on disseminating IAS/IFRS in developing countries.

Accounting practitioners and professional accountancy associations initiated the transnational endeavor and pushed for industry-led accounting standards within the IASC framework. Individuals and organizations from the Anglo-American countries were the main proponents of professional self-regulation. From the outset, they pursued a twofold strategy of developing general standards for voluntary use, on one hand, while forging a network of important alliance partners, on the other. Both tactics resulted in a strict alignment of the IAS with the information needs of capital market actors, which was a prerequisite for the IASC to evolve into the major international body for developing and setting international accounting standards. Until 2000, the Anglo-American actors had maintained the threat to allow the IASC to fail should their interests not be sufficiently considered. The developments described above are summarized in Table 3.1.

The comparison in the table underlines the differences between the three harmonization endeavors. The statist approaches pursued by the European Community and the United Nations could rely on state authority yet lacked significant support from the ranks of professional associations, multinational corporations, and the securities commissions. The attempts of Anglo-American association representatives to defend their conception of professional self-regulation in the international arena—marked by an aversion to state interference—were a major driving force for cross-border standardization to focus on financial disclosure only. Refraining from nonfinancial disclosure favored standards geared toward fair value accounting and enabled the accounting professionals to uphold their monopoly of interpreting all relevant accounting matters.

The comparison also shows that companies and auditors played the various initiatives off against one another. At the United Nations, independent experts were involved only at the beginning and were soon replaced by government delegates. In the European Community, Anglo-American association representatives took early action in defense of their interests. The influence of European associations, which was aimed at directing IAS toward a regulatory approach closely in line with capital market interests, prevented genuine harmonization of a specifically continental European type in the EU and was a factor in the European Commission's later decision to support the IASC. The representatives of the professional accountancy associations largely succeded in establishing their self-regulatory

*Table 3.1     Overview of the various initiatives for cross-border harmonization in accounting*

| | | European Community | United Nations | IASB |
|---|---|---|---|---|
| **Regulation** | Scope | Regional (Europe) | Global | Global |
| | Objective | Single Market To facilitate mobility of companies and capital | Control of multinational corporations in developing countries Today: establish-ment of minimum standards | Cross-border mobility of capital and companies Dissemination of capital markets principles |
| | Instruments | Hierarchical regulation (via EC Directives and EC Regulations) | Decisions by UN bodies (ECOSOC, UNCTAD) Issuing recommen-dations | Standards (initially voluntary) |
| **Disclosure** | Subject matter | Financial reporting and company law Companies (corporations) | Financial and nonfinancial reporting Multinational corporations | Limited to financial reporting only Listed companies |
| | Addressees | States | States | Companies (preparers and users of accounts, auditors) |
| | Rationale | Equivalence (comparability of company accounts across different countries) | Control of corporate activities in developing countries | Harmonization of information relevant to financial markets |

*Table 3.1*   (continued)

|  |  | European Community | United Nations | IASB |
|---|---|---|---|---|
| **Actors** | Proponents | European Commission European associations (FEE) | UNCTAD ECOSOC Developing countries | National professional associations, accounting firms Big corporations, stock exchanges, banks Anglo-American standard setters International organizations (IOSCO, OECD, World Bank) |
|  | Opponents | British accountancy association (ICAEW) Anglo-American standard setters (G4+1) National governments of member states | Multinational corporations International Chamber of Commerce International employers' federation | None |

approach. Their leverage was further enhanced by close ties to the major accounting firms, which had consolidated their market dominance in the 1980s and 1990s. Frequently, certain individuals were at the same time representatives of an association, partners or employees of an accounting firm, and delegates of a national standard setter. The gradual process of establishing the IASC as the major standard-setting body in preference to the other initiatives can be described in terms of forum shifting, as that term is used by Braithwaite and Drahos (2000, pp. 564ff.).

In addition, from corporations' point of view the IASC standards provided the most scope for handling company information. Especially for companies originating outside the Anglo-American countries, presenting financial statements based on international standards offered a way to convince analysts and investors that their company strives to live up to the high investor protection standards in force in the USA and codified in US GAAP. From the viewpoint of Anglo-American practitioners and their professional representations, IAS offered the most promising prospects for guaranteeing professional self-regulation. They were successful in limiting to a small group the number of actors involved in defining what was to be considered relevant expertise. In this way, they were able to consolidate the Anglo-American mode of professional self-regulation both nationally and, through the IASC, internationally.

In conclusion, I would like to stress not only that the three cross-border initiatives evolved at the same time, but that there was also some degree of immediate rivalry between the different forums involved in cross-border regulation. Company representatives, accountancy associations, and individual accounting firms were active in two respects. They prevented initiatives between states, on one hand, and supported and strengthened the IASC in response to far-reaching demands for disclosure, on the other. The IASC became the setting for meetings and negotiations in which private actors could bring their influence to bear and develop standards considered useful from the corporate perspective. As the EU and individual UN organizations turned to supporting the IASC in the 1990s, the move contributed to deciding the rivalry among the three initiatives in favor of the private organization.

In the following chapters, the development of the content of standard setting, the structures and procedures of the IASB, and the networks of persons and organizations taking part will be described and a detailed analysis provided of the interests and the attempts to exert influence by the various groups of actors involved. In a first step, we will address the content of standard setting.

## NOTES

1. In the years from 1973 to 2001, the private international standard-setting agency operated under the name International Accounting Standards Committee (IASC). Throughout this text, the acronym IASC will be used only when referring to the early developments. Since 2001, the organization has used the abbreviation IASB. In the light of organizational continuity, I nevertheless consider the early years of transnational standardization to be an integral part of IASB history.
2. Although Nobes's classification system enjoys fairly widespread use, it is not uncontroversial. D'Arcy (2001) questions the validity of his heuristics and, in the course of an empirical study, arrives at a different classification, which Nobes in turn has refuted (Nobes, 2004b). However, the fixation on the availability of investment capital leads to a

more fundamental point of criticism. By unlinking issues of accounting from the socio-economic context, Nobes falls short of the insights gained from his earlier, much more elaborate classification.

3.  The figures originate from a study by Grant Thornton of audits of the 3,300 largest listed companies worldwide with a market capitalization of over £340m (press release from June 15, 2007: See http://www.gti.org/Press-room/Press-archive/2007/G8-audit-concentration.asp (accessed June 7, 2011)). Grant Thornton is among the runner-up auditing companies that make up the so-called "second tier". Grant Thornton, however, achieves only a quarter of the turnover generated by the fourth largest competitor and has failed to catch up with the oligopoly.

4.  In 2006, a severe crisis occurred in Japan—largely unnoticed by Western media. Auditors working for the Japanese branch of PwC were accused of grave legal violations, the consequences of which could be contained only through direct intervention by PwC International (see *Financial Times*, international edition, May 16, 2006).

5.  The directive coordinates national provisions concerning the presentation and content of the annual accounts and annual reports. It defines the methods of valuation and publication requirements. The objective is to establish uniform standards of protection and minimum equivalent legal requirements for the publication of financial information by companies that are in competition with one another. In addition, the Fourth EC Directive determines that annual accounts must be audited by authorized persons. In the meantime, the directive has been supplemented and amended several times: http://europa.eu/legislation_summaries/internal_market/businesses/company_law/l26009_en.htm#amendingact (accessed June 6, 2011).

6.  The Seventh EC Directive defines the requirements for the preparation of consolidated accounts. Each company (parent company) legally authorized to control another company (subsidiary) is required to prepare a consolidated account. Consolidated accounts are to comprise the consolidated balance sheet, the consolidated profit-and-loss account, and the notes on the accounts. Consolidated accounts must give a true and fair view of the assets, liabilities, financial position, and profit or loss of the companies included in a consolidation taken as a whole. Amendments and supplements to the directive can be found at http://europa.eu/legislation_summaries/internal_market/businesses/company_law/l26010_en.htm#amendingact (accessed June 6, 2011).

7.  Only a brief outline of the historical development of the IASC can be provided here. For a comprehensive chronology, see IASplus, 2010. The summary presented here is based on Tamm Hallström, 2004; Botzem and Quack, 2006; Camfferman and Zeff, 2007; Gallhofer and Haslam, 2007; and Kirsch, 2007. Camfferman and Zeff (2007) give the most comprehensive account although their historical reconstruction adopts a strongly Anglo-American perspective (for a critical assessment, see Botzem and Quack, 2009).

# 4. Defining the content of international accounting standards

Since the mid-1970s, the IASB has pushed for the international standardization of accounting. Initially, standards development proceeded in an incremental fashion. The early International Accounting Standards (IAS) were compiled and edited from existing national standards. As a result, for a long time IAS were not a set of precise rules but rather an edited collection of diverse national regulations (see Sahlin-Andersson, 1996). The pragmatic approach gradually covered the different areas of regulation but created standards plagued by a lack of precision.

Revision of IAS began in the late 1980s by gradually reducing the variety of regulations and increasingly adjusting them to accommodate the information needs of capital market actors. This streamlining of standards was, above all, a prerequisite for the IASB to gain political recognition from state actors. The quest for recognition of IAS, renamed as International Financial Reporting Standards (IFRS) in 2001, has been a defining feature of standards development for more than 30 years. During this period, IAS/IFRS have been increasingly aligned with the fair value paradigm primarily championed by Anglo-American actors. The development of fair value accounting (FVA), in particular, evidences the priority given to the information needs of capital market actors. For most actors, above all those from continental Europe, FVA represents a paradigmatic shift: While in the past financial reporting took a number of different constituencies into consideration, today annual accounts are geared toward decision usefulness for financial market participants. FVA is a manifestation of an increased capital-market orientation, a development further fueled by IAS/IFRS.

In spite of its growing significance, the concept of fair value is by no means uncontroversial (Power, 2010). Other approaches, such as accounting based on replacement costs or historical costs, continue to play a role and sometimes express national differences: More conservative, continental European accounting systems, for instance, are characterized by large provisions, emphasis on creditor protection for the purpose of maintaining capital, and a linkage of financial statements with taxation.

International standardization is thus characterized by a rivalry between various national accounting traditions, which are closely tied to the historical peculiarities of different varieties of capitalism. In the domain of accounting, for the most part Anglo-American principles (especially the concept of decision usefulness) have come out on top in this rivalry. Today, assessing corporate performance on the basis of earnings per period and the distribution of dividends based thereon is just as uncontroversial as is tailoring standardization toward decision usefulness for market participants. The paradigm shift toward capital market orientation has cemented the dominance of financial market actors, especially of investors, shareholders, and managers in the financial sector and has bolstered the position of the major accounting firms, although replacement cost and historical cost accounting remain relevant in some areas.

This chapter traces the development of the IASB's standardization activities. The first two decades were devoted to setting and revising IAS. The period from the 1990s on was marked by efforts to align IAS/IFRS with US GAAP (Generally Accepted Accounting Principles). Apart from issues concerning the content of standards, political considerations also played an important role in advancing the capital market orientation of IAS/IFRS. The process leading to the adoption of certain standards, as can be demonstrated in the case of IAS 39, but also the debates surrounding the further development of the conceptual framework underscore the fact that transnational standard setting was largely influenced by a select group of actors.

## 4.1 THE DEVELOPMENT OF IAS

The IASB has been working on the development of international standards since 1973. While the initial approach based on compiling and editing national standards yielded quick results, it entailed the need to deal with issues of specification at a later point in time. Starting in the late 1980s, the existing standards were revised and alternative, in some cases contradictory, options were removed from the set of accounting rules. Setting new standards and revising existing ones both require the publication of exposure drafts. Official standards interpretations, containing specifications of IAS/IFRS and rules of application, have been issued since 1997.[1] The first standards draft was published in 1974, and IAS 1 was adopted the following year. The first revision of a standard occurred in 1992, and standards interpretations have been issued since 1997. The following figure shows IASB standards production over time.

If we take the number of exposure drafts issued as a measure, IASB

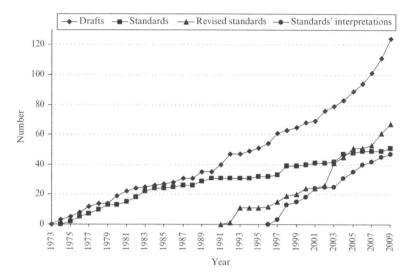

*Source:* Author's illustration based on IASplus, 2010; Camfferman and Zeff, 2007, pp. 513ff.; Kirsch, 2007, pp. 397ff.

*Figure 4.1 IASB standards production, 1973–2009 (cumulative)*

standardization activities show a steady output over the last three decades. In 1990, the adoption of new standards was suspended for a few years while existing standards were revised. By the close of 2009, more than 120 exposure drafts had been issued and debated. A total of 51 standards had been adopted (41 IAS and 10 IFRS) and more than 65 standards revised (that is, changed, amended, or superseded by other standards). The standards currently in force represent an extensive body of rules addressing all relevant areas of financial accounting.

Since 1997, the IASB has developed 47 standards interpretations to specify IAS/IFRS and ensure coherent application. The interpretations and standards together form the IASB's body of mandatory accounting rules. The International Financial Reporting Interpretations Committee (IFRIC) is responsible for devising interpretations while the final decision to adopt them is taken by the organization's board, as in the case of the standards themselves. The growing volume of interpretations is an indication of the increasing complexity of international standard setting: Standardization requires additional interpretative efforts to ensure global coherence by promoting a consistent application practice (see Czarniawska and Joerges, 1996 on issues of local adaptation; with regard to accounting, see Mennicken and Heßling, 2007).

### 4.1.1 Standardization as Elimination of Alternatives

The International Accounting Standards of the 1970s and 1980s were little more than a set of normative guidelines, which companies from various countries used in addition to their respective national standards (see Stolowy and Ding, 2003). In spite of the lack of precision that characterized its standards, the IASB demonstrated its ability to actively produce them early on. In contrast to international or European regulatory endeavors, standardization under private leadership quickly generated results. Despite few employees and meager financial means, the IASB has adopted an average of two standards a year since 1975. That level of activity was only possible because the organization continued to receive resources from the Accounting International Standards Group, the Anglo-American nucleus of the IASB (Camfferman and Zeff, 2007; Kirsch, 2007). Although the decision to emphasize the information needs of market actors was made early on, it was not uncontroversial. Initially, the standards also reflected continental European norms, such as creditor protection and commitment to long-term corporate strategies; IAS resembled a collection of different principles and lacked precision accordingly. The early phase of standard setting was characterized by the incorporation of various national standards, which were then discarded from the late 1980s onward.

Although the practice of harmonization by way of compilation (Thorell and Whittington, 1994, p. 224) enabled the rapid development of standards during the early, descriptive period of standard setting, it was insufficient to secure the approval of stock market oversight authorities. In their view, the lack of precision carried great risks for the companies applying the standards and subsequently for investors. Consequently, the authorities delayed recommending the use of IAS for a long time. Instead of pursuing an agreement with each individual national supervisory authority, the IASB decided to seek cooperation with the International Organization of Securities Commissions (IOSCO) as the international representative of the national securities commissions. The intent was to gain IOSCO's support so that the Organization would recommend its members to authorize the use of IAS by foreign companies. IASB's initial goal was to encourage the use of standards by companies listed on several stock exchanges (cross-border listings).

In the early 1990s, IOSCO was under the dominant influence of the US securities commission, which later became an outspoken adversary of IASB. The Securities and Exchange Commission (SEC) was the main player in determining IOSCO's strategy owing to the fact that it exercised regulatory responsibilities in the world's largest capital market. Initially, IOSCO only represented North and South American securities commissions and started admitting European and Asian members in 1984 (Camfferman and Zeff, 2007, p. 311). In the period following the broadening of membership, the SEC retained its dominant position and proved successful in pushing for major revisions of IAS and establishing that standards must be deemed appropriate before formally recognizing IAS. Accordingly, cooperation between IOSCO and IASB was of key significance in the 1990s since legitimation of the private standards through the securities commissions was crucial for IASB's development to become the sole transnational standard setter (see Tamm Hallström, 2004).

In the late 1980s, a decision was reached on two work packages involving a major revision of IAS to reduce the plethora of accounting options. The "comparability and improvements projects" lasted from 1987 to 1993 and resulted in the revision of ten standards.[2] In essence, accounting principles that were not in tune with the information orientation of capital market actors were discarded. This was accomplished by a hierarchical ordering of accounting options. The variety of options resulting from the process of collecting and systematizing various national standards was reduced by either eliminating some of the alternative accounting rules or declaring them exceptions to the preferred rule and requiring that, if chosen, specific reasons for doing so would have to be explicitly stated (see Thorell and Whittington, 1994, pp. 223ff.).

In areas where no single rule could be agreed upon, a primary option was determined and an additional option defined that would be accepted provided that reasons are given. Although options of the latter kind are permitted as *allowed alternative treatments,* they are considered to be exceptions to the preferred rule. This applies even in accounting matters that are consistent with the IASB's conceptual framework. The main criteria guiding the selection of alternatives were practical consequences and whether the provisions found acceptance among capital market actors. Accounting practices in line with those criteria were even declared *preferred treatments* or *benchmark treatments* in cases in which they came into conflict with the conceptual framework in which the IASB's normative principles were laid down.

> [T]he objective of enhancing the comparability of financial information on a timely basis is best achieved by choosing a treatment that follows current worldwide practice and trends rather than the one that conforms most closely with the definitions of, and the recognition criteria for, the elements of financial statements in the proposed framework. [. . .] The preferred treatment was justified on the grounds that it was the "most widely accepted practice" and because of the difficulty and subjectivity involved in deciding whether the costs met the recognition criteria for assets. The allowed alternative treatment was permitted because it was supported by the proposed framework. (Cairns, 2001, p. 11)

In the course of the comparability and improvements projects, ten standards were revised and numerous alternative accounting treatments eliminated. The amendments were nevertheless still not sufficient to prompt IOSCO to issue a recommendation in favor of IAS. While European representatives in the organization favored recognizing the standards, the SEC strictly opposed such a move (Camfferman and Zeff, 2007). It also prevented individual standards from being recommended and brought about a decision requiring the IASB to develop a set of "core standards" addressing all major issues before IOSCO would issue the desired recommendation.

It was not until 1998 that the IASB had completed the process of refining those core standards and the IOSCO recommended that its members permit listed companies to use IAS in preparing their financial statements (IOSCO, 2000). After the Asian financial crisis of 1997/1998 the European Commission, which had already advocated the introduction of IAS in 1995, again proposed making IAS mandatory in Europe (see European Commission, 1995; Martinez-Diaz, 2005). The SEC, however, remained reluctant. In spite of the IOSCO recommendation, it upheld demands for further revisions to IAS. Until IAS/IFRS are recognized in the USA, foreign companies listed on US stock exchanges are required to reconcile financial statements to US GAAP.

### 4.1.2  The Special Role of the USA in International Accounting

The EU's decision to require the use of IAS/IFRS in preparing consolidated accounts starting 2005 involved expectations of having a stronger voice in matters of transnational standard setting. The IASB, however, was predominantly interested in gaining recognition for IAS/IFRS in the USA. Once the EU had recognized IAS/IFRS, convergence between IASB standards and US GAAP became the major objective, which was also laid down in the organization's constitution (IASCF, 2002, para. 2c). After establishing IAS/IFRS in Europe, coming to terms with the FASB became the highest priority. In the Norwalk Agreement, named after the town in Connecticut where it was signed, the IASB and the FASB agreed to cooperate in the harmonization and future development of standards.

The aim of the Memorandum of Understanding (Norwalk Agreement) issued in 2002 is to achieve convergence of IAS/IFRS with US GAAP. This involves four key issues: 1) to quickly remove less significant differences between US GAAP and IAS/IFRS; 2) to remove other differences by coordinating the future work programs of both organizations; 3) to continue joint projects already under way; and 4) to encourage the respective interpretative bodies to reach agreement in matters of standards interpretation. In light of the accounting scandals involving Enron, Worldcom, and others, the Norwalk Agreement was applauded in Europe as well as the USA.

> The recent scandals have shown how important top quality accounting standards arc for the health of financial markets. Today's announcement [the Norwalk Agreement] is a very positive move towards a single worldwide set of high-quality, best of breed, principles-based financial reporting standards, which would dramatically improve the efficiency of global capital markets: costs would decrease, comparability would improve and corporate governance would be enhanced. (EU, 2002)

One of the reasons for the EC's favorable reception of the agreement was that it questions the rule-based standardization of accounting common in the USA. US GAAP are based on precedent like US case law, are legalistic, and thus represent a comprehensive set of detailed rules that are often applied in a formalistic fashion. In contrast, IAS/IFRS follow a more abstract, principle-based rationale, are organized in a more systematic manner, and require more exercise of judgment in applying and interpreting accounting norms.

In spite of expressed willingness to cooperate, there was intense struggle over the details of the standards. The SEC insisted that foreign companies listed on US stock exchanges be required to reconcile their financial statements to US GAAP. In February 2006, the IASB and the FASB renewed their intent to bring together the two sets of standards and agreed to accelerate the process.

> Shortly after the IASB was established in 2001, the IASB and the FASB agreed to cooperate on the convergence of US GAAP and international standards. After several years of convergence activity it became clear that the process would take way too long, so in 2006 the two boards agreed a Memorandum of Understanding (MoU) that described an acceleration of this work. Under the terms of the MoU, where the two boards agreed that either IFRSs or US GAAP had the better answer, then that standard would be adopted by both boards as a common standard. Where neither standard was deemed to be of sufficient quality, then the two boards would cooperate to develop a new standard. (Author's interview with IASB Chairman Sir David Tweedie)

The problem of ensuring coherent application of IAS/IFRS worldwide became the last major obstacle to the recognition of the standards in the USA: "It has been noted that the removal of this reconciliation requirement would depend on, among other things, the effective implementation of IFRSs in financial statements across companies and jurisdictions, and measurable progress in addressing priority issues on the IASB–FASB convergence program" (Roadmap IASB–FASB, 2006).

Twenty years after the comparability project between the IASB and IOSCO was initiated in 1987, the convergence program represented a major step toward final recognition of IASB standards in the USA. In summer 2007, the SEC issued a concept paper on allowing foreign and US companies to prepare financial statements based on IAS/IFRS (SEC, 2007). Robert Herz, FASB Chairman at the time, entered the debate outlining three potential paths for recognition of IAS/IFRS in the USA: 1) Recognition of financial statements based on IFRS for foreign companies only; 2) choice between IFRS and US GAAP for all companies; and 3) a single set of high-quality international accounting standards (Herz, 2007). Although the final decision has yet to be made, Herz and the FASB have expressed their preference for the third option, which would amount to the application of the IASB's standards to all listed companies whether foreign or domestic US. Introduction of IAS/IFRS in the USA would end long-standing US exceptionalism and the SEC's special role. Alignment of IAS/IFRS with the information needs of capital market actors was a crucial step for such a move to become possible and, in this respect, widespread acceptance of fair value was an important prerequisite. So, while the SEC's influence might formally decrease, Anglo-American logics prevail.

### 4.1.3   Fair Value Accounting as Dominant Paradigm

The increased significance of fair value in the preparation of annual accounts corresponds to a shift in the addressees of financial statements. This shift is a consequence of changed economic conditions but at the same time encourages greater attention to be given to capital market interests owing to the emphasis placed on the information function of financial reporting. Fair value accounting moves the information needs of capital market actors to the center of attention and reduces the range of potential addressees of financial statements. Initially, fair value accounting was mainly an Anglo-American accounting practice, primarily directed at indicating a firm's current market value, which also allows projected future profits that have not yet been realized to be taken into consideration. Important target groups—at least in the traditional continental European view—such as creditors, tax authorities, employees, and other societal stakeholders, lose significance.

The current fair-value orientation of IAS/IFRS largely goes back to Anglo-American influence since the 1990s but also has historical predecessors in other countries. Blaufus shows that fair value accounting was common practice in Germany up until the late nineteenth century (Blaufus, 2005). In the UK, it was quite common to combine the fair value approach with historical costs accounting, and in the USA, accounting

was also based on fair value early on, especially in periods of high inflation. Nevertheless, historical costs accounting, often recorded at purchase
price, had been dominant for a long time. Historical costs typically result
in more conservative valuation and reduce the tax burden. Historical costs
accounting, however, has limitations, especially in periods of high inflation or when derivative financial instruments are involved, which often
have no historical costs but may have a strong impact on future accounts.
Replacement costs accounting is one way of obtaining values closer to
market values although such figures remain approximations.

The purpose of fair value accounting is to disclose information that
reflects current market values as adequately as possible. The academic
debate on fair value is still far from coming to a close since valuation at
fair value raises a number of questions (see for instance Walton, 2007).
Assessment of market value essentially involves two problems: First, fair
value has a procyclical effect because it increases the volatility of company
valuations. Assets, such as real estate, securities, or patents, are included
at current market prices. The financial crisis has made this a particularly
pressing issue. Second, the problems in assessing fair value entail new
risks. Market value estimates are especially problematic in cases where
no markets exist (or no reliable market prices) or when markets have col-
lapsed, such as the interbank market during the financial crisis in 2007–08.
The difficulties are manifest in attempts to prevent subjective valuations,
such as value-in-use estimates left to the discretion of management,
although a clear distinction between value in use and fair value is not easily
drawn in practice.

As early as 2004, the European Central Bank (ECB) criticized the
introduction of fair value under IAS/IFRS for being a paradigm shift
in which capital market orientation poses heightened risks to banks and
consequently to economic stability:

> The move from the CAA [current accounting approach] to FVA can be truly
> qualified as a paradigm shift since backward-looking accounting measures
> based on the concepts of prudence and reliability give way to measures based
> on prevailing economic values. This fundamental shift explains the often heated
> and contentious debate regarding the pros and cons of the two accounting
> models. FVA may have positive consequences, such as a better reflection of
> economic reality. On the other hand, there are serious doubts as to how reliable
> the fair value estimates would be for instruments not traded on an active and
> liquid market, such as the vast majority of bank loans. (ECB, 2004, p. 79)

Although the doubts raised by the ECB primarily concern the reliability
of estimates, there are other conceptual reasons for the increasing volatility of corporate accounts. Apart from the fact that the concept of fair

value strongly relies on rationalized econometric models, the way in which total earnings per period are determined is another factor. The emphasis placed on change in value leads to a situation where less attention is paid to company operational performance; instead the focus is shifted to value creation in the statement of comprehensive income. In addition to net profit or loss, this includes components of other comprehensive income, such as revaluations, actuarial gains and losses on defined benefit plans, remeasuring financial assets that are available for sale, and the effective portion of gains and losses on hedging instruments.

In spite of the significance of fair value accounting, IASB rules do not provide an authoritative definition of fair value. Both the US standard SFAC 7 and the IASB standards contain slightly different understandings of fair value. In addition, concepts of fair value show considerable variation in their implicit assumptions of how fair value should be measured (cf. Bromwich, 2007). Such differences notwithstanding, there is common agreement that fair value refers to an exchange value between market participants. In the standards pertaining to financial instruments (IAS 32 "Financial Instruments: Disclosure and Presentation" and IAS 39 "Financial Instruments: Recognition and Measurement"), we encounter an identical definition according to which fair value is "the amount for which an asset could be exchanged, or a liability settled, between knowledgeable, willing parties in an arm's length transaction" (IAS 32.11).[3] This definition is predicated on the assumption of independent, rational market actors and an idealized notion of price formation in neoclassical markets. These assumptions, however, have been questioned both theoretically and empirically (Boyer, 2007).

Nonetheless, the IASB standards still attempt to approximate the ideal world of neoclassical economics. In the absence of market prices, hypothetical prices are estimated. This occurs in a three-step procedure: If a market price cannot be determined, reference prices are identified. In the event that no reference markets are available, the IASB allows price estimates based on econometric models to be used. This means that companies use calculated values in their annual accounts where reliable market values are absent.[4] To be sure, determining market value has priority ("mark to market"). However, if unsuccessful, the standards allow model-based price estimates ("mark to model"). The following illustration shows that this procedure results in three different conceptions of fair value (FV). FV can represent a real or a reference market value. It can also be a cash value determined using the discounted cash flow (DCF) method. The DCF method includes projections of future developments; the account thus takes expected values into consideration.

The valuation hierarchy for fair value measurement allows fair value

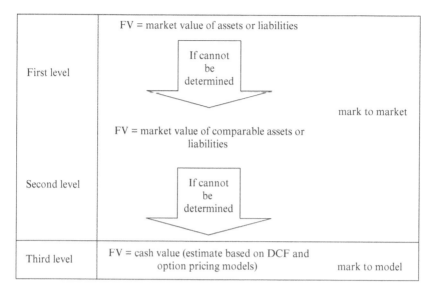

*Source:*    Adapted from Blaufus, 2005, p. 31 (author's translation).

*Figure 4.2    Valuation hierarchy for fair value measurement*

to be determined even where market prices are not available. The limitations of market information are overcome by recourse to mathematical models. The valuation hierarchy draws on logical reasoning, but doubts remain whether this corresponds with the initial assumptions. It remains contested whether econometric option-pricing models reflect the economic reality of a company more appropriately than, for instance, historical costs (for a detailed account of the genesis of option price theory, see MacKenzie and Millo, 2003).

Another source of increased volatility in annual accounts is the broadened application of fair value to reporting on comprehensive income. Comprehensive income covers a reporting period, not a value at a certain point in time, and consists of net and other types of income that do not have to be disclosed on the income statement because they have not yet been realized. Other comprehensive income, such as unrealized gains and losses on securities and currencies that are available for sale, gains and losses on derivatives, or certain actuarial gains and losses are not part of net income but are included to give a more complete picture of the business entity. The inclusion of other comprehensive income expands the traditional income statement, and add significance to those sections of the corporate account that are not part of the net profit and loss (P&L) account.

Although it initially has no effect on the income statement, other comprehensive income becomes a factor affecting the change in value of equity and contributes to an increased volatility of the financial statement. Fair value logics make reporting potential income—that is, income not yet realized—particularly promising because they allow numerical calculations even when market values cannot be identified. Subsequently, the widespread use of fair value facilitates the inclusion of items in the balance sheet that originally had no P&L effect. In Germany at least, changes in equity of this kind were largely unheard-of before the introduction of international standards (see Pellens et al., 2004, p. 430). Striving to report comprehensive income leads to the combining of earnings per period with period-specific changes in the value of other balance sheet items, thus undermining the significance of the P&L account (see Perry and Nölke, 2006). One consequence is that a company's operational activities lose significance compared to fluctuations in asset values. However, it is precisely this broadly conceived approach to recognition and measurement in determining company performance that the IASB was aiming for. As a result, international accounting standards contribute to shaping the image of and practices in corporations to favor capital investors over other interested parties when preparing financial statements.

From a conceptual point of view, FVA gives rise to a changed perception of what a corporation is: Companies are increasingly viewed as a bundle of capital flows that can be represented on balance sheets and in balance sheet items at market value. Operational management decisions are demoted to the back seat, behind financial decisions. Moreover, once FVA has been established, it is difficult to turn the clock back: Opting for fair value increases pressure to account for comprehensive income in future periods. The growing influence of this rationale rooted in the functioning of financial markets alters the nature of management tasks:

> [T]his primacy of financial management over the other functions of the firms (especially product design and development, productive organization and human resources management) may contribute to the hiding of the sources of profit in the long run. Finance theory tends to stress the role of substitution among different generic assets, whereas management theory points out that the real source of profit is the search for the strategic complementarity of firm-specific assets. (Boyer, 2007, p. 795)

Following Boyer's reasoning, this shift toward financial management contributes to obscuring a company's internal value-creation process and heightens vulnerability both at the individual company level and regarding the economy as a whole (Boyer, 2007, pp. 802ff.). FVA, aimed at measuring a company's value at market value, sets off a spiral that enhances the significance of financial management. Both the increased reliance on econometric models for estimating asset values and the extension of fair value rationale to a company's equity base are responsible for this dynamic.

At this point, neither academic debate nor the discussions within the IASB have come to a final conclusion as to what extent fair value should be incorporated into the body of IASB rules. In recent years, however, there has been a noticeable trend toward fair value, and there are voices demanding that full fair value accounting be adopted. However, the current extent of FVA already fuels tendencies toward redefining the purpose of entrepreneurial activity. Instead of accounts reflecting value creation based on producing goods or services, the overall change in value—measured by market values or econometric estimation—moves to the center of attention. This strengthens the role of capital providers in general and capital market actors in particular because corporations will be eager to present high earnings when reporting their comprehensive income to attract investment capital. This fosters short-termism and a fixation on shareholders' information needs. In contrast to historical costs, fair value can be more easily distorted and may lead to fueling a company's market volatility; a problem most evident during the financial crisis for banks holding unrealized securities, derivatives, and other financial instruments.

We may hold that FVA is a manifestation of an increasing focus on financial markets while at the same time reinforcing this trend. The growing attention paid to the principles governing the allocation of capital enhances the position of actors in the financial sector compared to those in the productive sector (Perry and Nölke, 2006, p. 575). In adopting fair value, the IASB greatly contributed to this paradigm shift. In spite of the IASB's leading role in establishing fair value accounting, the concept of fair value nevertheless remains controversial within the organization as the two selected examples, the standard for financial instruments and the drafting of a new conceptual framework, show. In the following section, both cases will be analyzed to demonstrate that the content of transnational standard setting is largely the outcome of controversy and compromise.

## 4.2  SELECTED CONTROVERSIES OF INTERNATIONAL STANDARDIZATION

The process of IAS/IFRS development is testimony to the fact that the process of defining accounting standards is not adequately explained in terms of simply attempting to find the most efficient solutions to coordination problems. Standard setting is far more contested than the technical arguments raised in the debate would have us believe (see Tamm Hallström, 2004; Camfferman and Zeff, 2007; Gallhofer and Haslam, 2007; Kirsch, 2007; Botzem, 2008). In this section, the conflictual nature of transnational standard setting will be illustrated by two cases: IAS 39 ("Financial Instruments: Recognition and Measurement") and IASB's conceptual framework are cases where considerable influence was brought to bear on the IASB in the process of standard formulation. The selection of examples is informed by a context-sensitive research design that focuses attention on critical cases (Pettigrew, 1990, p. 275). This allows me to demonstrate the tension between official, rationalist discourse and interest group politics.

### 4.2.1   IAS 39: Accounting for Financial Instruments

Accounting for financial instruments is one of the most controversial IASB provisions. The controversy came to a head twice, culminating in a clash of Anglo-American and continental European accounting principles: In the late 1990s, when IAS 39 was developed, and between 2003 and 2005, when the European Union only partly adopted the standard. IAS 39 defines provisions for the recognition and measurement of financial instruments. It was issued in 1998 and was one of the final standards to make up the IASB's set of core standards.[5] At the time of its adoption, IAS 39 already represented a compromise that was to be quickly revised. It is controversial for mainly two reasons. First of all, the standard determines the principles for recognition and measurement of financial assets and liabilities. The increasingly widespread use of financial instruments makes the standard particularly important for both the manufacturing industry and the financial sector. Second, IAS 39 is strongly shaped by the concept of fair value.

IAS 39 defines a financial instrument as follows: "A contract that gives rise to a financial asset of one entity and a financial liability or equity instrument of another entity" (IAS 39.9). Among such instruments are assets and liabilities, loans and receivables, debt and equity securities, mortgage-backed securities, and share buy-back agreements. Derivatives are of particular significance and are contested between some European actors and the IASB. Derivatives are financial instruments whose value derives from an interest rate, a foreign currency, or a security, which require low levels of investment, and the maturity date of which lies in the future (cf. MacKenzie and Millo, 2003). The question of how hedging activities, which serve the purpose of offsetting future fluctuations in interest rates, currencies, or stock exchange quotations, are properly recognized and treated in accounting is at the heart of the controversy surrounding IAS 39—an issue that 20 years later still has not been resolved.

On one hand, there are Anglo-American actors who view IAS 39 as a means of establishing fair value accounting for financial instruments as comprehensively and consistently as possible. They deem recognition and measurement of derivatives at fair value as necessary to disclose all liabilities so as to reflect expected performance early on. Although US GAAP contains similar provisions, in formulating IAS 39 the IASB could not have recourse to a coherent set of national standards as in other cases.

On the other hand, there are actors opposed to excessive hedge accounting at fair value. Among the opponents are Japanese businesses, a number of continental European banks, and the European Central Bank. They fear that fair value accounting for derivatives will entail an increased level of volatility and that businesses will be compelled to disclose the value of financial instruments even in cases where it is impossible to sell them—an issue that is at the heart of the financial crisis.

Both positions refer to different principles of accounting. Fair value advocates emphasize the reliability of market value as an indicator and warn against allowing management scope for manipulation. The proponents of historical costs believe that there should be more careful and conservative recognition and measurement of hedging instruments since increased levels of fluctuation pose considerable risk not only to banks and companies, due to the importance of credit financing in Europe, but to system stability overall.

Since both positions can hardly be reconciled, in the late 1990s the IASB decided on a compromise and opted for the so-called "mixed model". IAS 39 contains elements of fair value accounting and accounting at purchase price. The principles coexist but must not be mixed. Combining different accounting principles and incorporating a number of exceptions have rendered IAS 39 a highly complex standard that is difficult to comprehend. "In the meantime, international standards have evolved to such degree in terms of scale and complexity that they remain largely obscure to anyone without expert knowledge" (Ruhnke, 2005, p. 498—author's translation).

The IASB concedes that IAS 39 is way too complex and ever since it was adopted has been working on revising it. With regard to the standard's complexity, the *Financial Times* quoted IASB Chairman Tweedie as saying: "If you understand IAS 39, you haven't read it properly" (*Financial Times*, June 6, 2006). The inconsistencies and complexity are the result of the considerable time pressure involved in developing the core standards in the late 1990s (see Kirsch, 2007, pp. 313ff.), and the problem was further exacerbated by the clash of conflicting principles that gave rise to the mixed model compromise.

The history of IAS 39 began in the 1980s when the Canadian and Australian associations (in particular) along with the FASB sought to establish accounting for financial instruments at fair value. The Canadian Institute of Chartered Accountants (CICA) took the lead in developing a first draft in cooperation with the IASB. Exposure Draft E40 was issued in 1991. After amendments in response to criticism, it was again presented in January 1994 as E48. The debate already revolved around the introduction of fair value for financial instruments. The Canadian accountants discussed different alternatives that proposed adopting fair value accounting either as a benchmark treatment or at least as an allowed alternative. Along with US actors, they dominated the development process (Camfferman and Zeff, 2007, p. 362). Opposition to fair value came from French bank representatives, who mainly objected to fair value accounting for derivatives. Thereupon, the IASB assigned its staff the task of developing a revised draft (E62), which was issued in April 1998.

> E62 was a slimmed-down and slightly modified version of the lengthy compilation of US GAAP that had been rejected by the board in October/November [1997]. In a general sense, this meant that E62 reverted to the intent-based, mixed measurement model of E48, with many modifications in substance and style, reflecting the draft's origins in US GAAP. (Camfferman and Zeff, 2007, pp. 374ff.)

When a shortened deadline for the submission of comments expired, the Board adopted the standard in 1998 by the minimum of 12 votes (of 16 in total). There was one vote against the proposed standard and three abstentions. The Australian delegation, which favored full fair value, voted against the mixed model compromise. The British delegation abstained because of concerns that the interim solution might turn into a permanent one; the US delegation also abstained owing to objections to the shortened period for participation. The French delegation abstained as well, believing that the prudence principle had not been given due consideration. Adoption of IAS 39 paved the way for reaching an agreement on the core standards. As a result, the conditions were satisfied for IOSCO to recommend that the national securities commissions recognize IAS, thus facilitating the standards' global dissemination. This was also a precondition for the IASB's major organizational overhaul, which was completed in 2001.

The standards quickly found widespread use since the European Union determined (at the Lisbon summit in 2000) that IAS/IFRS would be mandatory for consolidated accounts starting 2005 (see Martinez-Diaz, 2005). The EU adopted a set of regulations requiring that every single standard be debated and put into effect individually. Except for IAS 39, all IASB standards have been implemented into European law without modification. Financial instruments were the first case in which exemptions ("carve-out") were defined, underscoring the EU's intention to take a more active role in cross-border standardization.[6]

In 2002, Regulation (EC) No. 1606/2002 was adopted requiring mandatory application of international accounting standards in the EU provided that they do not conflict with the Fourth and Seventh Directives. The standards are binding for the preparation of consolidated accounts and have been in force since 2005 upon approval under the comitology procedure as determined by the regulation. The final decision on putting individual standards into effect thus rests with the EC which, in accordance with Article 6 of Regulation 1606/2002, is assisted by the Accounting Regulatory Committee (ARC) in which the member states are represented. The regulation further requires that a technical committee provide support and expertise (paragraph (10), page (L243/2)). In practice, EFRAG (European Financial Reporting Advisory Group), a federation of European business organizations, has assumed this function.[7]

EFRAG advises the EC in matters related to accounting, gives recommendations, and issues position papers and opinions based on which it also participates in IASB consultation procedures. The group is in charge of conducting consultations and issuing requests for comments to guide opinion formation in the EU. After consultations with ARC and EFRAG, typically the EC unconditionally incorporates IASB standards and interpretations into the body of European standards (see Wüstemann and Kierzek, 2007a; for a critical view of IAS/IFRS recognition practice in Europe, see Chiapello and Medjad, 2007).

With the exception of IAS 39, as early as 2003 all IASB standards existing at the time were declared mandatory in the EU (Regulation (EC) No. 1725/2003). The provisions on financial instruments, however, were exempted from endorsement since they had prompted strong reservations from private European banks and the European Central Bank. After years of controversy, carving out certain controversial provisions paved the way for the adoption of the remaining parts of IAS 39. Therefore, from a formal legal standpoint, the standards in force in the EU today deviate from the IAS/IFRS endorsed by the IASB.

The dispute goes back to technical issues that had failed to be resolved in the late 1990s. Again it was continental European banks, especially from France, that sought to prevent provisions requiring hedge accounting at fair value. They exerted influence over the European Banking Federation and convinced the French President Chirac to send a letter to the President of the European Commission warning against the adverse consequences of IAS/IFRS in Europe. At the same time, some of these banks were trying to prevent the adoption of the provisions related to hedge accounting (see Armstrong et al., 2006). In their view, extending fair value accounting to their risk management practices would cause problematic volatility of corporate financial reporting. The IASB favors accounting at market value and therefore demands early disclosure of potential liabilities, thus creating an opportunity to draw attention to expected future profits and losses. The European Central Bank, in contrast, points out that, as far as financial instruments held to maturity are concerned—which particularly affects loan securitization—applying fair valuation may thus be inappropriate or even misleading. In this way, fair value contributes to volatility of the corporate value of banks (ECB, 2004, p. 74) and fuels criticism that the Anglo-American-dominated IASB fails to take lending adequately into account, which is of prime importance to many continental European banks.

Political controversy between the IASB, on the one hand, and the EC and individual member states, on the other, was sparked by two provisions: Fair value hedge accounting and the option to report all assets at fair value ("fair value option"), which was most prominently advocated by Anglo-American interest-group representatives. Adoption of the fair value option would have amounted to discarding the mixed model, and the Canadian accountants' original proposal of the early 1990s would have become reality. However, neither the member states nor EFRAG were able to muster a majority in favor of either the hedging provisions or the fair value option.[8] In November 2004, IAS 39 was implemented into EU law by Regulation (EC) No. 2086/2004, carving out the two controversial provisions. In the following year, the dispute over the fair value option was resolved. After several amendments of IAS 39 by the IASB in the summer of 2005, the revised fair value option was adopted in November 2005 to apply retroactively from January 1, 2005 (Regulation (EC) No. 1864/2005). The hedging issue remains controversial and the carve-out still applies in that area even though it is of little practical significance. A few continental European banks actually made use of the carve-out option. Most banks apply IAS 39 as the IASB intended, especially in cases where they are also listed on US stock exchanges. Among the eight banks that applied the carve-out option in 2007 are three French institutions (BNP Paribas, Crédit Agricole, Société Générale), two Belgian banks (KBC, Fortis), one German (Commerzbank), one from Luxembourg (Dexia), and one Swedish financial institution (Nordea Bank) (ICAEW, 2007, p. 78).

Apart from the different accounting requirements that Anglo-American and continental European banks face, cultural differences in accounting also play a role. Whether derivatives are viewed as hedging instruments or as a form of speculation also depends on motives imputed by standard setters. The notion that accounting standards must be restrictive to prevent abuse stirred irritation among continental European business representatives: "European preparers do not expect to have their good faith routinely called into question, and consequently have difficulty with standards that are heavily influenced by an anti-abuse approach. This is probably a feature of the IAS 39 debate" (Walton, 2004b, p. 13). The long-standing controversy over the regulation of financial instruments testifies to the fact that accounting standards are shaped by fundamental convictions, cultural habits, and material interests as well. In addition, the European Commission's carve-out moved IAS 39 into the spotlight of political debate. At the same time, this posed a challenge to the expert-driven mode of standard setting applied by the IASB. Interviews conducted with the organization's representatives show that they view the increasing role of European actors with skepticism and oppose this development as an exercise of inadequate political influence.

> Then in addition, you get people coming along who have a self-interest, like the French banks. I don't know what they were hiding or thought they were hiding, or what disaster was going to overcome them if they did hedge accounting in the form required but they obviously thought their interests were affected. They are going to lobby such committees [e.g. EFRAG] and put ideas in their heads and give them more opportunities for getting their hands on the standards, and they find it difficult to resist that temptation. [. . .] They just say, if it has a minor flaw in it, if it is not perfect it is against the European interest. That is not the test they should be applying. (Author's interview with Professor Geoffrey Whittington, former Board member)

Leading IASB representatives dismiss the greater role of political influence in standard setting procedures. In line with the Anglo-American world view, they insist on maintaining a separation between the political arena, on one hand, and standards development and standard setting as a realm of technical rationality, on the other (also see Porter, 2005). Those involved in the IASB nevertheless concede that, to the present, the decisions involved in determining standards have been strongly influenced by the need for compromise. The standardization process has been geared toward achieving widespread use of IAS/IFRS, which was not to be managed without recognition by national legislators. Priority was given to "fixing" existing standards.

The role of European bodies in shaping IAS/IFRS has not been limited to *ex post* endorsement. They are trying to play an active part in the development of new projects. Increasingly, however, European influence is viewed critically since it not only questions expert-driven standard setting but also holds the threat of leading to the development of separate European standards derived from IAS/IFRS:

[T]here is concern around the world that a single set of high-quality standards should be just that—one version of the standards. In some jurisdictions—Europe included—not all of the standards have been applied in full. In many countries the changes can be significant, whereas in Europe we are only talking about an option to ignore nine paragraphs in IAS 39, which less than 1 percent of European companies apply. [. . .] Nevertheless, the goal has to be to avoid future carve-outs and for everyone to apply the same standards on a consistent basis. (Author's interview with Tweedie)

However, as far as the content of IAS/IFRS is concerned, the EU still is in a weak position. The Anglo-American principles clearly dominate the IASB, but the Board has distanced itself from the rules-based approach predominant in the USA. Instead, the IASB has pursued a more principles-based approach and, in so doing, has strengthened the judgment of practitioners and experts. This is to ensure that IAS/IFRS not only cater to the needs of actors in industrialized countries but also aim to facilitate the global adoption of IASB's standards.

Developing global standards is not easy. In Europe, we are often criticised for being led by the US. In the US, there is concern that we are too heavily influenced by Europe, partly because Europe was one of the first jurisdictions to adopt IFRSs. And in Asia, there is concern that IFRSs are a bilateral arrangement between Europe and the US. The thing to keep in mind is that, while we are in the transition phase of constructing global standards, some imbalances will exist. These regional pressures should cancel each other out once everyone is using the same standard. (Author's interview with Tweedie)

Taken together, the controversy surrounding IAS 39 during the middle years of the last decade reveals key features of transnational standard setting. Despite the dominance of Anglo-American principles and the leading role of North American associations, establishing full fair value within the IASB has not been successful. Most resistance has come from the ranks of continental European banks, which were able to convince the EC of their position. Although the decision to drop provisions on hedge accounting from the catalog of mandatory standards is only a temporary solution, it slowed down the advance of fair value. At least for the time being, European banks are left the option to apply alternative accounting methods. The actual differences between IAS/IFRS and the modified, carve-out version of the standards applied in Europe may be minor, and only eight financial institutions make use of the carve-out provision, but the controversy has given the EU an opportunity to develop a profile of its own in the international arena of cross-border accounting standardization. This poses a challenge to the Anglo-American standard setters' notion of professional self-regulation.

In late 2008, at the height of the financial crisis, accounting for financial instruments became a focal point of criticism and triggered frantic activity on the part of both the US standard setter and the IASB. Reinterpretations of existing rules were included in the FASB provisions and IAS 39. After the FASB gave in to pressures (mainly from US financial institutions) to allow the reclassification of financial assets, the IASB followed suit in October 2008. Both organizations resorted to an interpretation of the financial crisis as a "very rare circumstance," which was a formula to allow for a temporary reclassification of assets. Essentially, this has to be interpreted as a violation of both the letter and the spirit of the standards. Given the severity of the drop in housing prices, the loss in value of many mortgage-backed securities, the failure of investment banks (among them most prominently Lehman Brothers), the freezing of the interbank market, and a stock market slump, banks were allowed to reclassify assets from the trading book to the bank book retroactively.

On October 13, 2008, the IASB discussed amendments to IAS 39 permitting reclassification of financial assets in a "response to requests by certain constituents to create a 'level playing field' in this area with US GAAP" (IASplus, 2008; see also IASplus, 2011b). Amendments allowed financial assets to be reclassified out of the category "at fair value through profit or loss" in certain cases. Contrary to the existing standard, banks were given the opportunity to reclassify assets held for trading as assets held for maturity. The intention was to avoid having to price these assets at their current value, which, at the time, was often nil since no market activity was taking place. In times of frozen markets, these assets had no market value. Ironically, while, until the bubble burst, the banks had happily displayed the increasing market values of their assets as an increase in comprehensive income, they now criticized accounting provisions for being procyclical and posing a threat to organizational survival and system stability as a whole.

After FASB had given in to pressures for reclassification and questioned the global approach that, until then, had informed both its and the IASB's standards, the European Commission became active. Immediately after the IASB had decided on October 13 to amend IAS 39 to permit the reclassification of financial assets *ex post* (effective from July 1, 2008, before the bubble burst), the EC adopted the changed provisions. Following a decision of the European Council of Economic and Finance Ministers (ECOFIN) and echoing meetings in Paris of European G8 member and euro-area countries the preceding week, the Commission supported changes in IAS 39 and IFRS 7 (including additional disclosure requirements) to mitigate the consequences of the turbulence in global financial markets. The EC stated immediately after IASB's decision: "The IASB's approach fully achieves the objectives set out by the ECOFIN Council of 7 October, i.e. to place EU companies at the same position as their competitors as far as reporting rules are concerned. The amendment would also be applicable as of the third quarter of this year (periods starting after 1 July 2008) as requested by ECOFIN" (European Commission, 2008).

Controversy over fair value accounting in general and the discrepancies between US and international decisions fueled discussions about the content and the governance structures of transnational accounting standardization. The G20 Summits became a forum in which criticism was articulated. The concluding document of the G20 Summit in Washington in November 2008 tasked the ministers and experts with reviewing and aligning global accounting standards, particularly for complex securities. In particular, summit members criticized a lack of transparency and accountability. They were asked to ensure that global accounting standards bodies enhance guidance on the valuation of securities and urged that regulators and accounting standard setters should improve the required disclosure of complex financial instruments. The G20 explicitly criticized the IASB:

> With a view toward promoting financial stability, the governance of the international accounting standard setting body should be further enhanced, including by undertaking a review of its membership, in particular in order to ensure transparency, accountability, and an appropriate relationship between this independent body and the relevant authorities. (G20, 2008, p. 6)

In the following years, the regulation of financial instruments remained a controversial issue, and the IASB amended IAS 39 a number of times before the standard was superseded by IFRS 9 ("Financial Instruments"). The new standard was divided into three sections: classification and measurement, amortized costs, and hedge accounting. The first package (covering classification and measurement of financial assets) was issued as IFRS 9 in October 2010 (to be effective on January 1, 2013). The standard now excludes the available-for-sale and held-to-maturity categories conceptualized in IAS 39. Furthermore, it calls for all debt instruments to be measured at fair value through P&L if they do not pass a business model and a cash flow characteristic test (IASplus, 2011c).

In sum, these new provisions solidify the fair value logic of IAS/IFRS. In Europe, however, criticism has been particularly intense, and the IASB's intention to address most of the EU's criticism of reporting on financial instruments, so far, has proven unsuccessful: "Nevertheless, in light of the financial sector's critical position *vis-à-vis* the proposal, the European Commission pressured the IASB to make the fair value rules even more flexible (i.e., allow more opportunities for financial institutions to use purchase prices, as opposed to market prices, in valuing financial instruments in order to limit volatility in the financial statements)" (Leblond, 2011, p. 456). As a result of the discontent of many European actors with the new IFRS 9 standard, the Commission is seeking more changes and has consequently decided to delay the endorsement of IFRS 9 until the remaining phases (amortize costs and hedge accounting) are published (Leblond, 2011). This decision is not as radical as a carve-out but indicates that the EC is willing to increase political pressure on the IASB. At the time of writing, a final decision on IFRS 9 is still pending.

At this point, the long-term consequences for the IASB are an open question. It is conceivable that the EC may again resort to carve-out decisions and little by little create a European version of IAS/IFRS. It can just as easily be imagined that the IASB will attempt to anticipate conflict and refrain from adopting standards that are unlikely to gain majority support in Europe. However, it remains a fact that fair value accounting is virtually irreversible. In fact, to maintain fair value accounting during the financial crisis, the IASB opted to temporarily suspend the dominant logic by arguing that the financial crisis was a "very rare circumstance" that justified abandoning fair value principles. It was this temporary retreat that has allowed fair value accounting to be rescued overall. It is likely that IFRS 9 will further bolster the information orientation of capital market actors and contribute to marginalizing traditional cost-based methods, which shield many actors from short-term price fluctuations.

### 4.2.2 Conceptual Framework: Defining the Addressees of Reporting Information

Apart from the standards and their interpretations, the IASB's authoritative statements also include a conceptual framework. This document came into effect in 1989, was confirmed in 2001, and is currently being redrafted. It consists of guidelines and basic norms and defines the purpose of standard setting. However, its status in the hierarchy of IASB norms is unclear. Board members are required to agree contractually to have regard to the conceptual framework when making decisions (IASCF, 2009, para. 29). In cases where the framework collides with individual standards, however, the latter take precedence.

The conceptual framework is considered to be a normative foundation, but its practical significance for accounting practice and standard setting is not clear. The framework is currently being reviewed in a joint process between the IASB and the FASB. The development of the new conceptual framework can be taken as an endeavor to define the fundamentals of one set of global accounting norms. The framework complements the IASB

constitution, which currently states four objectives: 1) to develop and disseminate global accounting standards; 2) to promote the use and rigorous
application of those standards; 3) to take account of the special needs
of small and medium-sized entities and emerging economies; and 4) to
bring about convergence of national accounting standards and IAS/IFRS
(IASCF, 2010, para. 2). The first objective, developing global accounting standards, has recently been amended and specifies IASB's goals in
concrete terms. The organization seeks

> to develop, in the public interest, a single set of high quality, understandable,
> enforceable and globally accepted financial reporting standards based upon
> clearly articulated principles. These standards should require high quality,
> transparent and comparable information in financial statements and other
> financial reporting to help investors, other participants in the world's capital
> markets and other users of financial information make economic decisions.
> (IASCF, 2010, para. 2a)

By contrast, the original conceptual framework of 1989 defined a much
wider circle of addressees of international accounting standards. During
the middle years of the last decade, redefining who should be the dominant
addressees of accounting standards proved to be highly controversial,
revealing a rift within the Anglo-American camp, which will be summarized here. The initial conceptual framework anticipated a wide array
of constituencies in accounting standardization, among them investors,
employees, customers, governments and regulatory agencies, and the
general public, specifying the information needs of each group.

The attention paid to the various target groups raises questions
concerning the hierarchy among the—to some degree conflicting—
information needs, which the conceptual framework leaves unanswered.
It is simply assumed that most information needs will be satisfied by
providing the information needed by investors.

> What the framework does say is that the provision of information that meets
> the needs of the providers of risk capital will also meet most of the needs of
> other users that financial statements can satisfy. If users other than providers
> of risk capital have other needs which can be met by financial statements, the
> IASC would consider addressing those needs. (Cairns, 2001, p. 8)

Subsumption of all information needs under the interests of investors provides the justification for concentrating on investors as the most
important target group. This development can also be traced in the US
academic debate (see Young, 2006) and is in line with the increasing focus
on shareholder value generally observed in recent years (see Froud et al.,
2000).

*Table 4.1*     *Addressees and their information needs according to the conceptual framework of 1989*

| Addressees | Information is needed |
| --- | --- |
| Investors | To help determine whether to buy, hold, or sell investments |
|  | to enable assessment of the ability of an enterprise to pay dividends |
| Employees and their representative groups | To assess the stability and profitability of their employers and their ability to provide remuneration and retirement benefits |
| Lenders | To determine whether their loans and interest will be paid when due |
| Suppliers and other trade creditors | To determine whether amounts owing to them can be paid when due |
| Customers | About the continuance of an enterprise and whether business relationships can be maintained in the long run |
| Governments and their agencies | To assess the allocation of resources and the activities of enterprises |
|  | to regulate the activities of enterprises |
|  | to determine taxation policies as the basis for national income and similar statistics |
| Public | To judge an enterprise's contribution to the local economy |

*Source:*     Framework, para. 9 (EU, 2003, p. 19).

Despite consensus that investors are the primary target group for IASB standards, it is apparent that the meaning of decision usefulness as the main objective of accounting is far from clear. Controversy over the responsibility of management toward company shareholders in the IASB–FASB joint review of the conceptual framework during the period between 2005 and 2010 bears witness to this. The dispute over how decision usefulness is to be understood reveals a conflict within the Anglo-American paradigm between US and British interests and beliefs. Specifically, the conflict revolves around the question whether facilitating the allocation of capital should be the sole purpose of accounting or whether control of management ought to be given equal importance.

At a joint meeting in October 2004, the IASB and the US standard setter decided to draw up a common conceptual framework to replace the two organizations' existing frameworks. The process was divided into eight phases; a discussion paper and a separate exposure draft would be prepared for each phase.[9] The first stage, "Phase A: objectives and qualitative criteria," was due to have been completed by the end of 2007. Instead, the two organizations scheduled the publication of a detailed draft for interested parties to comment on for the second quarter of 2008. The delay was caused by disagreement about the primary objective of cross-border accounting and on the question of who are the relevant addressees of decision usefulness. The discussion paper tends to favor US traditions and is skewed towards the idea of resource allocation as the objective of financial accounting:

> The objective of general purpose external financial reporting is to provide information that is useful to present and potential investors and creditors and others in making investment, credit, and similar resource allocation decisions. (IASB, 2006, p. 18)

That wording prompted two British Board members, Whittington and Chairman Tweedie, to write a dissenting opinion, which was added to the set of questions included in the discussion paper. In their view, the emphasis on resource allocation is a one-sided and simplistic interpretation of capital market orientation. Instead, they advocated that effective control of management by shareholders should not be subsumed under the principle of resource allocation. Limiting the objectives of accounting to addressing the needs of investors, who are mainly interested in future corporate performance, fails to live up to the idea of accountability. In their dissenting opinion, Whittington and Tweedie propose to consider stewardship as an objective of financial reporting in its own right:

> Stewardship is concerned with the accountability of the directors, or management board, of a business entity to its proprietors or owners. This is at the heart of the financial reporting process in many jurisdictions, where the financial statements are presented to the shareholders at an annual general meeting, which approves the financial statements, elects directors, approves dividends, and conducts other important business. The financial statements provide input into these decisions, by providing an account of past transactions and events and the current financial position of the business. These decisions concern not only the competence of the stewards of the entity (which is clearly an important consideration in resource allocation) but also their integrity. (IASB, 2006, p. 44)

The emphasis on stewardship can be read as criticism of a narrow conception of principal–agent theories (see Donaldson and Davis, 1991). The importance placed on responsible management questions the dominance of simple principal–agent approaches that conceptualize corporate governance issues solely as problems of coordination and control. "The call for transparency and disclosure, embodied in corporate governance codes and the International Accounting Standards (IASs), should improve the information asymmetry situation so that investors are better informed about the company's activities and strategies" (Mallin, 2004, p. 12).

The stewardship perspective opposes the separating of management responsibility from company performance. As the alternative view included in the discussion paper states:

> The two IASB members do not agree that stewardship requires management performance to be separated from entity performance [. . .]. The stewardship responsibility of the management board extends to all of the activities of the entity. Even if some risks are out of the control of management, the decision to be exposed to those risks (by the choice of activities, investments and hedging and insurance strategies) is within management control. (IASB, 2006, pp. 42ff.)

This view is supported by stewardship theory, which describes the role of management from a sociological and psychological perspective. "Stewardship theorists assume a strong relationship between the success of the organization and the principal's satisfaction. A steward protects and maximizes shareholders' wealth through firm performance, because by doing so, the steward's utility functions are maximized" (Davis et al., 1997, p. 25). It is nevertheless evident that the alternative view documented in the discussion paper remains in line with shareholder value considerations. However, it does not subscribe to the belief that there exists a fundamental discrepancy between the interests of management and those of shareholders. With regard to the objective of accounting, this perspective is predicated on the assumption that financial statements are important not just in view of future investment decisions but are also useful, and indeed should be, for the subsequent evaluation of past management strategies. The advocates of stewardship particularly emphasize the significance of information with regard to the past and the present.

This new cleavage is now separating important US actors from much of the rest of the world, led by the UK. To some degree this confrontation has displaced the former divide between continental European conceptions emphasizing precaution and protection of creditors, on one hand, and Anglo-American approaches focusing on capital market actors on the other. These differences remain but can no longer be simply attributed to national origin. The answers given to the questions posed in the discussion paper testify to such a shift. When asked, "What should be the interaction between financial reporting and management's perspective?" almost all significant European actors—both from the Continent and the UK—stressed the importance of stewardship. In contrast, North American representatives did not deem it necessary to address accountability of management in the conceptual framework as an issue in its own right.[10]

In the majority of the comment letters, stewardship was mentioned as an objective of accounting in its own right: Banks, industrial associations, and accountants from the UK have spoken in its favor, as have French industrial representatives, all German banks, the Institute of Public Auditors in Germany (Institut der Wirtschaftsprüfer—IDW), and the Accounting Standards Committee of Germany (ASCG). International organizations, such as IOSCO and the Bank for International Settlements, have also urged that stewardship be mentioned as an objective of financial reporting. The same is true of the accountants' associations of New Zealand, Australia, and South Africa, which have endorsed adopting it as a separate objective, as has the European Federation of Accountants (FEE). The Big Four have also consented to explicitly stress management responsibility since they, too, believe that decision usefulness alone fails to take this aspect sufficiently into account.

Positions advocating that stewardship be subsumed under the overarching goal of resource allocation almost exclusively originate from the USA. Among the advocates are the American Institute of Certified Public Accountants (AICPA) and Goldman Sachs, as well as the international associations of CFOs (Financial Executives International—FEI) and financial analysts (Chartered Financial Analyst Institute—CFA). The IASB has determined that 86 percent of the comment letters received are in favor of the alternative proposal, so has recommended that stewardship be adopted as a separate accounting objective (IASB, 2007).

In spite of the overwhelming support for the alternative proposal, discussions within the IASB and talks with the FASB show the difficulties of communicating that position in the USA. There, information needs are still derived from resource allocation as the primary objective. Although a compromise has been reached in the meantime, the notion of stewardship reveals that, as far as decision usefulness as the objective of accounting is concerned, the chasm between the USA and UK is deeper than between the UK and continental Europe. My interview with a former British IASB board member confirms this assessment:

> In chapter 1 [of the framework]—get off the ground—we have to agree what the financial statements are for. And some of us thought that stewardship was an important aspect of accounting, not just what the Americans call decision usefulness. Decision usefulness really means: Does it help you if you are an operator on a stock market to decide whether to buy and sell the shares, basically. Whereas in Europe in general, and in the UK certainly as well, there is this idea that the directors have a responsibility to the shareholders and the accounts of their statement of what they have done in the past—not just what they think they can do in the future—have they behaved properly, have they paid the money out to the right people? It connects to the use of tax purposes because that was why tax authorities thought that accounts were a good thing

to use because they were reliable audited records on what a company had done. (Author's interview with Whittington)

At the same time, it is quite evident that the stewardship approach would be misunderstood as taking the information needs of a wider range of stakeholders into consideration. Capital markets remain the focal point, the main difference being that the accountability of management is considered and decisions are not confined to resource allocation.

After a further round of revisions and comment letters, the principle of stewardship, labeled "accountability" in the new document, was incorporated in the conceptual framework. This resulted also from the fact that not just Board members but also representatives of the UK Accounting Standards Board (ASB) have become actively involved in the debate. European standard setters, together with EFRAG, have founded an interest group aimed at strengthening European initiatives. In June 2007, the ASB prepared a discussion paper on behalf of a new collaboration project among European standard-setting organizations called Pro-active Accounting Activities in Europe (PAAinE). The paper takes up again the numerous points of criticism advanced in the 179 comment letters and explains why management accountability should be included as a separate objective in the conceptual framework (PAAinE, 2007). The year before, PAAinE, in cooperation with the French Conseil National de al Comptabilité (CNC), had issued a discussion paper raising a number of basic questions regarding the nature of the framework.

A synopsis of the comment letters was presented to the Board on February 2, 2007 (IASB, 2007) and was discussed more extensively at the meeting on September 9, 2007. The audio documents of that board meeting underscore that the IASB members from the USA have great difficulty in accepting stewardship as an independent objective. Nevertheless, the FASB and the IASB continue to cooperate despite some differences:

> The two boards are in the process of completing work on their conceptual frameworks. There is not always uniformity in the views of each of the boards. For example, the concept of stewardship has greater support outside the US. The two boards are working through these issues to try to come up with a common approach. (Author's interview with Tweedie)

The debate on whether management accountability should play a prominent role in the conceptual framework underscores the shift in the underlying paradigm of transnational standardization. The continental European tradition of paying heed to the precautionary principle, protection of creditors, and the needs of other stakeholders has largely disappeared. Controversy over standardization revolves around issues that fall within the range of the Anglo-American paradigm as the widely accepted common denominator, even though it can hardly be considered homogenous (see Bush, 2005). The dispute about stewardship illustrates that the actors in the accounting field disagree about the concrete shape that capital market orientation should take. The object of debate is the role of management and how financial reporting can serve to appraise and control it.

In their activities, standard setters determine what kind of conception of an enterprise is embodied in accounting norms. Predominantly in the USA, the view of a firm is one of efficient resource allocation as the primary objective. The majority of the rest of the world argues in favor of giving equal importance to the objectives of decision usefulness and management accountability. The newly emerged alliance in Europe (PAAinE) and the long-standing ties to the Commonwealth countries have supported British accounting traditions as an alternative model to the US conception of a capital market centered on resource allocation. Although the latter remains uncontested within the USA, it is challenged almost everywhere else. In addition, the reputation of US accounting has taken a battering in the course of accounting scandals, the resulting regulatory efforts under the Sarbanes–Oxley Act, and the financial crisis.

## 4.3　CONCLUSION: CAPITAL MARKET-ORIENTED ACCOUNTING STANDARDS

In almost 40 years of its existence, the IASB has created an extensive body of rules. The standards and standards' interpretations currently in effect, along with the conceptual framework, make up the authoritative statements of international accounting. Over the years, what transnational standardization comprises has undergone substantial change; once a compilation of a variety of national rules, the body of standards has evolved into a strict set of requirements for capital market-oriented accounting, placing increasing significance on fair value accounting.

Contrary to the dominant rhetoric revolving around technical solutions, standard setting has always been far more than a technical endeavor. Political issues have permeated the IASB's efforts at standardization from the onset. Numerous interest groups seek to influence the contents of standards: Academics, preparers of financial statements, accountants, standard setters, regulatory agencies, and legislators attempt to feed their interests into the process in many ways. They engage in lobbying, draft comment letters and other written statements, make decisions concerning the application of standards, and enact laws. Controversy and dispute over the contents of IAS/IFRS is particularly frequent when veto power becomes concentrated. The latter is mostly in the hands of public supervisory and regulatory agencies, which decide on whether standards will be adopted. The European Commission has begun increasingly to assume such a role while the US Securities and Exchange Commission has actively filled that role during the past decades.

Consequently, the SEC has ensured that the rationale of capital market orientation has been inscribed into the standards. Once the course was set in the early 1990s, the international standards were gradually purged of elements reflecting other normative traditions, such as the principle of prudence, a sustainable long-term perspective, and the smoothing of earnings. From the onset, the SEC and other Anglo-American actors made acceptance of IASB standards conditional upon a specific mode of private standard setting that will be discussed in the following chapter. In their view, a private sector initiative that would ensure the primacy of market-oriented standards was the only acceptable approach. In the meantime, the fair value orientation of IAS/IFRS has certainly made the adoption of these standards in the USA much more probable.

The IASB's extensive cooperation with a wide variety of private and public actors has laid the groundwork for the widespread use of IAS/IFRS. They have been incorporated into national regulations in many countries, and companies use them in preparing accounts. At the same time, IASB standards are gaining importance for stock exchange listings or lending, which leads to network effects in disseminating IAS/IFRS.

The conceptual framework and the IASB standards now give priority to the information needs of capital providers over the needs of other stakeholders. Fair value accounting is essential for tailoring IAS/IFRS toward investors. Interestingly, the vague conception of decision usefulness does not impede the growing acceptance of the IASB's standards. Perhaps to the contrary, a high degree of ambiguity allows very different groups of actors to push for their interests—as long as they maintain a capital market orientation and rationalist patterns of "technical" decision making are respected.

In the debate about stewardship, another aspect of international standard setting surfaces, which the IASB largely fails to acknowledge: The need to adapt general rules to local conditions. Decision usefulness represents an objective that is sufficiently ambivalent to allow the development of global standards while at the same time leaving scope for local interpretation. The European case is an example of exhibiting autonomy in adopting IASB standards in the EU—even to the extent of potentially developing local standards and thus regionalizing standard setting. This illustrates the tension inherent in the task of specifying IAS/IFRS: While, on one hand, the process of tailoring standards to the particular needs of investors is on the advance, on the other hand they must be flexible enough for use across all different contexts if claims to global applicability are to be sustained. This also bears potential for future diversity: "The standards are part of a system of order that need not necessarily restrict the coexistence of different worlds for the systematic production of figures but can incorporate and even advance and strengthen them" (Mennicken and Heßling, 2007, p. 213—author's translation).

In the view of international standard setters, adapting IAS/IFRS to particular local conditions should not be problematic so long as their capital market orientation remains dominant. The general trend toward an increasing significance of financial indicators points in this direction. The more extensively the IASB incorporates fair value logic into its standards, the more likely it is that the dominant actors in international standard setting will have the main say in the future development of accounting requirements. General reference to the objective of efficient resource allocation allows Board members to pursue their activities in the name of the users of financial statements. Those users do not have to be actively involved in interest representation themselves. The IASB's scope is much larger when referring to an abstract definition of "user" derived from the rationalist patterns of reasoning found in economic literature. Chapter 6 examines the role of users as an interest group in IASB standard setting. Before we turn to this topic, I will first analyze the changes in the IASB's organizational composition.

## NOTES

1.  Since 1997, interpretations have been among the IASB's authoritative pronouncements. From 1997 to 2002, interpretations were issued by the Standing Interpretations Committee (SIC); since then, the International Financial Reporting Interpretations Committee (IFRIC) has been charged with this task. As of April 2010, the body has been called IFRS Interpretations Committee. The IFRIC's composition and responsibilities will be addressed in detail in Chapter 6.
2.  Officially, there were two revision projects. The "comparability project" was conducted from 1987 to 1990 with the goal of eliminating alternative accounting treatments (Cairns, 2001, p. 11). The "improvements project" (1990–1993) mainly focused on changes in format, "to ensure that they [IAS] were sufficiently detailed and complete and contained adequate disclosure requirements to meet the needs of capital markets and the international business community" (Cairns, 2001, p. 12).
3.  The standardization of financial instruments has been a key factor in advancing the debate on fair value since accounting based on historical costs is inappropriate in this area. The principle of fair value accounting, however, extends far beyond financial instruments.
4.  While the financial crisis unfolded, a response to the difficulties involved in the proper accounting treatment of derivatives was to relax regulations on the conditions under

which companies and banks could resort to internal calculations. The IASB was forced to relax its accounting rules once the FASB had granted companies greater scope for discretion in spring 2008 (see Nölke, 2009).

5. For a detailed account of the development of IAS 39, see Camfferman and Zeff, 2007, pp. 361ff.; Kirsch, 2007, pp. 313ff.; Walton, 2004b, pp. 13ff.; and www.iasplus.com/standard/ias39.htm.

6. So far, there is only insufficient documentation of the controversy between the EU and the IASB between 2002 and 2008. For this reason, I consulted the business press to complement the interviews conducted in 2007. The reconstruction of events in this section is based on an analysis of the English edition of *The Financial Times*. For the period from January 1, 2003 to April 1, 2008, the search term "IAS 39" yielded 310 articles, upon which the following account is based.

7. Among the EFRAG founding organizations are leading European business organizations: the Union of Industrial and Employers' Confederations of Europe (UNICE), European Round Table (ERT), European Federation of Accountants (FEE), Federation of European Securities Exchanges (FESE), European Federation of Financial Analysts Societies (EFFAS), European Insurance Association (CEA), European Banking Federation (FBE), European Savings Banks Group (ESBG), European Association of Co-operative Banks (EACB), European Association of Craft Small and Medium-sized Enterprises (UEAPME), European Federation of Accountants and Auditors (EFAA) (EFRAG, 2005, p. 20).

8. In the regulatory committee, the member states France, Spain, Italy, Belgium, and Portugal opposed the provisions. EFRAG was also divided on the issue and submitted an opinion to the EC weighing the pros and cons, but refrained from issuing a recommendation (EFRAG Endorsement, July 8, 2004). Of the eleven persons attending the EFRAG consultations, six opposed the provision, three of whom were French (Walton, 2004b, p. 6).

9. The following eight phases were decided upon: A. objectives and qualitative characteristics; B. elements and recognition; C. measurement; D. reporting entity; E. presentation and disclosure; F. purpose and status of the framework; G. application of the framework to not-for-profit entities; H. remaining issues, if any.

10. A total of 179 comments on the discussion paper were received. All comment letters can be accessed online on the IASB's homepage as part of the information concerning the Discussion Paper "Objectives and the qualitative characteristics" (Phase A) issued in July 2006: http://www.ifrs.org/IASCFCMS/Templates/Project/LetterList.aspx?NR MODE=Published&NRNODEGUID={A3EC74B1-0CA0-41DA-90F2-B6210F3930 DB}&NRORIGINALURL=%2fCurrent%2bProjects%2fIASB%2bProjects%2fConce ptual%2bFramework%2fDPJul06%2fComment%2bLetters%2fComment%2bLetters. htm&NRCACHEHINT=Guest (accessed June 7, 2011).

# 5.   Organizational characteristics of the International Accounting Standards Board

Developing and disseminating accounting standards form the core of the IASB's responsibilities. Use of IAS/IFRS must nevertheless be permitted by legislators, and private actors, such as stock exchanges or banks, have to recognize them for the standards to be effective. This situation affects the organizational structure of the IASB, which seeks to strike a balance between outside recognition and independent standard setting: On one hand, the organization relies on the support of political and administrative authorities as well as private actors and their willingness to cooperate. On the other hand, the IASB aims at conducting its standardization activities independently and, in the process, establishing itself as an autonomous standard setter not subject to any form of direct control.

The organization and procedures of standard setting are thus designed to promote the IASB's credibility and functionality. In this chapter, changes in IASB's organizational structure, funding, and the consultation procedures for standard setting will be described and analyzed. It will be shown how the IASB has developed to become a solution-oriented technical standard setter serving the needs of international capital markets and cooperating with practitioners in developing accounting standards for this purpose. Nonetheless, the organization analysis also demonstrates that the IASB's development has been subject to political influence from the very beginning and that its organizational structures and procedures cannot be accounted for in functional terms only. Recognition of the IASB as a legitimate standard setter has played an important role in organizational matters all along (see Tamm Hallström, 2004).

The empirical research is concerned with changes in the division of labor between oversight and decision making in standard setting, and the realignment of funding arrangements. Moreover, I will analyze the design and role of the consultation procedures employed in standard setting. The IASB constitution, first adopted in 2000 and subsequently revised in 2002, 2005, 2007, 2009, and 2010, provides the starting point.

# 5.1 CHANGES IN IASB'S ORGANIZATIONAL CONFIGURATION

The year 2001 marks an important turning point in IASB history. What was once a joint venture of national professional associations to develop voluntary standards became a foundation under US law aimed at developing a set of mandatory standards for global use. The IASC officially became the International Accounting Standards Committee Foundation (IASCF), and its board and secretariat, based in London, were put in charge of operations. The reform facilitated the transformation of a loose network of national association and business representatives into a professional, increasingly bureaucratic organization, which has put the task of standardization in the hands of a full-time staff of standard setters. In 2009, the IASB had 15 Board members, more than 110 employees, and an annual budget of roughly £20m sterling (IASCF-AR, 2009).

The organizational overhaul in 2000 resulted in the adoption of a structure modeled on the US Financial Accounting Standards Board (FASB). The FASB has long had considerable influence owing to the significance of the US capital market. In the wake of the amendments to the constitution in 2000, the IASB became an almost mirror image of the FASB. There, too, supervisory authority rests with the foundation, the trustees of which oversee the organization (Miller et al., 1998). FASB was established in 1973 after the former process of standard setting, which had exclusively been in the hands of the professional accountants' association, had come under attack. A lack of responsiveness to various interest groups in combination with a perception that standards for financial accounting too strongly reflected the influence of the companies using the standards prompted the Securities and Exchange Commission (SEC) to withdraw standard setting authority from the accountants' association and put the FASB in charge of standards development (see Mattli and Büthe, 2005 on FASB accountability).

The groundwork for the regulation of financial reporting in the USA was laid by the New Deal legislation in the 1930s. Since that time, the SEC has been responsible for regulating financial accounting, and it put the FASB in charge of standard setting in 1973. Accordingly, as a standard setting organization the FASB is formally subordinate to the SEC even though it operates as a foundation and its trustees represent various interest groups (in IASB terminology "constituencies"), such as companies preparing accounts, investors, and auditors. Although the FASB is free to make decisions on its organizational structure, ultimate political authority lies with the US Congress via the SEC, even though this has little significance in the day-to-day business of standard setting. Federal authority in matters of regulating financial accounting, deriving from competences over securities supervision and the principle of investor protection, is concentrated in the hands of the SEC. Those competences are entirely separate from matters of taxation, which mainly rest with the US states. In contrast to Germany or the UK, where the German Commercial Code or British company law respectively provide the legal framework for commercial activities, accounting standards for listed companies in the USA are the exclusive responsibility of the securities regulatory authority. Accordingly, the SEC and the FASB are oriented toward events on stock exchanges and make decisions with an eye to price formation in securities markets. Due to the federal distribution of power, in the first instance accounting standards in the USA are attuned to the needs of securities trading and protection of investor rights. This is rooted in a legal framework that is not specifically geared to shareholder needs but serves to regulate price formation on primary and secondary securities markets.

> The market pricing model of governance and financial reporting was intended to substitute the lack of shareholder rights in state law, as well as create a consistent framework for financial reporting. [. . .] The poor or non-existent reporting requirements of companies under highly protective and secretive state law, and weak rights of shareholders, were overlaid by one regulatory model. This was founded on a model of consistent financial reporting—not actually for shareholders as that was a protected state matter—but for those exchanging shares in secondary markets or for those subscribing to new share issues by companies. (Bush, 2005, p. 7)

Those US peculiarities have left their mark on transnational standard setting because of the SEC's major role in the International Organization of Securities Commissions (IOSCO). As Chapter 3 shows, the IASC's main goal in the 1990s was to gain recognition of IAS/IFRS by IOSCO. To this end, in the mid-1990s all organizational reform was postponed until an agreement with IOSCO on recognizing the standards was reached (Kirsch, 2007, p. 339).

### 5.1.1 The US Blueprint

The SEC made its approval of the constitutional reform in 2000 contingent upon the IASB adopting an organizational structure largely resembling FASB's organizational design. This was made a precondition for surrendering regulatory authority to a transnational body. In its daily operations, the IASB was to be independent of direct political influence. The Strategy Working Party (SWP) in charge of the IASC restructuring project faced the problem of having to deal with this precondition. In a first attempt, it proposed a compromise between a representative model, favored by the EU Commission, and the US expert-based model, which ultimately failed due to opposition from the SEC (Martinez-Diaz, 2005; Camfferman and Zeff, 2007). Some observers give a simplified account of the conflict as revolving around the question whether to install a one- or two-chamber system (see Kirsch, 2007). However, at the heart of the matter was the question of what the basis for the legitimacy of transnational standardization should be and the need to make a key strategic decision concerning the foundations upon which future standards development within the overall IASB framework should rest.

The European Commission (EC) preferred to put ultimate authority in matters of cross-border standards development in the hands of a body that would be independent of national standard setters thereby limiting Anglo-American influence. In its comment letter addressing the constitutional overhaul, the Commission wrote:

> [The] proposed structure is also quite close to the current structure of the US FASB (apart from the proposed IASC Board, the power of which would be greatly reduced). There are considerations applying to a potential global standard setter that do not apply to a national standard setter, for example international political legitimacy, and the IASC should not attempt to base its structure on any national model. For it to be trusted to safeguard the wider public interest, the IASC must be independent of, and be seen to be independent of, any one national standard setter or any group of national standards setters. (European Commission, 1999, p. 3)

By contrast, the SEC made it clear that it did not consider the dual structure compromise proposed by the SWP in 1998 an acceptable option. From its point of view, those in charge of standard setting should not be subject to any form of external control. The SEC stated in its comment letter:

> We strongly believe that the IASC should reject any proposal that does not grant the ultimate standard-setting authority to an independent decision making body consisting of expert standard-setters. The current SWP proposal [. . .] represents a mismatch between the IASC's objectives and pursuit of an efficient and effective structure for setting high-quality, internationally accepted accounting standards. (SEC, 1999, p. 6)

The SEC underscored its position by announcing that it would not recognize IAS/IFRS in the USA and would pursue alternative paths of cross-border standardization instead if its position were disregarded. It threatened to develop the informal working group comprised of the four Anglo-American standard setters (G4) into a global standard setter

(Camfferman and Zeff, 2007), which would draw on US GAAP as a foundation for cross-border standards. At the time, US GAAP was still considered to be the most demanding set of accounting rules although in the meantime the reputation of US standards has taken a severe battering in the wake of the accounting scandals involving Enron, Worldcom, and a number of other companies. Thus, the position adopted in the late 1990s aimed at establishing US GAAP as the global set of standards, would have had much lower prospects of success only shortly thereafter. Although there has been a tendency to attribute the accounting scandals to poor auditing instead of shortcomings in the rules as such, the rules-based US standards have nevertheless suffered from a loss of reputation.

Apart from questions relating to organizational design, the IASC reform was also characterized by the rivalry between different sets of standards. The EC, which had decided to support IAS early on, felt compelled to prevent the choice of US GAAP. To achieve that objective, the Commission was forced to make substantial concessions, giving the SEC considerable leverage in the 2000 constitutional reform.

### 5.1.2   The New IASB Structure in 2001

The transition from IASC to IASB was in the hands of the SWP, founded for this purpose in 1997, and the IASC Board. In March 2000, the IASC Board endorsed the constitutional amendments unanimously, and in May 2000, the International Federation of Accountants' (IFAC) general assembly also gave its approval for the restructuring proposal. Thereafter, a nomination committee began selecting trustees for the new foundation, who, in turn, were to appoint the members of the Board. The new organization commenced operations in spring 2001. In April, the first Board meeting was held in London under the chairmanship of Sir David Tweedie (for a detailed chronology of the transformation, see Camfferman and Zeff, 2007, pp. 447–99; and Kirsch, 2007, pp. 338–62).

Since that time, the IASB has been characterized by a two-tiered structure consisting of an oversight and a decision-making body. The oversight function rests with a group of trustees. They are responsible for the IASB's overall development, most notably for funding, selecting Board members, and representing the organization. The Board, on the other hand, has complete responsibility for preparing and issuing standards and other official releases—in the language of the IASB, this is referred to as responsibility in "technical" matters of standardization (IASCF, 2010, para. 37).[1]

The Board is the *locus* of IASB operations. The trustees are expressly bound to refrain from interference in the "technical" aspects of standardization (IASCF, 2010, para. 15e). As well as the Board and the trustees, the

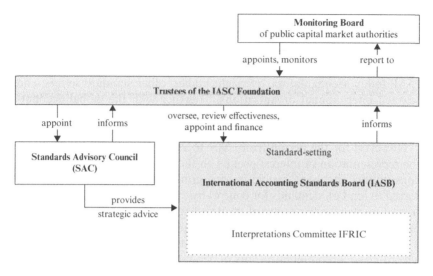

*Source:* IASCF, 2009, p. 2; tints are my own emphasis.

*Figure 5.1 IASB organizational structure, 2009*

constitution provides for an interpretations body charged with the task of specifying standards and preparing instructions for interpreting them, which must be submitted to the Board for final approval. The Standards Advisory Council (SAC) is the fourth body; its main task is to maintain liaison relationships with selected interest groups.[2] In 2009, a newly created Monitoring Board was set up to counter criticism questioning IASB's legitimacy. It is comprised of six members of national and international securities regulators. Given the Monitoring Board's short existence, it is not possible to assess its impact. However, its unclear mandate, its limited powers, and the requirement to reach all decisions by consensus (IASCF, 2010, para. 23) are conditions unlikely to allow the new body to play a significant and consequential role in IASB oversight. The most relevant competence will be to participate in appointing trustees, which is only an indirect means of improving accountability. The IASB's organizational structure as of late 2009 can be illustrated as above.

The illustration shows the overall structure of international standardization. The trustees and the IASB are at the heart of activities, but standard setting power rests exclusively with the Board; the Board makes all decisions in matters concerning the content of accounting standards. From 2012 onwards, at least 13 of the 16 members are to be employed on a full-time basis and are not permitted to maintain other commitments. The trustees are responsible for the organization as a whole, its funding, liaison activities, and the selection of Board members. In contrast to its predecessor, IASC, the IASB no longer maintains permanent contacts with national professional organizations. Of much greater significance to the IASB today are regulators, oversight bodies, other standard setters, and selected international organizations. Together with the global accounting firms, the national standard setters provide the bulk of the technical expertise outside of the IASB required in standard setting (Botzem, 2008).

However, for the period from 2001 to 2005, specific requirements for the representation of interest groups on the Board were laid down in the constitution. Involving certain interest groups based on statutory quotas served to fend off demands for control by the nation states. The introduction of quotas for the group of trustees and the Board was an important measure to ensure a smooth transformation from IASC to IASB. In 2000, a dual quota was adopted to ensure that the trustees were appointed according to a representative mix of geographic regions and professional backgrounds. Requirements were also determined defining the professional background of appointees to the Board. Those guidelines based the influence of various interest groups on formal foundations and marked the end of the influence of the national accountants' associations. In several places the constitution of 2001 makes express mention of constituency organizations that are to be involved. Among them are auditors, preparers and users of financial statements, and academics.

The board of trustees was initially composed of 19 persons, 5 of whom were to be nominated in consultation with the IFAC. One trustee each was to be appointed after consultation with international organizations of preparers, users, and academics. As regards the other 11 trustees, no criteria were defined regarding their professional backgrounds (IASCF, 2002, para. 7f.). Of the 14 IASB members, at least 5 were to have been practicing auditors, a minimum of 3 to have a background as users of financial statements, and at least 1 an academic background. The background of two other persons to be appointed remained unspecified (IASCF, 2002, para. 22). Unlike the trustees, it was explicitly stated that geographical origin was to play no role in selecting Board members.

However, another provision of the 2001 constitution extended special status to seven national standard setters, thus raising some questions as to the extent of the IASB's independence. Paragraph 23 of the constitution determined that seven of the twelve full-time members "will be expected to have formal liaison responsibilities with national standard-setters in order to promote the convergence of national [and international] accounting standards" (IASCF, 2002, para. 23). The constitution does not state which countries were to be considered; yet it is of little surprise that the seven standard setters on the Board represent the most important economies. Among them are the four Anglo-American standard setters that make up the Group of Four (standard setters from the USA, the UK, Canada, and Australia) as well as the national standard setters of Japan, Germany, and France.

In conclusion, we can identify four characteristic features of the transformation from the IASC to the IASB of 2001:

1. The organization is structured following the US model. The separation into an oversight and a decision-making body is modeled on the FASB, as is its legal design as a foundation under US law.
2. Including interest groups based on quotas both benefits private actors and strengthens the dominant position particularly of auditors among the group of trustees and on the Board.
3. A select group of national standard setters have managed to maintain their influential position via the special status that they were granted in proposing Board members.
4. The IASB is not accountable to any other entity—in this respect, it is in a different position to the FASB, which formally answers to the SEC. The trustees are not accountable to any superior body while the body is composed by coopting fellow members. Provisions to alter the mode of trustee appointment have since been introduced, including a nominating procedure now in coordination with the Monitoring Board.

The IASB's organizational structure in the period from 2001 to summer 2005 was primarily the outcome of an alliance of the SEC, national Anglo-American standard setters, and the Big Four. The alliance was able to establish an organization, the key features of which were modeled on the FASB, yet without any form of ultimate political or democratic accountability. The formal oversight function that once rested with the national professional associations was replaced by a group of trustees that answered only to itself. This arrangement has been changed only recently with the introduction of the Monitoring Board. The inclusion of certain interest groups, such as auditors, preparers and users of financial statements, and academics, is ensured via the constitution. The selection of individual Board members, however, rests with the board of trustees.

### 5.1.3 Abolishing Recruitment Requirements

The constitution must be reviewed at least every five years by the trustees, who appoint a Constitution Committee from their midst. To that end, they issue a set of questions and invite public comment from interested

| | |
|---|---|
| **November 2003** | Trustees issue consultation paper as the basis of the review process. Topics: |
| | • a future mandate to develop standards for small and medium-sized enterprises (SMEs) |
| | • composition of the trustee board |
| | • composition of the Board |
| | • changes in consultative arrangements (due process) |
| | • changes in the role of the Standards Advisory Council (SAC). |
| **by February 2004** | IASB receives 70 comment letters. |
| **May 2004** | The Constitution Committee identifies ten topics and issues "An update on the Constitution Review and information regarding public hearings". |
| **June–October 2004** | Four public hearings are held; 64 organizations either attend the meetings or submit comment letters: |
| | • New York, June 3, 2004 |
| | • Tokyo, July 13, 2004 |
| | • London, June 29, 2004 |
| | • Mexico City, October 6, 2004. |
| **November 2004** | Publication of "Review of the Constitution—Proposals for change." Topics resemble the paper of November 2003 and additionally include: |
| | • funding and the independence of funding arrangements |
| | • effectiveness of the interpretations body (IFRIC). |
| | Changes to the consultative procedure are postponed. |
| **by February 2005** | IASB receives 71 comment letters. |
| **June 2005** | Trustees follow the recommendations issued by the Constitution Committee and adopt the revised constitution. |
| **July 1, 2005** | Revised constitution is put in effect. |

*Source:* Author's illustration based on IASCF, 2004.

*Figure 5.2 Steps in the constitutional amendment process, 2003–05*

parties. The first constitutional review process was officially launched in November 2003 by publishing a 13-page document suggesting a list of issues for review. Interested parties were invited to submit comment letters by February 11, 2004. In a subsequent step, the committee charged with the constitutional review process developed cornerstones, which were subjected to debate in public hearings in summer 2004. This was followed up by a second consultation process, which involved the publication of another set of questions for comment. From the responses, the Constitution Committee derived a set of recommendations, which the trustees adopted in June 2005. After 19 months of consultations the revised constitution was put in effect on July 1, 2005. Figure 5.2 summarizes the steps leading up to the amendment of the constitution.

This synopsis shows that the trustees had a strong influence on the constitutional review process from the onset. They set the agenda and reviewed the responses provided in the comment letters. The first paper in particular had a strong formative influence. Most of its recommendations became part of the 2005 constitution. Only two topics were controversial, funding and the further development of the consultation procedure. Both are key factors affecting the IASB's credibility and both were postponed by the trustees to be addressed at a later date. They will be described in detail below.

Only a few modifications to the structure of the organization were implemented as a result of the constitutional reform of 2005. The trustees had already made it clear during the review process that they were in favor of retaining the IASB's basic approach:

> [T]he Trustees have concluded that the basic elements of the existing Constitution, first recommended by the former IASC's Strategy Working Party and then approved by IASC in 2000, have proved to be sound. However, some of the concerns raised by those parties responding to the possible approaches developed by the Constitution Committee, notably on the Trustees' oversight role, the composition of the Trustees and the IASB, and the IASB's operating procedures, are strongly held and warrant attention. The Trustees have considered and addressed those concerns in formulating their proposals. (IASCF, 2004, p. 6)

The result of the 2005 constitutional review was that the division of labor between the trustees and the Board was maintained and minor changes were made in the composition of the various bodies from 2005 on. Recruitment requirements for the trustee board were relaxed and those for the main Board completely abolished. This paved the way for the enhanced significance of "technical" expertise as a recruitment criterion (ultimately unspecified). Abolishing the recruitment requirements increased the autonomy of Board members since "technical" expertise became the sole criterion for membership. This gives the Anglo-American actors, who dominate the IASB, even more influence as they can more convincingly claim to have more of the necessary capital market expertise in their ranks than is possessed by many other actors.

The most striking difference between the 2001 and 2005 constitutions is the almost complete removal of formal quotas for specific interest groups. Instead of defining the composition of the bodies in detail, the goal has become to ensure balanced representation. The trustee board is only required to contain two members with practical auditing experience. Apart from that, only general criteria for the composition of the board of trustees are laid down: "The mix of Trustees shall broadly reflect the world's capital markets and a diversity of geographical and professional backgrounds. The Trustees shall be required to commit themselves formally to acting in the public interest in all matters" (IASCF, 2005, para. 6).

Similar provisions were adopted with regard to the Board. Instead of setting quotas for certain groups, the constitution states:

> The main qualifications for membership of the IASB shall be professional competence and practical experience. The Trustees shall select members of the IASB so that it will comprise a group of people representing, within that group, the best available combination of technical expertise and diversity of international business and market experience in order to contribute to the development of high quality, global accounting standards. (IASCF, 2005, para. 19)

Practical expertise and diversity become the key recruitment criteria while the constitution fails to specify precisely what qualities these terms are meant to indicate. Such imprecision strengthens the groups already represented in transnational standardization since it is left to them to determine the exact meaning of such unspecified terms. In practice, stressing "technical" expertise gives auditing professionals the opportunity to maintain their position even though professional associations do not play a significant role any more. And the position of individual experts is further reinforced by the removal of representation privileges initially granted to the seven national standard setters.

In February 2008, another routine constitutional revision was launched in accordance with the requirement to review the constitutional provisions every five years. The constitution was changed in several successive steps. The most relevant amendments were made to improve overall accountability by introducing the Monitoring Board, enlarging the IASB Board from 14 to 16 members, and increasing geographical diversity by introducing a fixed quota for members by geographical origin. Amongst other measures, additional consultation provisions were introduced, a commitment to the "principles-based" approach was codified, and the duration of a possible second term for Board members was reduced. Finally, the names of the Foundation, its operations, and its standards were streamlined (cf. IASplus, 2010; IASCF, 2010). From 2010 onward, the IASC Foundation became the IFRS Foundation. The interpretations committee and the advisory council were renamed the IFRS Interpretations Committee (IFRIC) and the IFRS Advisory Council, respectively. Only the Board kept its name: it remains the nucleus of transnational standard setting in accounting. Table 5.1 gives an overview of the changes in the IASB's structure over time. Most noteworthy are the changes in quota. Those adopted in 2001 were largely dropped, and unspecified "technical" expertise has become the key criterion for recruitment of the trustees and the Board. While geographical background has played a role in the composition of the trustee board in the past and continues to do so, such a provision was introduced to the Board for the first time in 2010.

*Table 5.1*   *Organizational structure of transnational standard setting*

|  | 2000 | 2001 | 2005 | 2010 |
|---|---|---|---|---|
| Organization | IASC | IASCF | IASCF | IFRS Foundation |
| Annual expenses (£ sterling) | 3.1m | 8.8m | 12m | 19m |
| Employees | 21 | 36 | 67 | 114 |
| Oversight body | IFAC | Trustees | Trustees | Trustees (advised by Monitoring Board) |
| Members | Formal decisions by IFAC | 19 | **22** | 22 |
| Recruitment principles | | Individual expertise | Individual expertise | Individual expertise |
| Composition | In practice, decisions largely determined by IASC | Quota: 5 IFAC, 3 interest groups, 11 unspecified Geographic quota: 6 Europe, 6 N. America, 4 Asia, 3 unspecified | 2 auditors, **no** other requirements Geographic quota: 6 Europe, 6 N. America, **6** Asia, **4** unspecified | 2 auditors, **no** other requirements Geographic quota: 6 Europe, 6 N. America, 6 Asia, **1 Africa, 1 S. America,** 2 unspecified |
| Term | Unlimited | 3 years, renewable once | 3 years, renewable once | 3 years, renewable once |
| Decision-making body | IASC Board | Board | Board | Board |
| Members | 16 delegations (56 individuals) | 14 | 14 | Up to 16 |
| Recruitment principles | Representatives of the national professional associations and other select interest groups | Individual recruitment, based on quotas for interest groups; representation of seven national standard setters | Individual recruitment, **no** interest group quotas; **no** representation of national standard setters | Individual recruitment |

*Table 5.1*    (continued)

|              | 2000 | 2001 | 2005 | 2010 |
|--------------|------|------|------|------|
| Composition  | 13 professional associations, 3 interest groups | 5 auditors, 3 preparers 3 users 1 academic, 2 unspecified | **No specific requirements** Mix of practical experience | **Geographic quotas:** 4 Europe, 4 N. America, 4 Asia, 1 Africa, 1 S. America, 2 unspecified |
| Term         | No limits | 5 years, renewable once | 5 years, renewable once | 5 years, **3 more years possible** |
| Voting rules | One vote per delegation | One vote per person | One vote per person | One vote per person |
| Majority     | 75% | 8 of 14 (57%) | **9** of 14 (64%) | 10 of 16 (62%) |

*Source:*    Author's illustration, major changes are indicated by bold text.

First of all, the table indicates a bureaucratization of transnational standard setting: Between 2000 and 2005, there was a continuous increase both in employees and in financial requirements. Both figures tripled over only five years. This development strengthened the IASB's operations branch, which is under the authority of the Board. However, it did not affect the division of labor between trustees and Board. It is notable that in both cases the quotas, which had just been introduced in 2000, were largely dropped. The move enhanced the autonomy of "technical" expertise, which was now hardly subject to any remaining restrictions. Although the trustees officially oversaw the Board, they lacked the authority to revise decisions in "technical" matters. The appointment of individual Board members could only be terminated on grounds of gross misconduct. The fact that the trustees, in turn, were not answerable to any other entity once they had been selected is a questionable arrangement in this division of labor between trustees and Board. The introduction of the Monitoring Board has not significantly altered this arrangement.

Moreover, a fourth objective was included in the 2005 constitution, which has so far been of no immediate significance but has extended the fundamentals of IASB's future operations. In addition to standards development, coherent standards application, and convergence of national standards, small and medium-sized enterprises (SMEs) were mentioned for the first time. This testifies to IASB aspirations to expand the scope of standards application to nonlisted companies as well. In accordance with the existing objectives, "the special needs of small and medium-sized entities and emerging economies" were to be taken into account (IASCF, 2005, para. 2c). The IASB thus gave itself the mandate to develop future standards for companies not listed on capital markets. Even if standards for SMEs are supposed to be less complex than IAS/IFRS, they still adhere to a rationale geared toward the information needs of capital markets (Nölke and Perry, 2007). Thus, the groundwork was laid for extending fair value to SMEs provided that no resistance arises. It is still too early to assess the impact of the latest (2009/2010) constitutional reform, but the changes, specifically the introduction of a formal geographical quota for Board membership, indicate that the IASB is eager to improve its accountability.

### 5.1.4 The Organization's Accountability Deficit

Formal oversight of the Board, which administers all standardization activities, rests with the trustees. For this reason, the composition of the board of trustees has increasingly come under attack. Whereas the Board's complete autonomy appears to be uncontroversial, the lack of clearly defined accountability for the trustees has been the target of criticism. Apart from geographical quotas, the only other requirements the trustees are bound by are a commitment to the public interest and a provision calling for regular reviews of the constitution. The constitution states that the trustees' accountability shall be ensured *inter alia* through: 1) a commitment made by each trustee to act in the public interest; 2) their commitment to report to and engage with the Monitoring Board; 3) their undertaking of a review of the entire structure of the whole organization every five years (IASCF, 2010, para. 17).

These and earlier, vaguely defined requirements have increasingly attracted criticism from political and private actors who, following the increasingly widespread use of ISA/IFRS, have higher expectations regarding the legitimacy of the organizational structure and procedures of standardization. Apart from the EC, which had pressed for more influence in the IASB early on, the European Parliament has also entered the debate on permitting the use of IAS/IFRS. A motion for a European Parliament resolution, authored by Alexander Radwan (a member of the European Parliament from the German Christian Social Union) in his capacity as *rapporteur*, points to the IASB's lack of credibility.

> Democratic legitimacy must ensure that the interests of all those affected are suitably represented and balanced in a transparent procedure using fair

rules. Up to now, these requirements are not adequately met in the system of the IASCF. The organisation's highest decision-making body, the Board of Trustees, shows particular shortcomings: the trustees are selected mainly on the basis of a criterion designed to ensure proportionate representation for the regions, so that no account is taken of other key interests (such as different sectors of the economy, forms of undertaking, the interests of employees and employers and, in particular, of political leaders). (Radwan, 2008, p. 14)

However, it is also the users of financial statements, such as investors and analysts, that have come to criticize the organization's lack of accountability. The Bruegel Institute,[3] a private think tank with ties to preparers and users, draws attention to the fact that the IASB's increased influence also attracts heightened demands for accountability:

> Only now is the IASB gradually discovering the full extent of the responsibility that its success has imposed upon it. [. . .] This means unprecedented political pressure. The IASB now needs to understand the interests of its various constituencies—multinational corporations, audit firms, investment banks, fund-management companies, various public authorities in the EU, China, the US and elsewhere, international organisations, central banks, and many others still. It needs, crucially, to strike the right balance between these interests, to fulfill its mandate and to ensure its own survival. (Véron, 2007, p. 35)

In contrast to the European actors, who demand a greater voice for state institutions, the users seek greater involvement of their own representatives. Véron, for instance, suggests reserving 40 percent of the trustee appointments for the users of financial statements. He underscores this reasoning by referring to the rhetoric employed by the IASB itself, which elevates those users—analysts and investors in particular—to the status of primary stakeholders (Véron, 2007, p. 50). A decision of that kind would most likely further increase the emphasis on fair value within the IASB and its standards.

Despite mounting criticism of the recruitment of trustees, the IASB has so far proven successful in fending off demands for greater control. Warnings of political influence have been the key to that strategy; they are justified on grounds of the need to secure a realm of freedom for "technical" expertise. In response to the criticism from Europe, Chairman Tweedie points out that the IASB's scope is not European but global:

> Europe remains an important stakeholder, given that it was Europe's decision to embrace international standards that provided encouragement for others to do the same. In general, we have a good relationship with the European institutions, including the Parliament and the Commission. The European Parliament among others expressed concern that the IASB lacked sufficient public accountability given that it is, in effect, setting law in over 100 countries. (Author's interview with Tweedie)

The underlying concern is that tolerating greater influence of political actors on the trustees might jeopardize the structure of the entire organization. In general, fear of political influence, which is equated with state influence, has a long tradition, especially in UK accounting. The anti-state impetus can be explained with reference to the sociology of professions where professional self-regulation is traditionally justified on the basis of "technical" requirements (see Macdonald, 1995; Sugarman, 1995). A similar view is encountered in works of political economy where different spheres of expertise are distinguished. Porter (2005) distinguishes between private, public, and technical authority and justifies that distinction on grounds of the IASB's effectiveness in matters of transnational standard setting. In the view of the dominant actors, this currently high level of functionality is the mainstay of the IASB's legitimacy. "Technical" experts make the best "technical" standards. Instead of representation and democratic participation, the IASB relies on the widespread recognition and use of IAS/IFRS as testimony to the quality of its standardization efforts, thus extending output-driven legitimacy to its work (see Scharpf, 2004). In this regard, the Monitoring Board is an attempt to square the circle: The IASB wants to react to its critics without making any substantial changes to its structure and by leaving "technical" decision making untouched.

In a nutshell, the IASB organization structure is best described as technocratic. The principles laid down in the 2001 statutory document to ensure the autonomy of a standardization process orchestrated by pre-defined interest groups were further refined in 2005 and 2009. The IASB continues to rely on a division of labor between trustees and Board that gives the latter utmost autonomy. The elimination of most quota requirements is another step in that direction. Nevertheless, the newly introduced regional quota for Board members is a new development, the consequences of which for standard setting are not yet clear. We can, however, expect the greater diversity on the Board to aid the global diffusion of standards.

The constitution secures an arrangement of autonomous Board members and trustees within a dual structure that largely evades any type of control. Only the Monitoring Board, which consists of regulatory agencies and oversight bodies at the national and international level, is given some formalized influence. However, its weak mandate and the need for consensus are likely to make it little more than a paper tiger. Real power arises from the interpretation of "technical" expertise and practical experience that secures the position of the dominant actors in transnational standard setting, first and foremost of auditing professionals.

The key component in this mode of technocracy is expertise, or more precisely, the power to define what is to be considered relevant expertise. Expert knowledge is an especially important means of securing the position of experts in the field of accounting (see Reed, 1996). In the IASB, the power to define relevant expertise rests with the standard setters themselves. At the same time, the IASB taps expert knowledge from the ranks of stock exchange operators, regulatory authorities, and preparers and users of financial statements through cooperation. The expertise required for transnational standard setting is thus to a much lesser degree in the hands of the national accounting professions, which to a large extent have been replaced by national standard setters, auditors, and the IASB as the bearers of expertise. Apart from organizational challenges and a lack of resources to build transnational structures, this is another factor explaining the associations' loss of influence. The large auditing firms, in contrast, have gained great importance. They have emerged as a *locus* of expertise—not least because of their role in defining what is considered relevant expertise in practice.

Calls for change are targeted at the greater influence of European actors and certain interest groups but do not question the IASB structure in principle. This may change once the first accounting scandals in the wake of the use of IAS/IFRS begin to surface, but even the financial crisis does not seem to have prompted a challenge to the IASB as a whole (Nölke, 2009). In spite of modest criticism (Véron, 2007; Radwan, 2008), the division of labor between trustees and Board is an arrangement that for the most part has gained the trust of the preparers of financial statements and national legislators. In essence, the privileged position of "technical" expertise is uncontested. Alternative modes of legitimation, such as democratic participation or greater legal regulation, play hardly any role and, if at all, are most likely to be discussed in the European Parliament.

Moreover, one also needs to bear in mind that the IASB is subject to a permanent process of organizational development. The aim is not to determine the final structure of the organization but to continuously adapt it. The provision requiring the statutory document to be reviewed every five years underscores the IASB's intent to reconsider its organizational composition and subject it to an ongoing process of development. The prominent role given the trustees in the process of constitutional reform at the same time serves to channel and control criticism and, in so doing, allows Anglo-American dominance to be maintained even after the latest constitutional revision.

During the statutory overhaul in 2005 there were, however, two issues of particular significance in the eyes of the trustees, which were postponed to a later date. The question of organizational funding and the role of consultative procedures were considered to be of major importance to the IASB and its credibility as a transnational standard setter. I will now turn to these two topics.

## 5.2 BROADENING THE FINANCIAL BASE

The nature of the IASB as a private organization is underlined by the fact that since 2001 it has mainly relied on voluntary contributions for funding. Initially, this funding arrangement was allowed to alleviate the financial constraints that had characterized the work of its predecessor organization. The IASC's 1999 budget was just above £2m sterling, 40 percent of which came from publications, approximately 25 percent from contributions, and about 30 percent from the membership fees of national professional associations (Kirsch, 2007, p. 378). In 1999, there were 16 employees, 6 of whom were responsible for accounting issues (Kirsch, 2007, p. 8). Since they were only able to handle part of the task, additional staff were seconded to the IASC by accounting firms and national standard setters (Camfferman and Zeff, 2007). The once-common procedure of assigning staff to the IASC strengthened the influence of the originating organizations. Professionalization of operations and financial autonomy were thus also objectives of the transformation of IASC to IASB. The increase in staff also required a considerable expansion of financial resources.

When the 2001 constitution came into force, the trustees were able to secure funding of about £12m sterling annually for the first five years based on voluntary contributions. The chairman of the trustees, Paul A. Volcker, who had been the Chairman of the US Federal Reserve between 1979 and 1987 and later worked for a number of banks and finance companies, managed to generate the major share of contributions made to the IASB. His successor, Tomasso Padoa-Schioppa from Italy, acknowledged Volcker's fundraising efforts during the early years of the IASB:

> With Paul Volcker I share only one thing, which is the past as a central banker. The difference is that Paul Volcker is a walking central bank himself. He can create money by just picking up the phone and asking donors to contribute to a good cause like the IASC Foundation. (Padoa-Schioppa, 2006, p. 2)

Industry contributions accounted for more than 80 percent of the IASB's funding from 2001 to 2005 and allowed the organization to demonstrate independence from state actors. Approximately 180 companies, contributing between US$100,000 and US$200,000 annually, provided the bulk of funding. The Big Four auditing firms, each providing US$1m annually, accounted for one-third of the budget (see IASCF–AR, 2002–05). The companies made those financial commitments for five years only, after which the financial base was to be realigned.

Initially, the question of funding was attached to the statutory reform since many of the comment letters received in winter 2003–04 raised the issue and urged greater transparency and an independent financial base. Although the trustees included the question of funding in a second round of invitations for comment, they suggested only marginal changes and postponed the solution of the problem (IASCF, 2004, p. 25). Instead of entering into a fundamental debate about the funding arrangement, the contribution-based system was extended for another two years. A total of roughly 280 companies and some central banks participated. The Big Four increased their contributions to US$1.5m each in 2005 and 2006 (IASCF–AR, 2006, 2007). Table 5.2 shows the development of IASB revenue in recent years.

After initial success in 2001, the trustees managed to obtain contributions of between £9m and £16m sterling in subsequent years as well. The organization covered an additional 10–20 percent of its budget needs through its own publications. Although broadening the financial base generated an increase of up to 16 percent in a few years, growth in revenue was matched by increased expenses, creating heightened pressure to set funding on more stable foundations. Table 5.3 illustrates the development of expenditure.

The IASB's largest single cost item is staff costs. These have risen steadily and, having reached £13.6m sterling in 2009, account for close to 70 percent of the IASB's total budget. Another 6.5 percent are costs incurred for office space. Comparison of revenue and expenditure shows an imbalance in 2004 for the first time, which was offset by surplus funds from previous periods.

In 2005, the trustees defined benchmarks for future funding in 2008 and beyond, thus responding to growing criticism, especially from Europe, of the short-term and insufficient funding arrangements that threatened to undermine the IASB's credibility (see ECOFIN, 2006, pp. 11ff.). The trustees suggested funding should be placed on a broader basis, to make financial contributions compulsory and open-ended, and to collect contributions on a country-specific basis (see IASB, 2008). These principles aim at protecting the IASB's autonomy and its independence of state actors and individual interest groups. From 2009 on, the newly established mode of funding was to come into effect and contain the role of special interests.

In 2009, the financial burden of approximately £16m sterling in contributions is distributed according to the economic potential of the participating countries. The USA supplied £1.85m, Japan £1.74m, Germany £1.24m, and the UK £800,000 (IASCF–AR, 2010). The specific financing mechanism varies from country to country. In the USA, about 30 companies and the US Federal Reserve Bank have provided contributions while in Germany 90 were willing to do so. In Japan, companies are involved in IASB funding while industrial associations play an important role

*Table 5.2  IASB revenue, 2000–2009*

| Revenue | 2000 | | 2001 | | 2002 | | 2003 | | 2004 | |
|---|---|---|---|---|---|---|---|---|---|---|
| | £m sterling | % | £m sterling | % | £m sterling | % | £m sterling | % | £m sterling | % |
| Contributions | 0.93 | 45.1 | 12.80 | 90.5 | 11.70 | 92.0 | 9.68 | 86.0 | 9.32 | 84.0 |
| Publications | 1.11 | 53.9 | 1.29 | 9.1 | 1.03 | 8.0 | 1.56 | 14.0 | 1.23 | 11.0 |
| Other | 0.02 | 1.0 | 0.06 | 0.0 | 0.02 | 0.0 | 0.02 | 0.0 | 0.50 | 5.0 |
| Total | 2.06 | 100.0 | 14.15 | 100.0 | 12.75 | 100.0 | 11.26 | 100.0 | 11.05 | 100.00 |
| Change to previous year | – | – | 12.10 | 588.3 | -1.45 | -10.2 | -1.47 | -11.5 | -0.21 | -1.9 |

| Revenue | 2005 | | 2006 | | 2007 | | 2008 | | 2009 | |
|---|---|---|---|---|---|---|---|---|---|---|
| | £m sterling | % | £m sterling | % | £m sterling | % | £m sterling | % | £m sterling | % |
| Contributions | 9.37 | 80.1 | 10.38 | 79.2 | 11.28 | 78.8 | 12.75 | 76.4 | 16.58 | 85.5 |
| Publications | 1.76 | 15.0 | 2.14 | 16.3 | 2.37 | 16.6 | 3.35 | 20.0 | 2.39 | 12.3 |
| Other | 0.57 | 4.9 | 0.59 | 4.5 | 0.66 | 4.6 | 0.59 | 3.6 | 0.41 | 2.1 |
| Total | 11.70 | 100.0 | 13.11 | 100.0 | 14.30 | 100.0 | 16.69 | 100.0 | 19.39 | 100.0 |
| Change to previous year | 0.65 | 5.9 | 1.41 | 12.1 | 1.19 | 9.1 | 2.38 | 16.7 | 2.70 | 16.2 |

*Source:*  Author's illustration, based on IASCF-AR, 2002–10, values may differ due to rounding.

*Table 5.3  IASB expenditure, 2000–2009*

| Expenditure | 2000 | | 2001 | | 2002 | | 2003 | | 2004 | |
|---|---|---|---|---|---|---|---|---|---|---|
| | £m sterling | % | £m sterling | % | £m sterling | % | £m sterling | % | £m sterling | % |
| Staff costs | 1.24 | 40.0 | 5.30 | 60.5 | 7.27 | 67.8 | 7.90 | 69.4 | 8.20 | 68.3 |
| Accommodation | 0.19 | 6.1 | 0.86 | 9.8 | 0.95 | 8.9 | 0.95 | 8.3 | 1.03 | 8.6 |
| Board costs | 0.31 | 10.0 | 0.69 | 7.9 | 0.85 | 7.9 | 0.85 | 7.5 | 0.81 | 6.8 |
| Trustees' costs | 0.36 | 11.6 | 0.41 | 4.7 | 0.49 | 4.6 | 0.49 | 4.3 | 0.65 | 5.4 |
| Other | 1.00 | 32.3 | 1.50 | 17.1 | 1.16 | 10.8 | 1.19 | 10.5 | 1.31 | 10.9 |
| Total | 3.10 | 100.0 | 8.76 | 100.0 | 10.72 | 100.0 | 11.38 | 100.0 | 12.00 | 100.0 |
| Change to previous year | – | – | 5.66 | 182.6 | 1.96 | 22.4 | 0.66 | 6.2 | 0.62 | 5.4 |

| Expenditure | 2005 | | 2006 | | 2007 | | 2008 | | 2009 | |
|---|---|---|---|---|---|---|---|---|---|---|
| | £m sterling | % | £m sterling | % | £m sterling | % | £m sterling | % | £m sterling | % |
| Staff costs | 8.31 | 69.1 | 9.20 | 68.0 | 9.74 | 67.1 | 10.98 | 68.0 | 13.61 | 69.1 |
| Accommodation | 0.98 | 8.2 | 1.24 | 9.2 | 1.32 | 9.1 | 1.30 | 8.1 | 1.29 | 6.5 |
| Board costs | 0.78 | 6.5 | 0.82 | 6.1 | 0.73 | 5.0 | 0.83 | 5.1 | 0.94 | 4.7 |
| Trustees' costs | 0.54 | 4.5 | 0.63 | 4.6 | 0.75 | 5.1 | 0.76 | 4.7 | 0.87 | 4.4 |
| Other | 1.41 | 11.7 | 1.64 | 12.1 | 1.99 | 13.7 | 2.28 | 14.1 | 3.00 | 15.2 |
| Total | 12.02 | 100.0 | 13.53 | 100.0 | 14.52 | 100.0 | 16.16 | 100.0 | 19.70 | 100.0 |
| Change to previous year | 0.02 | 0.2 | 1.51 | 12.6 | 0.99 | 7.3 | 1.64 | 11.3 | 3.54 | 21.9 |

*Source:*  Author's illustration, based on IASCF–AR, 2002–10.

114

as well. In the UK, and also in Italy and the Netherlands, the financial commitment agreed upon is collected via a levy on listed companies.

In spite of the expanded financial base, auditing firms continue to play a major role. The largest single contributions still come from the Big Four and these have even been on the rise, reaching US$2m annually. In addition, central banks and international organizations provide US$375,000 annually (see IASB, 2008). In conclusion, it can be noted that the IASB has made some efforts in the recent past to solve its funding problems and establish sustainable funding arrangements. Initially, certain individuals played a crucial role in the acquisition of funds, the chairman of the trustees, Paul Volcker, in particular. Although the financial base was eventually broadened, it still remained dependent on private actors. In the future, however, Europe has committed to providing more than €4 million annually directly from the European Commission to finance the IASB's further expansion (IASB, 2010) but also to increase the Commission's weight in transnational accounting standardization. However, this amount would still be less than what the Big Four contribute on a yearly basis.

In giving a green light for central banks to participate, state actors gave legitimacy to the IASB and acknowledged its activities while government representatives abstained from exercising direct influence.

Spreading the financial burden among a large number of companies while allotting the shares to be borne according to each country's economic potential is intended to reduce dependence on special interests. This is especially true for those countries that collect contributions via a levy on listed companies. The one remaining exception is the special influence of the Big Four, which continue to play a prominent role in funding. They account for a total of US$8 million, which continues to cover roughly one-third of the IASB's financial needs. This commitment not only documents their support of the IASB but also underscores their claim to a special role in the transnational standardization of financial accounting.

## 5.3 CONSULTATION AS CORE ELEMENT OF STANDARD SETTING

The IASB constitution not only defines the structure of the organization but also the process of standard setting. It provides that no standards or revision of standards may be adopted without a consultation process. The consultation procedure requires the publication of documents for public comment (see IASCF, 2010, para. 37b). It follows the US model in requiring a number of predefined steps of public participation. Adherence to due process is to ensure that the Board members familiarize themselves with the views of interested actors and that standards are in line with constitutional objectives.

Standards development proceeds along a sequence of designated steps centered on organizing communication with outside actors. In 2006 the trustees approved a formal *Due Process Handbook for the IASB* on which much of the following section is based (IASCF, 2006). The guidelines for due process derive from the IASB constitution and the preface to the IFRS. The procedure involves both mandatory and recommended elements. While the mandatory elements are compulsory, the recommended steps are subject to a comply-or-explain approach. The Board is required to state reasons whenever it decides to omit recommended steps.

The mandatory steps the Board is required to follow in compliance with due process are a) developing a technical agenda, b) preparing and issuing standards and exposure drafts, which should include any dissenting opinions, c) establishing procedures for reviewing the comment letters that are submitted, d) consulting the SAC on key issues, and e) publishing recommendations and conclusions with standards and exposure drafts. The recommended but nonmandatory steps include f) publishing discussion papers at the beginning of the consultation process, g) establishing working groups or other types of specialist advisory group, h) holding public hearings, and i) undertaking field tests to assess individual provisions on a trial basis (IASCF, 2006, p. 15).

Amendments to the consultative arrangements were initially discussed with reference to the first round of comment letters submitted in the course of the constitutional review process in winter 2003–04. In spite of calls to specify the individual steps of the standard setting process in greater detail, the trustees decided against provisions that might substantially limit the Board's discretion and merely recommended some minor changes in wording instead (IASCF, 2004, p. 35). In the trustees' view, the consultation process primarily serves to facilitate the Board's discussions and standardization activities.

> The IASB is tackling difficult conceptual issues on which there is little or no consensus. Some of the more challenging topics already on the IASB's agenda include insurance accounting, leasing, pensions and financial instruments. Reaching a common international standard on these and other topics will not be easy. Therefore, the Constitution Review has highlighted the need to reinforce the IASB's consultation process in order to engage fully those affected by standard-setting and to evaluate the many options in an even-handed manner. (IASCF, 2004, p. 6)

In the course of the review process, the trustees decided to postpone changes to the consultation process, to be handled separately at a later point in time. In 2006, they assembled a handbook containing a comprehensive set of guidelines on due process (IASCF, 2006). The underlying principles were derived from the constitution, the preface to IFRS, and from previous comment letters addressing issues of due process.

### 5.3.1   The Formalized "Due Process"

The consultation procedure comprises six steps oriented toward the following five principles: transparency, accessibility, extensive consultation, responsiveness, and accountability (IASCF, 2006, p. 4). The purpose of consultations is to provide the Board with a comprehensive overview of the issues involved in standard setting.

> [T]he IASB has full discretion in developing and pursuing its technical agenda and in organising the conduct of its work. In order to gain a wide range of views from interested parties throughout all stages of a project's development, the Trustees and the IASB have established consultative procedures to govern the standard-setting process. [. . .] The IASB uses many steps in its consultation process to gain a better understanding of different accounting alternatives and the potential impact of proposals on affected parties. (IASCF, 2006, p. 3)

The primary goal of the due process is not participation but to provide the Board with an instrument for collecting information on issues relevant to standard setting. The Board has full decision-making authority. The consultation procedure provides a channel of communication with the interested public. Opinion formation takes place in the course of presentations, discussions, at road shows, and at meetings with national standard setters and other organizations. Standards development nonetheless requires that the protagonists adhere to the six stages defined in the handbook. The IASB staff assist the Board by preparing documents and performing other preliminary tasks. The Board instructs the IASB staff, which largely carry out the assigned tasks independently. They prepare synopses of current research and expert opinions and lay the groundwork for the discussions informing Board decisions. In so doing, the staff influence the course and outcome of the debates of the Board.

The approach pursued in standards development emphasizes transparency of IASB operations. However, Table 5.4 also shows that the full-time staff play a crucial role in standards development. They draft documents for discussion by the Board, analyze comment letters, and again prepare summaries for discussion. The details of how the staff go about performing those tasks remain hidden from outside view.

Although the operating procedures to be observed in standards development are spelled out in great detail, a number of questions remain: It

*Table 5.4   The six stages of the consultation procedure*

| Stages | Staff responsibilities |
| --- | --- |
| *Stage 1: Setting the agenda* (preparing procedures) | |
| Identification of new issues | Staff makes |
| Assessment of the relevance of potential projects | preparations and |
| Consultations with other IASB bodies | recommendations |
| Adding an item to the agenda is decided by simple majority | |
| | |
| *Stage 2: Project planning* (preparation of consultations) | |
| Decision is made whether to conduct project alone or     jointly with another standard setter | Director of Technical Activities |
| Consideration whether to establish working groups | deploys staff |
| IASB Director of Technical Activities selects a project team | |
| | |
| *Stage 3: Publication of a discussion paper (may be omitted)* (initial round of public comment) | |
| Preparation of discussion papers (DPs) | Staff prepares |
| DP reflects staff's assessment, outlines subject matter,     and presents the Board's preliminary view | discussion papers and advises the |
| Board discusses DPs in public meetings and decides     on publication | Board; analysis and summary of |
| DPs are published to invite public comment; comment     period is usually 120 days | comment letters |
| Staff analyzes and summarizes the comment letters     for the IASB's consideration | |
| | |
| *Stage 4: Publication of an exposure draft* (mandatory round of public comment) | |
| The Board, supported by staff, SAC, and other     organizations, develops exposure drafts (EDs) | Staff draws up ED; analysis and |
| The Board discusses EDs and sets out specific proposals | summary of |
| EDs are published to invite public comment; comment     period is usually 120 days | comment letters |
| The staff analyzes and summarizes the comment letters for     consideration | |
| | |
| *Stage 5: Development and publication of a standard* (consultations and balloting) | |
| Decisions on standard setting are considered in     public meetings | Staff makes proposals and takes |
| Staff drafts IFRS | the vote |
| The standard is subject to review by the interpretations     committee (IFRIC) | |
| The near-final draft is posted online     (limited access for paying subscribers only) | |
| After consultation is completed, staff circulates     the balloting package to the Board members individually | |

*Table 5.4*   (continued)

| Stages | Staff responsibilities |
|---|---|
| *Stage 6: Procedures after a standard is issued* (follow-up) | |
| After standards are issued, unanticipated issues related to practical implementation and potential impact are to be considered | Staff has no defined role |
| The Board may review decisions at any time | |

*Source:*   Author's illustration, based on IASCF, 2006.

is not clear when issues are removed from the agenda, what projects are conducted jointly with national standard setters and how they are organized, how staff treat dissenting comment letters, and what criteria are used in determining that deliberations have been exhaustive and it is time to take the vote. It is further unclear why balloting does not take place during Board meetings but under the aegis of the IASB staff in written form (IASCF, 2006, p. 12).

Like the treatment of minority opinions in the legal domain, any dissenting opinions of Board members are included in the exposure draft. We cannot rule out that this practice might pose an additional impediment to dissent and keep Board members from voting against a ballot draft for fear of their opposition being exposed and possibly becoming a target of debate. Moreover, a collective mindset is fostered that encourages conformity in thinking and reasoning (see Janis, 1972).

The heuristics employed by the Board in decision-making practice favor an incremental evolution of IAS/IFRS. IASB Chairman Tweedie explains that Board members should only consent to a new or changed standard where the proposed standard represents a superior solution to the status quo. Voting practices are such that the Board only rarely decides against proposals that have undergone extensive preparation and consultation, even when they fail to offer fully satisfying solutions:

> When Board members vote, they are asked to consider if the new standard represents an improvement over the previous one. Board members should vote against only if they feel that the existing standard is superior. When 80 percent of a proposed standard is improvement and 20 percent isn't, it has to be balanced. Is it worth having the 20 to get the 80? (Author's interview with Tweedie)

Although the detailed guidelines require a comprehensive consultation process in which the IASB's full-time staff are hardly mentioned, the organization's personnel play a major role in standards development. Not

only the structure of the organization but also the consultative arrangements are clearly aligned with the principle of "technical" expertise, which
is additionally legitimized through the consultation procedures.

### 5.3.2   Legitimizing IASB through Consultation

Although in principle the consultation process is open to all parties,
private organizations are the main participants. In addition, regulatory
agencies and sometimes individuals send in comment letters stating their
opinion on IASB discussion papers or exposure drafts published by the
organization in preparation for issuing a standard or other authoritative
statements.

> Undoubtedly it [the due process] is a valuable tool. You have to have a process
> by which you develop the standards. I guess on one extreme you could have
> someone sitting in private writing a standard and then issuing it without
> consulting anybody. That would probably not win a lot of support for the
> standards. It may be possible to do that if everything is happening through
> the government [ . . . ] But it's not likely to happen in the private sector where
> you've got to win support for what is going to come out. (Author's interview
> with David Cairns, former IASC Secretary-General and now a consultant)

A similar assessment is found in accounting literature, where some
authors stress the opportunities for interested actors to exert influence in
addition to the legitimation function:

> The design of the formal [consultation] procedure thus testifies to the IASB's
> efforts at involving, as far as possible, all groups interested in matters of
> accounting in IFRS development. Those groups are given the opportunity
> to exercise immediate influence either by participating in the Standards
> Advisory Council or by writing comment letters in response to the discus-
> sion papers or exposure drafts. (Pellens et al., 2004, p. 85—translated from
> German)

Conversely, the IASB protagonists have a less positive view of the
due process. Whittington, who sat on the Board from 2001 to 2006,
expresses skepticism about the possibility of influencing standard setting
via comment letters. Since the Board thoroughly debates the respective
issues in advance of the consultation process, the comment letters rarely
provide additional insight, in his opinion. Often the process of exploring the subject matter for new knowledge to further advance standards
development has already been completed at that point. Moreover, the due
process is frequently misunderstood as a participatory procedure. From
the Board's perspective, which is perfectly in line with the organization's

constitution, the purpose of the due process is to improve knowledge even though that objective is not easily accomplished.

> At that [rather late] stage you are pretty clear in your ideas and you have taken a lot of evidence already and it would be in some ways surprising if some startling new evidence available emerged that would make you change your mind [. . .]. When we were taking comment letters, we were seeking evidence. We weren't doing an opinion poll. It wasn't a Gallup poll. We weren't saying 51 percent of the constituency think that what we were doing on business combination is wrong so we shouldn't do it. It is not a general election. We don't set standards that way. We make the judgement, but we do it on the basis of evidence. So when the Board says no new ideas were advanced, that is often true. [. . .] I can see the frustration people have when they have written a carefully argued comment letter but [it] is often an argument that has been rehearsed before. (Author's interview with Whittington)

This perception of the due process underscores the Board's claim to be able to make what it considers to be the "technically" most appropriate decision on its own. Contrary to the technocratic bias implied in this perception, standard setting is by no means nonpolitical. We can safely assume that actors engage in lobbying and strive to ensure that their interests are given due regard in standards development. However, this does not necessarily take place via the formalized and transparent channels provided by the consultation procedure; rather, the toehold for such influence is contacts with individual Board members. Thus, the Board has laid down the rule that no more than five members shall attend an event together, otherwise it will be considered a Board meeting, which is required to be held in public.

The formalized consultation process tends to underestimate the role the staff play in standard setting. In fact, the IASB staff, who assist the Board and are familiar with details of the subject matter, play a major part. IASB Chairman Tweedie stresses their independence:

> The IASB is fortunate to have highly skilled and capable technical staff. The staff do the research and draft the standards for consideration by the Board. In the past there has been some criticism that the IASB has not consulted widely enough in developing new standards. [. . .] Some of this criticism reflects a need to make hard choices that will rarely be universally popular. However, we have significantly upgraded our outreach and communications activities to make sure the views of many are taken into consideration while we are developing new standards. (Author's interview with Tweedie)

The staff's high level of expertise and close cooperation with the decision makers make the IASB employees an important factor in transnational standard setting—albeit one that has received little attention so far.

However, their growing significance and the related process of supplanting academic expertise is increasingly coming to attention and being criticized:

> The discussion papers prepared by the private accounting bodies are replacing academic scrutiny. Scholarship's retreat from this terrain is increasingly perceived as inappropriate, both domestically and internationally, in the light of the urgent problems of financial reporting, the satisfactory illumination of which would require the use of scientific methods. (Wüstemann and Kierzek, 2007b, p. 4—author's translation)

The IASB staff's influence extends beyond the boundaries of the organization. Their working style, resembling the academic exchange of arguments, promotes the concentration of expertise within the organization. This entails a shift in interpretative power in favor of the IASB, further strengthening its autonomy and influence. The IASB has become a *locus* of knowledge production in its own right and—due to its prominent position—the leading global standard setter in the field of accounting. Since the consultation process cannot be expected to provide substantial insights on "technical" issues, this suggests the conclusion that the primary purpose of the due process is to be found in the legitimation of private standard setting. Instead of bringing in external opinions, the due process allows the IASB to disseminate its view on how to regulate certain issues by acquainting the general public and special interest groups with its line of reasoning. In addition, we can expect traditional lobbying to take place outside of the formal consultation process.

At the same time, we can observe a spread of consultation procedures in general. The use of the due process originally applied by the FASB and later adopted and further refined by the IASB is also spreading. Consultation procedures modeled on those used by the IASB are found at the national and European level as well. The British Accounting Standards Board employs them as does the Accounting Standards Committee of Germany (ASBG). They also play a role at the European level. For instance, the European Financial Reporting Advisory Group (EFRAG), a private organization recognized by the EC, also invites public comment on discussion papers issued as part of its own due process. However, interested parties must command considerable resources and expertise to be able to participate across the whole range of procedures.

Since national standard setters also publish the IASB discussion papers and exposure drafts and invite public comment aimed at developing a national position, this not only provides additional opportunities for exercising influence but also creates a participatory landscape that is difficult to follow. Small businesses have particular difficulty in identifying the institution potentially most responsive to their interests. However, it is not just small businesses that face difficulties: The situation poses a challenge to associations as well. Participation in all of the consultation procedures is even a burden to the large UK accountancy association ICAEW. A member of the ICAEW staff described the amount of work involved for the organization in the case of standards for small and medium-sized companies as follows:

> Like the IFRS for SMEs which is taking place at the moment, we will establish working parties that will review those accounting standards and we are actually doing one response to the ASB, we'll do another response to the IASB and then probably also do a response to EFRAG, because they also have a view in terms of what they think about that standard. So there is quite a lot of consultation, quite a lot of responses to that consultation. (Author's interview with Marianne Mau, staff member, ICAEW)

An overall appraisal of the consultation procedures reaches a mixed verdict. Although they are an indispensable part of standard setting, they are of little actual relevance in the development of the concrete content of the standards. Instead, they serve to protect IASB credibility by providing a platform for communication with third parties. For the IASB, the due process is not so much the instrument for collecting information that it claims to be as a channel for informing interested parties about its preferred solutions to accounting issues. In the process, the IASB also benefits from other standard setters feeding their proposals into the discussion as well. This replication of consultative arrangements at the national and European level serves as a crucial reinforcement mechanism that not only leads to multiplication of procedures but also contributes to establishing the IASB as the uncontested authority in the field of transnational standardization.

## 5.4 CONCLUSION: EXPERT-BASED SELF-REGULATION WITHOUT ACCOUNTABILITY

The IASB is closely modeled on the US example in terms both of organizational structure and of the procedures employed in standard setting. This resemblance was the prerequisite for the SEC to consider surrendering responsibilities in the field of standard setting. Even so, the actors that dominated the IASC and were put in charge of the constitutional review process in 2000 secured the positions of the various interest groups by installing quotas and granting influence to a select group of national standard setters. The provisions to that end can be interpreted as a substitute for sovereign oversight. In contrast to the FASB, which answers to the

SEC and thus ultimately to the US Congress, there is no such oversight of the IASB. The Board is accountable to its trustees only, for the appointment of whom the criteria have been changed yet still remain insufficient in the eyes of many critics.

The constitution review of 2005 reaffirmed the division of labor between oversight and decision-making bodies and enhanced the Board's autonomy. Shortly thereafter, the trustees successfully broadened the IASB's financial base although the moves made have not affected the key role that the Big Four continue to play in funding the organization. Apart from other standard setting organizations, the auditing firms are the only actors that command a high level of expertise. For the IASB, they represent an important reference point in "technical" matters. In the meantime, the Big Four have all established "technical" offices in London, and their level of involvement in consultation procedures exceeds that of any other group (Perry and Nölke, 2005). The large auditing firms are important consultants to the IASB and have direct influence on standards development due to their material and nonmaterial resources—especially their expertise, which is considered highly relevant.

In case of the IASB, the national—particularly Anglo-American—roots are a major factor. In recent years, however, the institutionalized cord linking it to the national professional associations has been almost completely cut. Instead, the IASB has sought cooperation with national standard setters and regulators and has discovered their usefulness as "channels of communication" since they disseminate the Board's ideas through their own consultation procedures. With the exception of the FASB, which occupies a special status, the relationship between the IASB and the national standard setters can be described as one of cooptation. The national–international tandem structure in standard setting has mainly evolved from the top down. Professionalization and bureaucratization of the IASB, with its annual budget of approximately £20m sterling, have been important factors in the process. The organization not only utilizes outside know-how but also provides "technical" expertise of its own by way of its staff.

In principle, the current IASB structure is of course also subject to future constitutional reviews. Yet, since the trustees remain in charge of preparing and structuring the review process, few surprises should be expected. The appointment of the trustees has attracted much criticism, which has been countered by establishing the Monitoring Board and increasing the size of the Board from 14 to 16 members to represent a broader range of interests. These measures can be expected to further increase the Board's autonomy. In spite of establishing the Monitoring Board to coordinate the selection of trustees, it seems unlikely that any form of effective outside control of standard setting will be instituted. The worldwide dissemination of participatory procedures certainly increases the chances of influencing standard setting in principle. Yet, since such activities are quite demanding and also taxing in terms of the resources required, the odds are that the opportunities for involvement will not be seized. The IASB's main concern is ensuring transparency not participation. And this will not change as long as the Board employs its due process procedures for generating information and above all for legitimation purposes. Recent attempts at amending those procedures to include social and environmental sustainability issues are likely to remain futile endeavors for some time to come (see Gallhofer and Haslam, 2007).

Summing up, the fact that both the IASB's organizational structure and its consultation procedures have their roots in the USA catches the eye. At the early stage, the IASB was modeled on the US standard setter FASB, but it has shown the ability to adapt. In recent years, the organization has evolved incrementally but has maintained a high level of continuity in its basic principles. This is evidenced by the appointments to the Board and other bodies of the organization analyzed in more detail in the next chapter.

## NOTES

1. Reference to the notion of "technical" matters is set in quotation marks to indicate that, contrary to usage in IASB documents and the opinions voiced by some of the protagonists in the course of the interviews, the standardization process cannot be exhaustively accounted for in terms of rational, unambiguous, or technically necessary decisions. As I have argued in the introduction, accounting standards are a product of social and political negotiations. Accordingly, decisions reflect actor interests and acts of bringing influence to bear. Casting this process in technical terms indicates an understanding of standardization predicated on Anglo-American premises that emphasize the apolitical nature of transnational standardization.
2. The membership of the various organizational bodies will be addressed in detail in Chapter 6.
3. As the self-portrayal of the institute states, "Bruegel is a European think tank devoted to international economics. It [. . .] is supported by European governments and international corporations. Bruegel seeks to contribute to the quality of economic policy-making in Europe through open, fact-based and policy-relevant research, analysis and discussion" (Véron, 2007, p. 71) The author, Nicolas Véron, has ties to the International Corporate Governance Network, an interest group representing financial investors. In addition, he is also a consultant to the Association of French Asset Managers and the Association of French Insurers (Véron, 2007, p. 4).

# 6. The role of individuals and organizations in transnational standard setting

The individual actors and organizations involved in international standard setting have a crucial impact on the process. They participate actively in the IASB's various bodies in order to influence both standard setting and the development of the IASB's organizational structure. For the most part, these actors are affiliated either with the preparers of financial statements, with the accounting profession, or with the users of financial statements, such as financial analysts or investors who base investment decisions on those statements. In addition, there are other groups that get involved in the process, for instance by submitting comment letters, issuing position papers, or requesting information. Among them are academics, public agencies, regulatory authorities, national standard setters, and professional associations. In this chapter, I will analyze the influence of individual persons and key organizations on international standard setting.

The analysis of the role of individual and collective actors follows the IASB's organizational design and is divided into two main parts: The first addresses the composition of the Board as the IASB's main decision-making body while the second is devoted to the organizations participating in the other IASB bodies. The study's structure thus matches the IASB's two-tiered structure, as laid down in its constitution, consisting of the Board, on one hand, and the set of complementary oversight, advisory, and interpretations bodies, on the other. The empirical findings confirm the division of labor between the Board as the *locus* of authority in matters of "technical" decision-making and the other bodies that perform advisory functions and, serving as a buffer, shield the Board from outside demands. At the same time the other organizational bodies are expected to influence the long-term course to be followed in matters of transnational standard setting. The investigation of the Board will focus on its individual members whereas in the analyses of the other bodies attention will be directed to the influence of organizations. Both strands of the analysis underline that the interest groups representing accounting professionals have a major influence on the IASB: Auditors make up the large majority of Board members while the Big Four dominate the network of organizations involved in its operations. Moreover, it will be shown that investors and financial analysts are much less prominently represented than today's dominant rhetoric of decision usefulness would have us believe.

The following analysis will demonstrate that, over the years, the trustees have pursued a Board appointment practice that has cemented this closure of the decision-making body to outside influence. The Board has been marked by a homogeneous and stable composition of membership while the other bodies have experienced much greater fluctuation.

## 6.1 THE CENTER OF DECISION-MAKING: THE BOARD

Prior to the 2000 constitutional review, all the main decisions were made by the IASC Board, which was appointed in line with geographic origin. This was a suitable arrangement in the early days. National professional associations ensured the integration of divergent interests, provided funding, and promoted the dissemination of IAS. In the mid-1990s, the decentralized structure ran into severe problems. Most notably, the development of precise standards proved difficult since a growing number of participants having different status were involved in the debates while formal decision making rested with the delegations of the national associations only (Tamm Hallström, 2004; Kirsch, 2007). The gap between voting and speaking rights led to protracted consultations and the unequal treatment of IASC Board members cast shadows of doubt on the legitimacy of standard setting. Before 2000, the constitution laid down that the delegations may consist of two delegates and a technical assistant. Each delegation was entitled to cast a single, collective vote, which led to each delegation developing its own voting rules. Where differences of opinion arose, some delegations abstained from voting while others voted for the option favored by the majority of their members. The situation was further complicated in the 1990s by the admission of observers who were granted speaking but not voting rights. This mostly involved the representatives of the regulatory agencies in charge of recognizing the IAS. By the end of the 1990s, the Board comprised 16 delegations with voting rights and up to 60 individuals participating in the consultations. Figure 6.1 gives an overview of the number of members on the IASB decision-making bodies since the organization's inception.

This illustration shows the increase in the number of individuals sitting on the IASC Board. The number almost tripled over a span of close to 30 years. Elected representatives, the delegations' technical advisers, and observers

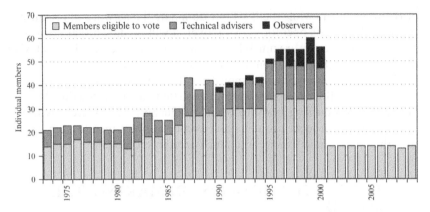

*Source:* Author's illustration, based on Camfferman and Zeff, 2007, pp. 506ff.; IASC, 1987–2000; IASCF–AR, 2002–10.

*Figure 6.1*    *Number of Board members for the IASC and the IASB, 1973–2009*

accounted for the increase. From the late 1980s, the number of advisers grew steadily, and observers began to attend the meetings for the first time in 1990. The reasons for this development lie in efforts to advance the specification of IAS and the involvement of interest groups deemed instrumental in winning political recognition for the IASB. The year 2001 marked a turning point. The new Board was a standard setting body of a manageable size with wide-ranging authority. The following aspects characterize the composition of the former board in the period between 1973 and 2000:

1.  *Professional background of its members:* The majority of its members were drawn from either the accountancy profession, representatives of companies or associations, or academia, and most were seconded by their employers.
2.  *Composition of the delegations:* In addition to the 13 delegations from the national professional associations, 3 of the interest groups coopted onto the Board were also granted voting rights (the International Coordinating Committee of Financial Analysts' Associations in 1986; the Federation of Swiss Holding Companies in 1995; and the International Association of Financial Executives Institutes in 1996). They were accorded the same status as the professional accountancy associations. The inclusion of interest groups is already a first step toward abandoning the principle of geographic representation.
3.  *Dominance of the auditing profession:* Auditors were the most

important interest group represented in transnational standard setting during the entire period. Their organizational affiliation varied by national origin: In the early years of the IASC, auditors from continental European countries, especially Germany, Italy, and France, were often partners in small accounting firms. This changed with the increase in concentration within the auditing market. In the wake of the mergers of the 1980s and 1990s, most auditors involved in the IASC were employees and partners of the major accounting firms.

4.  *Representation of developing countries:* All of the representatives from developing or newly industrializing countries who participated in the IASC as delegates of their national professional associations (Mexico, South Africa, and Nigeria) were employed by Western corporations or the major accounting firms.

5.  *Observers:* Starting 1990, national institutions that played a crucial role in the legal recognition of IAS began to be coopted onto the Board as observers who were given the right to speak but were not eligible to vote. The US standard setter FASB and the European Commission (both 1990), the People's Republic of China (1995), and IOSCO (1996) were all granted observer status.

Before 2001 the composition of the Board manifested the organization's attempt to secure the participation of a wide range of actors in standard setting. In this way, it sought to advance standard setting and began increasingly to tailor international accounting standards to the information needs of capital market actors. At the same time, it aimed to involve state institutions to ensure the dissemination and legal recognition of IAS. The Board strategy also led to its coopting selected private interest groups, national standard setters, the EC, the FASB, and IOSCO. The IASC Board, responsible for making all major decisions, was complemented by additional consultation and advisory bodies in order to provide channels for discussions with other interest groups. The Consultative Group was created in 1981 and the Advisory Body in 1994 (see Camfferman and Zeff, 2007).

In September 1996, the IASC Board decided to appoint a working group charged with reviewing the IASC's organizational structure once an agreement with IOSCO about the recognition of standards had been reached (Camfferman and Zeff, 2007, p. 448). As Chapter 5 shows, the constitutional review of 2000 initially required the Board to be staffed according to quotas for certain professional backgrounds (SWP, 1998). Since 2005, the trustees have been required to appoint the Board, as the key decision-making body in issues of standard setting, based on individual qualifications only (IASCF, 2005, para. 19). The official wording of the IASB constitution demands that up until 2009 "professional competence and practical experience"—further specified as "technical expertise" and "international business experience"—be the sole criteria for the recruitment of Board members. Appointment of Board members is one of the main tasks assigned to the trustees. The following section will demonstrate that they have used their discretion primarily to appoint Board members with an Anglo-American professional background.

### 6.1.1 Anglo-American Dominance

Table 6.1 gives an overview of the Board members as of June 30, 2009. The fact that almost all members are full-time employees of the IASB is one of the main differences that stands out in comparison to the period before 2001. In summer 2009, members from Anglo-American countries dominated the Board (8 out of 14 members, not including an Indian member who is also a member of the American Institute of Certified Public Accountants), and the majority were trained accountants and had either been employed by or had been partners in auditing firms at some point in their career. More than two-thirds had previous experience in national standard-setting bodies, mostly in Anglo-American countries. An aspect that strikes the eye in this respect is the fact that the cooperation between the national standard setters from the USA, the UK, Canada, and Australia initiated by the Group of Four has been continued. This will be addressed below.

A detailed look at the Board membership as of June 2009 gives the following picture: The only part-time member of the Board was Mary Barth from Stanford University. She left the Board in the summer of 2009 but remains an academic adviser to the IASB. Among the 13 full-time members are 2 who had been employed by preparers of financial statements prior to working for the IASB. Robert Garnett had been Executive Vice-President Finance for the UK-South African mining company Anglo American plc and Jan Engström had served as Chief Financial Officer for Volvo. Two others had worked for financial institutions before joining the IASB (Thomas Jones had held the position of Chief Accounting Officer with the US bank Citicorp and Stephen Cooper had been head of valuation and accounting research at UBS). Prior to their appointment to the Board, four members had been partners of global accounting firms: Gilbert Gélard had been with KPMG in France and Tatsumi Yamada with a Japanese affiliate of the PwC network, John Smith had been a partner with Deloitte and India-born Prabhakar Kalavacherla with KPMG. Three individuals had worked full-time for national standard setters before joining the IASB, all of them with an Anglo-American background: Sir David Tweedie with the Accounting Standards Board of the UK, Jim Leisenring as FASB's Director International Activities, and Warren McGregor as head of the

*Table 6.1    Board membership as of June 30, 2009*

| Position/name | Previous employer | Accounting experience | Experience in standard setting |
| --- | --- | --- | --- |
| Chairman Sir David Tweedie, UK | ASB (UK standard setter) | TA: Yes A: KPMG | N: ASB (UK), full-time I: IASC Board; G4+1 |
| Vice-Chairman T. E. Jones, USA | Citigroup | TA: Yes A: No | N: Trustee FASB (USA) I: IASC Board, in 2000, Chairman |
| Member, part time M. E. Barth, USA | Stanford University | TA: Yes A: Arthur Andersen | N: Advisory Council of FASB (USA) I: No |
| Member S. Cooper, UK | UBS | TA: Yes A: No | N: Advisory group to ASB (UK) I: IASB's Analyst Representative Group |
| Member P. Danjou, FR | AMF (French securities regulator) | TA: Yes A: Arthur Andersen | N: No I: IASB; Standards Advisory Council |
| Member J. Engström, SE | Volvo | TA: No A: No | N: No I: No |
| Member R. P. Garnett, ZA | AngloAmerican Corp. | TA: Yes A: Arthur Andersen | N: Accounting Standards Board (ZA) I: IASC Working Group |
| Member G. Gélard, FR | KPMG | TA: Yes A: Arthur Andersen, KPMG | N: CNC (FR) I: IASC Board |
| Member P. Kalavacherla, IN | KPMG | TA: Yes A: KPMG | N: No I: No |
| Member J. J. Leisenring, USA | FASB, Director of International Activities | TA: Yes A: Bristol, Leisenring, Herkner | N: FASB (USA) I: G4+1 |

*Table 6.1* (continued)

| Position/name | Previous employer | Accounting experience | Experience in standard setting |
| --- | --- | --- | --- |
| Member W. J. McGregor, AU | Australian Accounting Research Foundation, Director | TA: Yes A: Stevenson McGregor | N: Accounting Research Foundation (AU) I: IASC Board; G4+1 |
| Member J. T. Smith, USA | Deloitte and Touche | TA: Yes A: Deloitte and Touche | N: FASB working group I: IASC Board (in 2000) |
| Member T. Yamada, JP | PwC | TA: Yes A: PwC | N: No I: IASC Board |
| Member W.G. Zhang, CN | China Securities Regulatory Commission (CSRC) | TA: Yes A: No | N: China Accounting Standards Committee I: IOSCO |

*Notes:* TA = Trained accountant; A = Auditor; N = National; I = International.

*Source:* Author's illustration, IASCF, 2009; Camfferman and Zeff, 2007, pp. 497ff.; http://www.iasplus.com/restruct/boardhistory.htm (accessed May 4, 2011).

Australian standard setter's research foundation. More recently the Board has embraced national regulators. Philippe Danjou joined in 2005; prior to this engagement, he had been the director of the accounting division of the French securities regulator (Autorité des Marchés Financiers, AMF). In 2007, Wei-Guo Zhang, from China, became the first Asian member from outside Japan. He had previously been Chief Accountant and Director General of the Department of International Affairs at the China Securities Regulatory Commission (CSRC).

If we consider geographical origin, it stands out that 8 of the 14 members come from countries with Anglo-American accounting traditions. Four members of the Board are from the USA, two from the UK, and one each from Australia and South Africa. Some of the Board members have either received professional training or have worked in more than one of the countries with such accounting traditions. Indian Kalavacherla received his education in the USA and has worked in India, Europe, and the USA. He is a member of both the Institute of Chartered

Accountants of India and the American Institute of CPAs and therefore can be considered to be the ninth "Anglo-American" representative on the Board. In addition, the Chairman of the Board is British while the Vice-Chairman is a US American born in the UK. Of the five members who are not from countries with Anglo-American accounting traditions, three are from continental Europe (France and Sweden) and one each from Japan and China respectively.

A professional background in accounting is another striking common characteristic of the Board in 2009. Of its 14 members 13 had been trained as accountants in the course of their professional careers and 10 of them were partners in auditing firms, 8 with the big firms. This suggests that in their daily work the Board members draw on a foundation of experience rooted in an Anglo-American philosophy marked by an appreciation for private sector self-regulation and skepticism toward state intervention. We can also expect this background to favor an approach geared toward pragmatic problem solving. The experience of working for globally active accounting firms constitutes a common denominator in the professional background of this group. Having worked for the big firms also involves experiences (soft skills) that can only be gained in that specific environment (see Ramirez, 2007). The only person who was not a trained accountant had been employed with a large continental European auto manufacturer (Engström, Volvo); his main role on the Board was to represent the perspective of the preparers of financial statements. Kalavacherla was the only other member to have no institutional experience in national or international standard setting.

A glance at the previous involvement of individual Board members in standard setting gives evidence that considerable knowledge of national and international standard setting is represented on the Board. Ten of the fourteen Board members had been involved in national standard setting in their countries of origin. Except for the Frenchman Gélard and the Chinese Zhang, all of them had gained experience in standard setting in Anglo-American countries. Three Board members, from the USA, UK, and Australia, had worked in the field of national standard setting on a full-time basis prior to employment with the IASB. Moreover, the majority of Board members had previous experience in international standard setting. Eleven had been engaged in activities related to IASB. Apart from participating in the various IASB bodies, this included involvement in the Anglo-American coordination group G4+1.

Three of the members who had worked in the field of standard setting on a full-time basis had already been acquainted with one another via their joint participation in the G4+1 coordination group. That group was established in the early 1990s to pool and focus Anglo-American interests in standard setting and pursue them more effectively at the international level (Kirsch, 2007, p. 281). Initially, when the first Board convened in 2001, the influence of the G4+1 was even more dominant because, in addition to those three members with ties to it, two more of the decision makers with full-time experience in national standard setting had also been members of the G4+1. Both served on the Board of the IASB from 2001–07: Tricia O'Malley had previously chaired the Canadian Institute of Chartered Accountants' Accounting Standards Board (AcSB) and Tony Cope had served on the Board of FASB.

At the time, the G4+1 comprised leading representatives of four national standard setters from the USA, the UK, Canada, and Australia (Group of Four), plus the IASC (+1), which had been invited to the Group's meetings as an observer. Over the years, "G4+1 had evolved from 'think tank' to 'embryonic standard setter'" (Street, 2006, p. 116). The Anglo-American standard setters used the group as a means of putting pressure on the IASC at a time when the European Commission, in the context of the constitutional review in 2000, had expressed its interest in continuing to base board appointments on geographic representation. During the review process at the close of the 1990s, the four national standard setters repeatedly made it clear what they expected from transnational standardization and threatened to move forward and develop G4 into an international standard setter should the IASB be shaped in ways grossly departing from the Anglo-American tradition (Camfferman and Zeff, 2007; Street, 2006).

Aside from expectations concerning the structure of the organization, the standard setters' demands also included the attuning of standards to the principles of fair value accounting, which was part of the agenda pushed by the G4+1 early on. It thus seems justified to argue that the coordination group represented the nucleus of today's IASB both in institutional structure and in terms of the substance of the standards. The representation of former G4+1 members on the Board was the product of deliberate influence over appointment. In 2002, the decision was made to discontinue the G4+1, which can be interpreted as a sign of the group's success. It had managed to accomplish all of its major goals: The Anglo-American paradigm has prevailed, both over the IASB's organizational structure and in terms of the philosophy embodied in its standards. For this obvious reason, there was no longer any need for independent, interest-group politics inside the IASB.

The IASB Chairman traces the strong Anglo-American influence on the Board to the agreement reached between the IASB and the FASB, which was one of the objectives to be accomplished. In his view, this required a board to be appointed that represented as much experience and professional competence as possible, which the FASB would be ready to accept on equal terms and which would be able to hold its ground against the US standard setter:

> In the beginning the Trustees chose a Board, quite deliberately, of experienced standard setters to ensure that the IASB is on a par with FASB. There was a solid group of individuals that established IFRSs as high-quality accounting standards. (Author's interview with Tweedie)

In conclusion, it seems safe to characterize the composition of the 2009 Board as biased—at least if we take the organization's claims to global representation as a yardstick. Most notably, the high degree of homogeneity among the group strikes the eye. Not just the dominance of Anglo-American actors stands out but also the similarity of the career paths, including employment with the Big Four, previous involvement in national standard setting, and collaboration in the G4+1. The Board of 2009 is evidence of a skewed interpretation of the constitution currently in effect. In paragraph 21 the statutory document states: "The Trustees shall select IASB members so that the IASB as a group provides an appropriate mix of recent practical experience among auditors, preparers, users and academics" (IASCF, 2010, para. 27). Instead, trained accountants and standard setters from countries with Anglo-American accounting traditions dominated the Board while only two members represented preparers of financial statements from industry. Based on these findings, we may characterize the group of "accounting policy bureaucrats" that Power refers to (2009, p. 329) as follows: They have been recruited from within a very narrow network of mainly male, Anglo-American individuals with extensive previous experience in standard setting who have gained much of their practical knowledge by working in big auditing firms. Only recently the Board had been opened up to also integrate national standard setters and a few individuals from outside the OECD world.

In this light, a look at the groups that are hardly represented or not represented at all is quite instructive. Among the underrepresented groups are the users who base their investment decisions on IAS/IFRS financial statements. In June 2009, only two of the Board members (Jones and Cooper) had previously been employed with a large bank. Cooper's recruitment, however, can be taken as an indicator of the increased importance of users of financial statements. In the second half of 2009, two other members were included to replace Jones and Barth: Patrick Finnegan, with experience in the Chartered Financial Analysts Institute, and Patricia McConnell of Bear Stearns' Equity Research group; both are from the USA.

For most of its existence, the IASB's global claim was highly questionable, as almost no experience rested with countries in the developing world. Only recently have individuals from India and China (and Brazil, starting in 2009) been included. As the lack of geographical diversity is increasingly addressed, other open questions remain. This becomes clear when we look at the IASB's attempt to issue standards for small and medium-sized enterprises (IFRS *light*). There is no one on the Board who can claim to have any relevant experience of working in a SME environment. Although extending IAS/IFRS to nonlisted companies is one of the major projects for the future, the Board members in charge of pursuing the endeavor lack any hands-on experience pertaining to the particular reality of SMEs.

### 6.1.2   The Board Composition over Time

So far, the analysis has largely been based on a snapshot of the Board's composition. This approach will now be complemented by a longitudinal perspective to trace the development of the key decision-making body over time. When adopting such a perspective, the first thing to strike the eye is the degree of continuity. Seven of the fourteen members of the Board in 2007 had been on the IASC Board in the late 1990s. The first constitution of 2001 contained no provisions limiting terms of office so that later constitution reviews had no effect on the tenure of the initial personnel making up the Board. In the meantime, Board membership has been limited to a maximum of eight years.

An overview of length of Board membership underscores this continuity. If we also take IASC membership before 2000 into account, we see that some individual Board members have assumed an active role in transnational standardization for almost two decades: Initially as members of the respective delegations involved in standard setting, today as members appointed by the trustees. By summer 2007, six of the fourteen Board members had served on the boards of the IASC and IASB for at least twelve years. Apart from working together within the IASB framework, individual members also cooperate in other contexts, such as European, international and bilateral bodies, so that we may speak of a closely knit network of individuals who have become well acquainted with one another over many years. Table 6.2 documents IASB membership from 2001 to 2009, including former membership on the IASC Board.

Comparison of the Board of 2001 with that of 2009 reveals only some change in the composition of the two bodies, most notably in 2007. During the first six years, only three persons were replaced. Herz resigned after a few months to become Chairman of the FASB. In 2004, Engström replaced the outgoing Harry Schmid, a former Senior Vice-President of Nestlé and IASC member since 1995. Upon the end of his term of office, the Briton Geoffrey Whittington, professor of accounting at the University of Cambridge, left the Board and Philippe Danjou took his place toward the end of 2006.

*Table 6.2  Length of service on the Board of the IASB, 2001–09 (including IASC Board membership)*

| | Before 2000 | 2001 Name | 2002 | 2003 | 2004 | 2005 | 2006 | 2007 | 2008 | 2009 Name (years' service) |
|---|---|---|---|---|---|---|---|---|---|---|
| | | | Years of membership — Name of newly appointed members | | | | | | | |
| Chair | 6 | Tweedie | 8 | 9 | 10 | 11 | 12 | 13 | 14 | Tweedie (15) |
| Vice Chair | 6 | Jones | 8 | 9 | 10 | 11 | 12 | 13 | 14 | Jones (15) |
| Member | | Barth | 2 | 3 | 4 | 5 | 6 | 7 | 8 | Barth (9) |
| Member | | Bruns | 2 | 3 | 4 | 5 | 6 | Cooper | 2 | Cooper (3) |
| Member | 5 | Cope | 7 | 8 | 9 | 10 | 11 | 12 | – | Kalavacherla (1) |
| Member | | Garnett | 2 | 3 | 4 | 5 | 6 | 7 | 8 | Garnett (9) |
| Member | 12 | Gélard | 14 | 15 | 16 | 17 | 18 | 19 | 20 | Gélard (21) |
| Member | | Herz | Smith | 2 | 3 | 4 | 5 | 6 | 7 | Smith (8) |
| Member | | Leisenring | 2 | 3 | 4 | 5 | 6 | 7 | 8 | Leisenring (9) |
| Member | 14 | McGregor | 16 | 17 | 18 | 19 | 20 | 21 | 22 | McGregor (23) |
| Member | | O'Malley | 2 | 3 | 4 | 5 | 6 | Zhang | 2 | Zhang (3) |
| Member | 6 | Schmid | 8 | 9 | Engström | 2 | 3 | 4 | 5 | Engström (6) |
| Member | | Whittington | 2 | 3 | 4 | 5 | Danjou | 2 | 3 | Danjou (4) |
| Member | 6 | Yamada | 8 | 9 | 10 | 11 | 12 | 13 | 14 | Yamada (15) |
| Mean period in office (yrs) | 4.9 | | 5.9 | 6.9 | 7.2 | 8.2 | 8.9 | 9 | 9.8 | 10.1 |
| Max. period in office (yrs) | 15 | | 16 | 17 | 18 | 19 | 20 | 21 | 22 | 23 |

*Source:* Author's illustration; Camfferman and Zeff, 2007; IASCF–AR, 2002–10; IASC, 1987–2000.

137

If we direct our attention toward the individual members' length of service on the boards (total years of service as of 2009 in brackets), we come across some astonishing figures. Two persons have been members of the decision-making bodies since the 1980s. McGregor first attended IASC Board meetings in 1986 and Gélard in 1989; four others joined in 1995 (Tweedie, Jones, Schmid, and Yamada). In 1996, Cope followed as the international organization of financial analysts' first representative on the IASC Board. When the Board was set up in 2001, it could already draw on an average five years of experience per member. The length of Board membership has steadily increased and due to low levels of fluctuation mean membership reached close to ten years by 2007. Comparing the length of membership on the IASB with average periods of service on the executive boards of companies brings to light a striking difference: Whereas nonexecutive directors of listed companies in the UK spend an average 4.5 years in office—and chief executives 5.3 years (cf. SpencerStuart, 2010, p. 21), the average figure for IASB Board members was 10 years and the Chairman and Vice-Chairman had served 15 years each.[1] This is also more than double the mean tenure of a member of the FASB during the period between 1973 and 2007, which amounts to 4.25 years (Allen and Ramanna, 2010). Compared to the management boards of companies, the composition of the IASB Board displays a remarkable degree of stability.

Summing up, we may conclude that a longitudinal perspective exacerbates the impression of bias in Board composition. The longitudinal view brings to the fore that the lack of social diversity on the Board is a stable characteristic over time. We can identify a group of individual members who have been responsible for key strategic decisions for many years. Among them are the IASB Chairman Sir David Tweedie, his Vice-Chairman Tom Jones, and the Australian Warren McGregor. The ties among the group extend beyond the IASB, as the G4+1 exemplifies. From the perspective of the trustees, the seamless transition in 2001 was to ensure the continuity of ongoing projects:

> I think they [the trustees] did that on purpose because they had a number of projects still coming through and if you change the board members then you suddenly get a new debate on subjects and you know . . . I think it was deliberate. They renewed a lot of the original terms, but from now on, I think you see turn-over. (Author's interview with Ian Macintosh, Chairman, UK Accounting Standards Board)

This assessment underlines the fact that, apart from the formal requirements for the appointment of Board members spelled out in the constitution, the course pursued in filling these positions stands for a certain orientation in standard setting. The stability that marked the first seven years amounted to securing the dominance of Anglo-American accounting traditions and continuity in the pursuit of the agenda and principles of the G4+1 group. The group could afford to disband in 2002 because Anglo-American standard setters no longer needed separate channels of influence. Capital market interests were solidified within the IASB and this predominance remains uncontested within the organization. This can hardly be expected to change, even after the composition of the Board is restructured in the future to accommodate the interests of the newly industrializing countries China, India, and Brazil. For the emerging markets, attracting investment capital is a core requirement of their development model. That is why they want to ensure that investors are provided the types of financial statement they are used to. At the same time, IAS/IFRS diffusion to these jurisdictions is crucial for the IASB to become a standard setter with a truly global reach.

With regard to the long-term continuity of the IASB decision-making body, we can point out two findings: First, there is a small group of individuals that has played a crucial role in shaping the IASB over many years. Some of that group, such as Tweedie, who was a member of the Standing Working Group (SWG), were directly involved in developing the 2000 constitution and subsequently in staffing important positions. Second, a stepwise process of opening up the Board has been initiated, and its enlargement to 16 members is planned. In accordance with previous practice—and the provisions laid down in the constitution—we can expect future members from countries outside the Anglo-American nexus to show the same commitment to capital market orientation as the representatives from the USA, the UK, and Australia. This will ensure that the predominant Anglo-American paradigm will continue to prevail on the Board even as the composition of the decision-making body changes to include individuals from various parts of the world. Today, capital market orientation is the norm outside of the Anglo-American world as well. So, even if the constitution introduces geographic quotas, we can assume that these will be less consequential than in the past since the fair value orientation of the respective Board member might be much more significant.

The Board is the most important but of course not the only organizational unit that makes up the IASB. It is complemented by oversight and advisory bodies that support the transnational standardization activities and help achieve the standards' global diffusion. The following section is devoted to an analysis of the other bodies actively involved in transnational standard setting.

## 6.2 CHARACTERISTICS OF THE STANDARD SETTING NETWORK

In this section, the focus is on the network of transnational standard setting and the changes it has undergone in the period from 2001 to 2009. The aim of the empirical analysis is to identify the organizations whose representatives take part in and influence the various IASB bodies. For this purpose, I have analyzed the publicly available annual reports that have been regularly issued by the IASB since its inception for the reporting periods ending on December 31 of each year. This research is concerned with the composition of the three IASB bodies charged with supervising the Board and assisting it in its tasks.[2] All of the organizations involved in the oversight, advisory, and interpretations bodies together form the transnational network of standardization in the field of accounting. The organizational representation is analyzed using descriptive statistics and UCINET to track and visualize the network effect (Borgatti et al., 2002). The methodology allows both to identify dominant players and to shed light on the missing actors in a social network.

The analysis of the organization network focuses on the organizations delegating representatives to participate in the three constituent bodies of the IASB, which are in charge of overseeing IASB operations (the trustees), advising the Board (the Standards Advisory Council), and interpreting standards (the International Financial Reporting Interpretations Committee). Unlike the Board, membership in these bodies is not full-time, as they convene only a few times a year.

In contrast to the analysis of the Board, the structures of representation that characterize the three bodies in question are not studied at the individual level but rather in terms of identifying the organizations that form the transnational network of standardization. Although formally it is individuals who are appointed, their organizational affiliation in fact plays a key role. Both the annual reports and the academic literature testify to this (see Perry and Nölke, 2005). The following overview illustrates the responsibilities of the various bodies and underlines the crucial part that the trustees play in the appointment process.

The trustees who are charged with overseeing the Board influence the course and development of the entire organization, which is formally a US foundation located in the state of Delaware (the International Accounting Standards Committee Foundation, IASCF). The trustees are responsible for securing funding and for the organization's overall strategic orientation. In addition, they organize and oversee the process of reviewing and amending the constitution that has to take place every five years. One of the most important powers given the trustees is the appointment of the

*Table 6.3 Appointment rules and responsibilities of the IASB bodies*

|  | Responsibilities | Number of members according to the constitution | Constitutional provisions for recruitment | Appointed by |
|---|---|---|---|---|
| Trustees | Securing the financial base, overseeing the Board, constitutional amendments | 22 (until 2005: 19), 3-year term, renewable once | 6 Europeans, 6 N. American, 6 Asian, 1 African, 1 S. American, 2 unspecified | Cooptation (a Trustees' Nominating Committee to be appointed for this purpose), Monitoring Board |
| International Financial Reporting Interpretations Committee (IFRIC) | Interpretation of standards; final approval of interpretations rests with the Board | 14 members eligible to vote, 1 IASB member, 2 observers | None (IASB member appointed by trustees) | Trustees |
| Standards Advisory Council (SAC) | Advising IASB SAC serves as forum for individuals and organizations with an interest in international financial reporting | 30 or more, 3-year term, renewable once | Geographic and organizational diversity | Trustees |

*Source:* Author's illustration, based on IASCF, 2010.

Board and the Standards Advisory Council (SAC). In cooperation with the Monitoring Board, they also coopt individuals onto the Board of Trustees after the end of term or early resignation. There are no precise requirements with regard to the qualifications of the trustees. The constitution merely sets the number of individuals to comprise the group at 22 and defines geographic quotas: Six individuals each from North America,

Europe, and Asia-Oceania, one from Africa, one from South America, and two persons from other parts of the world. In terms of further requirements for the recruitment of trustees the constitution states:

> All Trustees shall be required to show a firm commitment to the IFRS Foundation and the IASB as a high quality global standard-setter, to be financially knowledgeable, and to have an ability to meet the time commitment. Each Trustee shall have an understanding of, and be sensitive to, the challenges associated with the adoption and application of high quality global accounting standards developed for use in the world's capital markets and by other users. [. . .] The Trustees shall be required to commit themselves formally to acting in the public interest in all matters. (IASCF, 2010, para. 6)

IFRIC is in charge of specifying and interpreting standards. Decisions are made by 12 voting members after consultations, which are also attended by a Board member and 2 observers (representatives of the EU and IOSCO respectively). Publication of official standards interpretations is conditional upon approval by the Board (IASCF, 2010, paras. 39–43).

The SAC has only consultative functions. It comprises 30 or more members representing organizations that are to provide their views on core issues concerning the work and the course of the IASB. The SAC's three main tasks are advising the Board in matters of priority setting, informing the Board of the views of the respective organizations, and advising the trustees (IASCF, 2010, paras. 44–6). The members and chairperson of the SAC are appointed by the trustees.

The overview given in the table above demonstrates the trustees' key role in staffing the IASB bodies. However, the analysis of the Board's composition across time has also shown that the trustees' formal powers do not automatically translate into an active personnel policy. For this reason, a network analysis has been conducted in order to identify changes in the participation of the various organizations. The membership of the three bodies for each of the past nine years will be documented for this purpose.

### 6.2.1   Composition of IASB Bodies over Time

Table 6.4 displays data of the organizational relationships that constituted the IASB network during the period from 2001 to 2009. For this purpose, the numbers of members of the three bodies are totaled. The values thus determined vary between 76 and 90 organizations represented each year. A total of 750 memberships was calculated for the three IASB bodies over the nine-year span under study.

There are only minor changes in the size of the respective bodies in the period under study. During the first four years, the number of members

*Table 6.4  Number of representatives on the three IASB bodies, 2001–09*

| | 2001 | | 2002 | | 2003 | | 2004 | | 2005 | |
|---|---|---|---|---|---|---|---|---|---|---|
| | total | % | total | % | total | % | total | % | total | % |
| Trustees | 19 | 22.1 | 17 | 20.2 | 20 | 22.7 | 19 | 21.8 | 19 | 24.4 |
| SAC | 52 | 60.5 | 52 | 61.9 | 53 | 60.3 | 53 | 60.9 | 44 | 56.4 |
| IFRIC | 15 | 17.4 | 15 | 17.9 | 15 | 17.0 | 15 | 17.3 | 15 | 19.2 |
| Total | 86 | 100.0 | 84 | 100.0 | 88 | 100.0 | 87 | 100.0 | 78 | 100.0 |

| | 2006 | | 2007 | | 2008 | | 2009 | | Total members reported | |
|---|---|---|---|---|---|---|---|---|---|---|
| | total | % | total | % | total | % | total | % | | |
| Trustees | 21 | 27.6 | 22 | 27.5 | 22 | 27.2 | 22 | 24.4 | 181 | |
| SAC | 40 | 52.6 | 43 | 53.8 | 42 | 51.8 | 51 | 56.7 | 430 | |
| IFRIC | 15 | 19.7 | 15 | 18.7 | 17 | 21.0 | 17 | 18.9 | 139 | |
| Total | 76 | 100.0 | 80 | 100.0 | 81 | 100.0 | 90 | 100.0 | 750 | |

*Source:*   Author's illustration, based on IASCF–AR, 2002–10.

remains mostly constant. Only after 2005 are there significant changes in the size of the SAC. IFRIC comprises 15 individuals every year up until 2007 and is enlarged to 17 voting and nonvoting individuals starting 2008. There is also little variation in the number of trustees, which ranges between 17 and 22. SAC membership declines from 52 to 40 between 2001 and 2006 but increases again in 2009.

The nine annual reports for the period list 181 trustees, 430 SAC members, and 139 persons participating in IFRIC. This is the number of individuals active in the IASB bodies. However, this number by far exceeds the number of organizations that are represented due to the fact that some individuals originate from the same home organization. The 750 individuals stem from 144 organizations, which already indicates an uneven distribution of positions within the network. The importance of assuming a central position in the IASB network is twofold: First, being represented in a number of bodies, and perhaps even by more than one person, allows organizations to coordinate internally and therefore address issues more strategically. Second, being a core participant in the network is also an indication of the relevance ascribed to an organization by the IASB as it selects members for its bodies and is most likely to choose those that can contribute expertise, material resources, or legitimacy.

The 750 members of the three bodies over a nine-year period constitute the population of the network analysis. The Appendix provides a complete list of all 750 relationships. It also shows that the total number of relationships involves only 144 organizations. This poses the question which organizations are most strongly represented in the IASB network. The UCINET software allows a network analysis to be performed, which provides answers to those questions (see Borgatti et al., 2002; Hanneman and Riddle, 2005). The visual representation of the organizations that are part of the IASB standardization network enables conclusions to be drawn with regard to their significance for transnational standard setting. We may assume that a central position within the network holds a host of opportunities for exercising influence.

### 6.2.2 Properties of the IASB Network

In terms of methodology, the analysis of the IASB network is modeled after the study by Perry and Nölke (2005). However, they did not assess membership of the various bodies but participation in the due process. They compiled and analyzed data from letters commenting on 16 exposure drafts from April 2002 to August 2004. The findings indicate a strong influence attaching to financial market actors and accounting firms (Perry and Nölke, 2005). As mentioned above, their network analysis documents the degree of participation by way of comment letters but, as pointed out in Chapter 5, we must not mistake submitting comment letters for exercising actual influence. Such letters do nevertheless indicate the desire to make one's interests heard.

The most significant methodical difference between this analysis and the work of Perry and Nölke lies in the temporal dimension. Whereas their study is based on a single analysis for all activities across a 28-month period, I performed individual network analyses for nine 12-month periods, ending on December 31 of each year, in order to trace shifts in the network structure over time. In the following, I will focus on the visual representation of the networks using Netdraw (see Borgatti et al., 2002). The graph will then be analyzed and interpreted in more detail. Although centrality measures for the IASB network can be calculated in principle, in this particular case it does not make much sense to do this since the IASB constitution limits the total number of representatives.[3]

As of December 31, 2001, a total of 61 organizations—visualized as dots in the graph, the abbreviations in which are spelled out in the Appendix— were represented on the IASB bodies. The lines connecting the trustees, the SAC, and IFRIC with the organizations indicate membership in those bodies. Figure 6.2 illustrates the 15 organizations represented on IFRIC, the 41 on the SAC, and the 19 organizations by which the trustees are currently (or were formerly) employed. Multiply represented organizations (i.e. by more than one member) are indicated by a bold line; such cases are mostly encountered on the SAC. The UCINET software calculates the visual arrangement of the organizations in such a way that the actors with the most connections are placed at the center of the illustration.

The graph visualizes the entire network of organizations that were represented by at least one member on one of the IASB bodies in 2001. In 11 of the 61 cases, an organization was represented on 2 or more bodies: The EC, IOSCO, General Electric, KPMG, and Arthur Andersen each sent delegates to IFRIC and the SAC. The Bank for International Settlements, Pfizer, and the US Federal Reserve occupied positions on the board of trustees and the SAC. Three organizations were represented on all three bodies. All three were accounting firms: PricewaterhouseCoopers (PWC), Deloitte Touche Tohmatsu (DTT), and Ernst & Young.

The graphs for the following four years (not illustrated) are essentially a mirror image of the situation in 2001. We may thus conclude that the structure of the network for the period from 2001 to 2004 is marked by a high degree of stability. There are only a few minor changes. In 2003, JP Morgan was represented on the board of trustees and in 2004, the financial analysts' federation Chartered Financial Analysts (CFA) was given a seat on the IFRIC and on the SAC. Morgan Stanley became a member of the

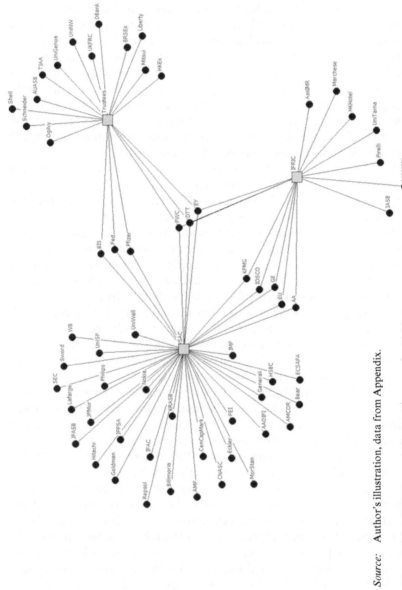

*Source:* Author's illustration, data from Appendix.

*Figure 6.2 IASB organizational network, 2001*

SAC and IFRIC in 2002 and has also been represented among the trustees since 2007. After the Enron scandal Arthur Andersen was dismantled and subsequently does not appear in the network afterward. The picture changes slightly in 2006. The differences in the graphical arrangement are the result of changes in the sizes of the bodies. The key organizations are visualized in the same manner as in the previous illustration.

In 2006, the constitutional amendment expanding the number of trustees took effect. There are now 21, where there were 19 trustees. While IFRIC still contains representatives of 15 organizations, the SAC is now made up by only 36 different organizations sending a total of 40 representatives. Looking at the entire network, the group of key organizations became smaller still in 2006 since the EC was now only represented on IFRIC. Eight organizations enjoyed multiple representation: IOSCO, the World Bank, Morgan Stanley, and Deloitte were members of the SAC and IFRIC, and the Bank for International Settlements was represented on the board of trustees and the SAC as in previous years. Again, the accounting firms were the key organizations in the network. Three of them were represented on all IASB bodies (PWC, Ernst & Young, and for the first time KPMG).

Figure 6.4, showing the situation in 2009, completes the picture. In that year, the total number of 90 memberships in all three IASB bodies was distributed among 71 organizations. Eleven organizations sent persons to more than one forum. The Australian Financial Reporting Council was represented on the SAC and the board of trustees; Bombardier and Sumitomo, two preparers of financial statements, enjoyed membership of IFRIC and the board of trustees; and five organizations, four of which are international organizations with regulatory competences (the European Commission, IOSCO, the World Bank, and the SEC) were members of the SAC and IFRIC. Deloitte was also represented on these two bodies while the rest of the Big Four participated in all three bodies.

For the period from 2001–09, graphical network analysis yields the following particularly noteworthy results:

1. The number of yearly representations decreased in the middle of the first decade of this century but then in 2009 increased by more than 10 percent over the previous year.
2. The core group also decreased to eight in 2006 but rose again to eleven three years later. While industrial corporations and national standard setters have recently joined the inner circle, accounting firms, and international organizations still play the dominant role.
3. The globally operating accounting firms are the main pillar of the network. They have formed the stable inner circle every single year and, in addition, account for one-third of the IASB budget.

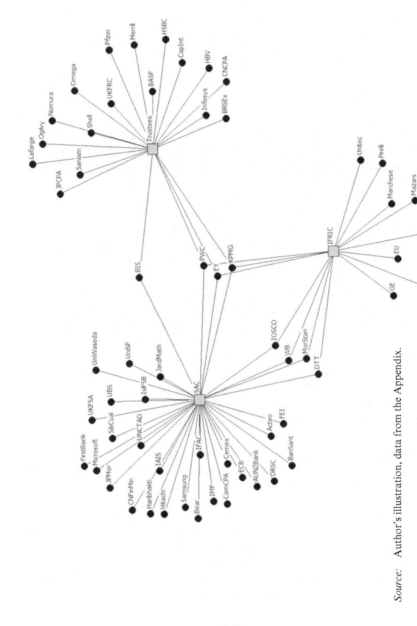

*Source:* Author's illustration, data from the Appendix.

*Figure 6.3    IASB organizational network, 2006*

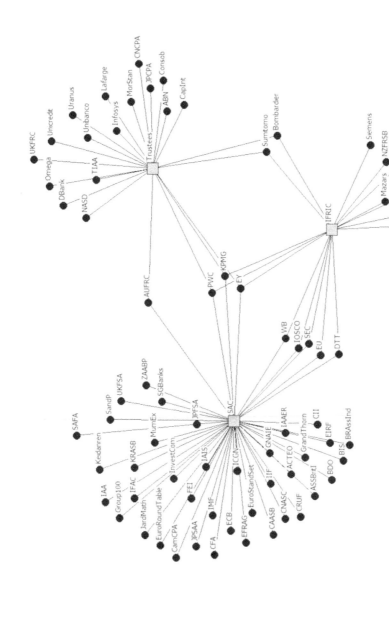

*Source:* Author's illustration, data from the Appendix.

*Figure 6.4 IASB organizational network, 2009*

### 6.2.3　Interests and Actors Dominating the IASB

The graphical analysis of network relations over a nine-year period evidences the dominance of the international accounting standardization network by a few organizations. In a second step, this allows conclusions to be drawn about the organizations that are not represented. Before we do this, let us first take a systematic look at all organizations that were represented on at least two bodies during the whole period from 2001 to 2009 to gain a more comprehensive picture of the network structure and its stability over time. On the whole, what we see is a small, exclusive circle of organizations. By 2009, only eleven organizations were represented on more than one of the IASB bodies. Table 6.4 charts this development and shows that over the entire period under study only 18 organizations have belonged to this core group for at least one year.

The table lists the organizations that are represented on the board of trustees (T), the SAC (S), and IFRIC (I). Based on membership, we can make out a threefold division of the IASB core network. First, there are seven organizations on the margins, each of which were represented on two or more of the IASB bodies for more than one year. Pfizer, Arthur Andersen, the Chartered Financial Analysts, Sumitomo, and the Australian Financial Reporting Council were represented for only one year. JP Morgan, the SEC, and Bombardier were involved for two years and General Electric for four. The investment bank Morgan Stanley enjoyed continuous representation from 2002–08. The second group comprises international organizations involved in international financial regulation that were actively engaged during most of the period under study (IOSCO, the EC, and the Bank for International Settlements as well as the World Bank, which has become a stronghold since 2006; cf. Tsingou, 2008). Lastly, the inner core of the network is exclusively dominated by auditing firms: The Big Four have been represented over the entire period—and mostly in all of the three bodies. In particular, Ernst & Young and PricewaterhouseCoopers have been dominant.

The table highlights three characteristics of the core standard-setting network, which comprises the 18 organizations listed:

1.　In the period from 2001 to 2009, the number of organizations that are multiply represented ranges between eight and eleven.
2.　The variety of organizational types is also remarkably low; there are essentially only five different types of organization present: Auditors and international organizations clearly dominate, complemented by investment banks, a few preparers, and, since 2008, national standard setters.

*Table 6.5   Organizational core of the transnational standard-setting network*

| | 2001 | | | 2002 | | | 2003 | | | 2004 | | | 2005 | | | 2006 | | | 2007 | | | 2008 | | | 2009 | | | Type of organization |
|---|---|---|---|---|---|---|---|---|---|---|---|---|---|---|---|---|---|---|---|---|---|---|---|---|---|---|---|---|
| | T | S | I | T | S | I | T | S | I | T | S | I | T | S | I | T | S | I | T | S | I | T | S | I | T | S | I | |
| Ernst & Young | ✓ | ✓ | ✓ | ✓ | ✓ | ✓ | ✓ | ✓ | ✓ | ✓ | ✓ | ✓ | ✓ | ✓ | ✓ | ✓ | ✓ | ✓ | ✓ | ✓ | ✓ | ✓ | ✓ | ✓ | ✓ | ✓ | ✓ | Auditor |
| PWC | ✓ | ✓ | ✓ | ✓ | ✓ | ✓ | ✓ | ✓ | ✓ | ✓ | ✓ | ✓ | ✓ | ✓ | ✓ | ✓ | ✓ | ✓ | ✓ | ✓ | ✓ | ✓ | ✓ | ✓ | ✓ | ✓ | ✓ | Auditor |
| Deloitte Touche Tohmatsu | ✓ | ✓ | ✓ | ✓ | ✓ | ✓ | ✓ | ✓ | ✓ | ✓ | ✓ | ✓ | ✓ | ✓ | ✓ | ✓ | ✓ | ✓ | ✓ | ✓ | ✓ | ✓ | ✓ | ✓ | ✓ | ✓ | ✓ | Auditor |
| KPMG | ✓ | ✓ | | ✓ | ✓ | | ✓ | ✓ | | ✓ | | | ✓ | | | ✓ | ✓ | | ✓ | ✓ | | ✓ | ✓ | | ✓ | ✓ | | Auditor |
| Arthur Andersen | ✓ | ✓ | | | | | | | | | | | | | | | | | | | | | | | | | | Auditor |
| IOSCO | ✓ | ✓ | | ✓ | ✓ | | ✓ | ✓ | | ✓ | ✓ | | ✓ | ✓ | | ✓ | | | ✓ | ✓ | | ✓ | ✓ | | ✓ | ✓ | | Int. organization |
| EC | ✓ | ✓ | | ✓ | ✓ | | ✓ | ✓ | | ✓ | ✓ | | ✓ | ✓ | | | ✓ | | ✓ | ✓ | | ✓ | ✓ | | ✓ | ✓ | | Int. organization |
| Bank for International Settlements | ✓ | ✓ | | | | | ✓ | ✓ | | ✓ | ✓ | | ✓ | ✓ | | ✓ | ✓ | | ✓ | ✓ | | | | | | | | Int. organization |
| World Bank | | | | | | | | | | | | | | | | ✓ | ✓ | | ✓ | ✓ | | ✓ | ✓ | | ✓ | ✓ | | Int. organization |
| Morgan Stanley | | | | ✓ | ✓ | | ✓ | ✓ | | ✓ | | | ✓ | ✓ | | ✓ | ✓ | | ✓ | ✓ | | ✓ | | | | | | Investment bank |
| JP Morgan | | | | ✓ | ✓ | | ✓ | ✓ | | | | | ✓ | ✓ | | | | | ✓ | | | | | | | | | Investment bank |

151

*Table 6.5*  (continued)

| | 2001 | | | 2002 | | | 2003 | | | 2004 | | | 2005 | | | 2006 | | | 2007 | | | 2008 | | | 2009 | | | Type of organization |
|---|---|---|---|---|---|---|---|---|---|---|---|---|---|---|---|---|---|---|---|---|---|---|---|---|---|---|---|---|
| | T | S | I | T | S | I | T | S | I | T | S | I | T | S | I | T | S | I | T | S | I | T | S | I | T | S | I | |
| GE | ✓ | ✓ | | ✓ | ✓ | | ✓ | ✓ | | ✓ | ✓ | | | | | | | | | | | | | | | | | Corporation |
| Sumitomo | | ✓ | | | | | | | | | | | | | | | | | | ✓ | | | | | | ✓ | | Corporation |
| Pfizer | ✓ | | | | | | | | | | | | | | | | | | | | | | ✓ | | | ✓ | | Corporation |
| Bombardier | | | | | | | | | | | | | | | | | | | | | | | ✓ | | | ✓ | | Corporation |
| SEC | | | | | | | | | | | | | | | | | | | | ✓ | | | ✓ | | | ✓ | | Standard setter |
| Australian Financial Reporting Council | | | | | | | | | | | | | | | | | | | | | | | ✓ | | | ✓ | | Standard setter |
| CFA Analysts | | | | | | | | | | ✓ | ✓ | | | | | | | | | | | | | | | | | Analysts' assoc. |
| Total organizations | 10 | | | 9 | | | 10 | | | 10 | | | 9 | | | 8 | | | 9 | | | 10 | | | 11 | | | |

*Source:*  Author's illustration, based on data from the Appendix.

152

3. Representatives of users (analysts and investors) are largely absent from the inner core of the network; financial analysts are only included in 2004.

The variety of organizations peaked in 2009 when four different types of organizations were represented in the core network; among them national and international regulators, preparers and auditors. There has been recent change—notably the inclusion of industry and national regulators, probably as a reaction to the criticism leveled against the lack of accountability.

Contrary to the emphasis placed on the private nature of transnational standard setting, it is quite evident that international organizations are important. They are needed to ensure the global dissemination and national adoption of standards. This goes to show that the IASB today still holds on to the strategy adopted in the early 1980s of systematically involving actors considered instrumental in securing legitimacy for IAS/IFRS with public authority (Camfferman and Zeff, 2007). This can also explain the recent inclusion of national standard setters. The question of what independent interests of their own must be attributed to those international organizations cannot be answered based on this study. On one hand, we can expect bureaucrats to have a greater role in those organizations, especially in cases where they have long been entrusted with certain tasks and thus have become important players in negotiations (on the role of the European Commission, see van Hulle, 2004). On the other hand, it is plausible to assume that they see themselves as stewards of the public interest. The position of international organizations in transnational regulation remains an issue for further research.

The further characteristic is the notable absence of users of financial statements from the inner core of the IASB network. Neither independent financial analysts nor investors are significantly represented in this segment if we leave aside the CFA in 2004. Among the core group, investment banks—in their capacity as analysts—are the only organizations representing the users of financial statements. However, they also prepare their own financial statements. Chapter 4 clearly demonstrated the far-reaching consequences that, for instance, accounting for financial instruments (IAS 39) has had, especially for banks.

The network analysis has confirmed Perry and Nölke's study (2005) while going beyond their work to deliver more precise results. Whereas Perry and Nölke also showed the dominance of the Big Four and the strong engagement of capital market actors, they missed the role that other actors play. My analysis fills the gap caused by focusing on the comment letters submitted to the IASB, which leads to the influence of private actors being overstated. Contrary to their results, my inquiry into the composition of the IASB bodies shows that public actors—in this case, most importantly international organizations—indeed play an important part in the network. IOSCO, the Bank for International Settlements, the EC, and the World Bank are a core part of the wider IASB structure. Interestingly enough, this is not true of the users of financial statements whose absence will be subjected to closer scrutiny in the next section.

To summarize the conclusions as concerns the core network actors, I have shown that the representation of the various organizations involved in the IASB network deviates from the IASB's own self-conception in two ways:

1.  In spite of constant emphasis on private sector self-regulation, international and public organizations play a significant role. IOSCO and the EC in particular have belonged to the inner core of the standard setting network from the outset. The Bank for International Settlements ceased to be part of the inner core in 2007; the World Bank has been represented instead since 2006. The increasing significance of the growing volume of international capital transactions and the realignment of cross-border financial regulation, but also the recent financial crisis and the need for international coordination, make IOSCO, the federation of national securities regulatory authorities, a key player linking national and international regulatory ambits.

2.  Despite all attempts to ensure adequate representation for various constituencies, the playing field is clearly tilted in favor of the accounting firms. Although the official IASB documents stress the commitment to maintaining a proper balance in the representation of preparers, auditors, users, and academics on the IASB bodies—and all of those groups are indeed involved to some degree—the analysis of the entire network reveals the clear dominance of accounting firms, especially the Big Four. Not only has employment with the latter been an important step in the individual careers of Board members, but the major global players in the auditing market play a crucial role for the IASB as a whole. The Big Four account for a third of the IASB's total budget and are the main sources of external expertise. Each of them sends their technical partner, who is in charge of "technical" decisions within the firm, to act as a delegate on the interpretations committee (IFRIC). This testifies to the importance that the Big Four assign the decisions made by the IASB in matters of standard setting. And it also indicates their efforts at maintaining their oligopoly. Although IFRIC today comprises only 17 members, all of the Big Four are represented.

Coordination among the Big Four and with the IASB is necessary to ensure a common understanding of standards and comparable practice in auditing. The edge of the Big Four over their competitors derives primarily from their reputation. For this reason, they must make sure that accounting and auditing rules are applied in a coherent manner worldwide. This requires in-house knowledge management and leads to a concentration of expertise in the hands of the Big Four that formerly, to a far greater degree, had been under the control of the national associations of professional accountants (see Ramirez, 2007; Botzem, 2008). Professional expertise and the ability to determine the relevant body of knowledge are the basic pillars upon which the Big Four's business operations rest. This also stresses the role of the partners responsible for "technical" issues of standard setting who are involved in the IASB. To gain a more complete picture of how the dominance of the Big Four within the IASB network relates to the absence of users of financial statements from the core network, we will now turn attention to the absence of certain interest groups.

### 6.2.4  The Absence of Users of Financial Statements

The historical development of transnational standard setting outlined in Chapter 3 has shown that the decision to put international standard setting in the hands of private actors has fostered tendencies towards excluding certain societal interests. The IASB is dominated by private sector actors who subscribe to a positive view of global accounting standards with a clear capital market orientation. By contrast, the interests of developing countries have traditionally played a minor role as have the needs of employees, unions, environmentalists, and consumer protection activists (see Gallhofer and Haslam, 2007). Much more surprising in light of private sector dominance and an organizational philosophy marked by state skepticism is that the users of financial statements are also barely present in the inner circle of the organizational network.

I will now discuss this aspect systematically and examine the representation of users throughout the entire IASB network. The analysis will draw on the classification system employed by the IASB, which in its documents mentions as interest groups auditors, preparers, academics, and users alongside certain association representatives and national standard setters. In practice, drawing a clear line between preparers and users is no easy task. Banks, for instance, are both preparers and users of financial statements. The same holds true for some listed companies, especially when they engage in financial management activities. For the analysis of interest group participation, the interest groups under study shall be defined in the following manner: "Auditors" shall be taken to

*Table 6.6    Individuals represented by interest group affiliation, 2001–09*

|  | Trustees | | SAC | | IFRIC | | Total | |
|---|---|---|---|---|---|---|---|---|
|  | total | % | total | % | total | % | total | % |
| *Auditors* | | | | | | | | |
| Accounting firms Associations | 31 | 17.1 | 114 | 26.5 | 49 | 35.3 | 194 | 25.9 |
| *Regulators* | | | | | | | | |
| Regulatory authorities, standard setters International organizations | 40 | 22.1 | 137 | 31.9 | 35 | 25.2 | 212 | 28.3 |
| *Preparers* | | | | | | | | |
| Preparers of financial statements | 41 | 22.7 | 84 | 19.5 | 24 | 17.3 | 149 | 19.9 |
| *Academics* | | | | | | | | |
| Faculty of institutions of higher education | 9 | 5.0 | 12 | 2.8 | 8 | 5.8 | 29 | 3.9 |
| *Users* | | | | | | | | |
| Investors, financial analysts, banks, insurers, stock exchanges Associations | 60 | 33.1 | 83 | 19.3 | 23 | 16.5 | 166 | 22.1 |
| Total | 181 | 100.0 | 430 | 100.0 | 139 | 100.0 | 750 | 100.0 |

*Source:*   Author's illustration, based on data from Appendix, values may differ due to rounding.

mean employees of accounting firms and representatives of the national organizations of the accountancy profession. National and international regulatory agencies and standard setters are grouped under the designation "regulators". Representatives of companies engaged in the business of preparing financial statements will be called "preparers". "Academics" are defined as faculty members of institutions of higher education.

The category "users of financial statements" is employed in a very broad sense to rule out the possibility that their lack of representation might be an artifact of how the group is defined. Among the users of financial statements I count banks, insurance companies, and the associations that represent them, as well as investors, analysts, stock exchanges, and companies that originated in the manufacturing sector but have increasingly become involved in the financial sector, such as General Electric. Table 6.6 gives an overview of the entire IASB membership classified according to the IASB bodies and the interest group category their organization of origin falls into based on the above definitions (for a comprehensive list for the whole IASB network, see the Appendix).

As the table illustrates, the distribution of interest groups across the three bodies differs slightly from the aggregate distribution. These effects are caused by variations in the size of the different IASB bodies, which in turn are partly due to the different tasks they have been assigned. The composition of the SAC comes closest to resembling the aggregate distribution. In the case of the trustee board, the most notable deviations are the low representation of auditors and the higher share of members from the ranks of preparers and users. The interpretations committee displays an opposite pattern. There, the users of standards are underrepresented. The accounting firms are dominant while the share of all other groups is low compared to the aggregate distribution.

A look at the distribution of interest groups over time reveals only minor changes. There is a slight trend toward a declining number of auditors and academics while the proportion of regulators has remained constant and a small increase in the number of user representatives, with some degree of fluctuation, can be observed (see Table 6.7).

Despite the variation in some of the individual values, the longitudinal data testify to the stability of the organizational network. This holds for the representation of user interests as well, the share attributed to which fluctuates between 17.4 percent in 2001 and a maximum of 27.8 percent in 2009. This prompts the conclusion that the strong representation of the users of financial statements on the board of trustees—where they account for 33 percent of the membership and thus constitute the single largest group—does not translate into similar levels of representation on the other bodies. A reason for this may be found in the heterogeneity of the users, which comprise representatives from banks, insurers, associations, stock exchanges, and users in the narrow sense. If we break down the group of users in more detail, we can see that two-thirds of the user representatives come from banks and insurers (see Table 6.8).

Only 35 individuals (or 21.1 percent of all users) represent user organizations in the narrow sense (institutional investors, representatives of funds, and financial analysts). This amounts to only 4.7 percent of all representatives in the IASB network during the period from 2001 to 2009. In comparison, each of the Big Four has been represented by at least 33 members over the nine-year period under study (KPMG and E&Y 36, DTT 37, and PwC 43). The four accounting firms together account for 149 of the 750 delegates recorded for that period. Thus, the Big Four have roughly the same number of members of the IASB as the user organizations altogether (166 in total).

Weak user representation contradicts the emphasis given to the importance of users—at least at the rhetorical level—for the development of

*Table 6.7  IASB membership by interest group affiliation, per year, 2001–09*

|  | 2001 | | 2002 | | 2003 | | 2004 | | 2005 | |
|---|---|---|---|---|---|---|---|---|---|---|
|  | total | % | total | % | total | % | total | % | total | % |
| Auditors | 26 | 30.2 | 25 | 29.8 | 25 | 28.4 | 27 | 31.0 | 18 | 23.1 |
| Regulators | 23 | 26.7 | 23 | 27.4 | 26 | 29.5 | 24 | 27.6 | 22 | 28.2 |
| Preparers | 17 | 19.8 | 14 | 16.7 | 16 | 18.2 | 14 | 16.1 | 15 | 19.2 |
| Academics | 5 | 5.8 | 4 | 4.8 | 4 | 4.5 | 5 | 5.7 | 3 | 3.8 |
| Users | 15 | 17.4 | 18 | 21.4 | 17 | 19.3 | 17 | 19.5 | 20 | 25.6 |
| Total | 86 | 100.0 | 84 | 100.0 | 88 | 100.0 | 87 | 100.0 | 78 | 100.0 |

|  | 2006 | | 2007 | | 2008 | | 2009 | | Total | |
|---|---|---|---|---|---|---|---|---|---|---|
|  | total | % | total | % | total | % | total | % | total | % |
| Auditors | 19 | 25.0 | 18 | 22.5 | 17 | 21.0 | 19 | 21.1 | 194 | 25.9 |
| Regulators | 19 | 25.0 | 23 | 28.8 | 25 | 30.9 | 27 | 30.0 | 212 | 28.3 |
| Preparers | 17 | 22.4 | 18 | 22.5 | 19 | 23.5 | 19 | 21.1 | 149 | 19.9 |
| Academics | 3 | 3.9 | 3 | 3.8 | 2 | 2.5 | 0 | 0.0 | 29 | 3.9 |
| Users | 18 | 23.7 | 18 | 22.5 | 18 | 22.2 | 25 | 27.8 | 166 | 22.1 |
| Total | 76 | 100.0 | 80 | 100.0 | 81 | 100.0 | 90 | 100.0 | 750 | 100.0 |

*Source:*  Author's illustration, based on data from Appendix; values may differ due to rounding.

*Table 6.8     Users of financial statements by type of organization, 2001–09*

| User organizations in the IASB network | Total | | Total share of representatives (% population 750) |
|---|---|---|---|
| | number | % | |
| Banks (and banking associations) | 78 | 47.0 | 10.4 |
| Insurers (and insurance associations) | 32 | 19.3 | 4.3 |
| Companies with significant involvement in the financial sector | 14 | 8.4 | 1.9 |
| Stock exchange representatives | 7 | 4.2 | 0.9 |
| Users in the narrow sense (funds, financial analysts, and their respective associations) | 35 | 21.1 | 4.7 |
| Total | 166 | 100.0 | 22.1 |

*Source:*   Author's illustration, data from Appendix.

IAS/IFRS and in the discussions surrounding the conceptual framework. In both cases, the decision usefulness of standards is the core argument advanced in the debates on matters of accounting. Detailed analysis of user representation, however, shows that the significance assigned to this group in IASB documents is not reflected in the actual reality of standard setting. Each of the four firms forming the accounting oligopoly is more strongly represented on the IASB bodies than all the users in the narrow sense—investor representatives, financial analysts, and their associations—together.

The results of the network analysis are confirmed by the expert interviews, which all consistently testify to the absence of the users of financial statements. As possible reasons for this, the respondents identify a lack of monetary incentives for high-earning financial analysts and difficulties in organizing user interests. This seems to be a problem not limited to the IASB:

> Every standard setter I have come across has sought to get the analysts involved in the process and it has always been difficult because they often say they are not paid to think about these things. [. . .] But there ought to be a range of interests involved in the process. It is more difficult to get industry, preparers and users thinking about these things. But if you just left it to the auditors, I think that would be wrong. (Author's interview with Cairns)

Similar experiences are reflected in statements made by members of the Board whose main contacts with users are with the Chartered Financial Analysts and investment banks from important countries:

> Users are particularly important in accounting and traditionally have been
> particularly difficult to access because there aren't so many of them . . . and
> they spend a lot of time making money. They are very highly paid, their time is
> valuable. [. . .] They are a growing profession. And the problem is if we don't
> talk to the individuals, we have to go to their representative bodies, and there
> is only one real body that speaks for them . . . the CFA (Chartered Financial
> Analysts Institute). [. . .] We tend to have contact with big companies—just as
> we have with big auditors—the ones who do straddle the continents. Big invest-
> ment banks and people like that, they have analysts. (Author's interview with
> Whittington)

However, the growing and, to some extent, controversial debate on the
incorporation of user interests is also about not losing sight of other interests and thus revolves around the question of balancing the participation
of all interested parties.

> And now, I think we've got to get not too carried away because some would say
> all that matters [are analysts] . . . some would say follow your concepts, what
> are financial statements for? They are for decision usefulness . . . the objective
> is the decision-useful needs of users. [. . .] But, I think that's over-simplistic and
> we are a little bit in danger at the moment only because they [users] have been
> hanging back for so long. [. . .] There is great enthusiasm at the moment but
> I still think you have to listen to preparers, you still have to listen to auditors,
> you still have to listen to regulators and all the other groups around as well.
> (Author's interview with Macintosh)

Tweedie points to the IASB's intention to more actively integrate users
of financial statements.

> The primary purpose of financial statements is to articulate the financial per-
> formance of companies to their ultimate owners—investors. It is therefore
> appropriate that investors are closely involved in the development of financial
> reporting standards. One of our priorities is to find ways to increase investor
> participation in our work. (Author's interview with Tweedie)

In conclusion, the analysis underscores the remarkably weak representation of the users of financial statements both on the Board and throughout the entire IASB network. The interviews conducted as part of this
research confirm that finding. Although the absence of users can hardly
be claimed to be a completely new phenomenon, it has increasingly begun
to draw the attention of the principal players. While the importance of
users in standard setting is acknowledged in the abstract, it is a striking
observation that a specification is nowhere to be found of precisely which
users are meant when speaking of *decision usefulness* or the *users of financial statements*. The diversity of users and the problems of organizing user

interests render interest representation more difficult in this case while making it all the easier for the dominant actors of the IASB network to close the gap by giving their own spin to what they conceive of as user interests.

The IASB took the initiative in 2003 and began organizing the interest representation of financial analysts on its own. For this purpose, it set up the Analyst Representative Group (ARG), which consists of fifteen financial analysts who convene three times annually with five Board members for meetings in order to voice their interests. While banks, insurers, and the associations of financial analysts play a role in this setting, a number of funds and institutional investors are also represented. In addition, the Board has recently been joined by individuals who had previously been active as analysts. Stephen Cooper, in fact, had been a member of ARG before becoming a part-time and now full-time member of the Board. In July two more individuals with previous experience as analysts joined the Board: Patrick Finnegan, who was with the CFA Institute, and Patricia McConnell, a former analyst with Bear Stearns.

In spite of such efforts at integration, the heterogeneity of user representatives remains a defining feature of this interest group. In practice, the IASB's attempts at intensifying contacts with parties representing users has resulted in the Board determining who is to be considered the legitimate representatives of user groups. This suggests that the auditors, as the dominant group within the IASB, have succeeded in interpreting what is to be conceived as user interests instead of actually involving users in the process of defining those interests. There are some weak signs of change, but so far there is no substantial evidence suggesting that the integration of individuals with specialized analyst knowledge could in any way offset the influence that the auditing firms are able to exercise. Ironically, even if they did set up a counterpoint to some degree, most likely an increasing focus on the users of financial statements would further spur the fair value orientation of IAS/IFRS and heighten criticism directed against the IASB in that respect.

The analysis has demonstrated that it is primarily auditors and accounting firms that dominate both the IASB Board and the extended organizational network of transnational standard setting. They provide the channel by which user interests enter the standard setting arena so that we can expect those interests to be filtered and interpreted in accordance with the accountants' perspective. This is but another means working in favor of maintaining the auditors' dominance. They have strengthened the principle of decision usefulness, on one hand, while they—instead of the users themselves—determine what the concept actually means, on the other.

## 6.3    CONCLUSION: DOMINATION OF INDIVIDUALS AND ORGANIZATIONS

The longitudinal analysis of the regulatory power of the individuals and organizations involved in the IASB's standard setting activities demonstrates the strong position of accountants within the IASB. This is due both to the significance assigned to "technical" expertise as a necessary prerequisite for appointment to the Board and the prominent role of the globally operating accounting firms, which represent the most significant type of organization among the IASB network. The Board has for a long time been dominated by a small group of individuals who have known one another for many years and have been involved in the development of the IASB and its standards. They combine previous experience both as auditors and in the field of national standard setting.

For a substantial part of the period surveyed the Anglo-American coordination group G4+1 formed the nucleus of the Board. It has not only made its mark on the IASB's organizational structure but, above all, has also been instrumental in promoting the capital market orientation of the standards. The G4+1 has played a considerable role in overcoming resistance from inside and outside the organization to modeling the IASB according to Anglo-American preferences and has laid the groundwork for a development that still defines the organization today. The group's decision to formally disband in 2002 can be interpreted as a consequence of its success.

Dominance by a small group of organizations and the absence of the users of financial statements are key characteristics of the IASB organizational network. Both the network analysis and the expert interviews attest to the absence of this interest group. In the meantime, even the IASB itself has come to view this as a problem, which has led to creating the Analyst Representative Group (ARG) to fill the representational gap and advance the integration of users, i.e. financial analysts and investor representatives in particular. This mode of integration at the same time serves as a venue to select users: Instead of offering already existing organizations, such as Chartered Financial Analysts, the opportunity to represent their constituency on the IASB, the Board itself organizes a body in the form of the ARG to represent the users. In this way, the IASB defines who the legitimate stakeholders are, thus retaining the power to define which user interests are considered legitimate claims to representation. The ambiguity of the concept of decision usefulness, demonstrated in Chapter 4, provides scope for the key actors of the IASB network to take advantage of their powerful position and construct user interests from their own perspective.

A look at the academic debate in the USA shows that this mode of constructing user interests is a familiar phenomenon. There, academics in particular have been involved in painting a picture of users based on a specific conception of rational behavior:

> In stressing the *rational*, users can be seen more as hypothetical readers of financial statements than as actual readers. Hypothetical, as we can presume that they behave in particular ways (otherwise they are irrational) and that they are therefore interested in only particular types of information. [. . .] The rational economic decision maker that is the current focus of standard-setting is primarily concerned with economic events and transactions and with predicting their impacts upon an entity's future cash flows, future profitability and future financial position. [. . .] In these ways, this conception/construction of the financial statement user works to embed accounting and accounting standard-setting more deeply within an economic discourse that holds efficiency and growth as the appropriate ends for organizations. (Young, 2006, p. 596, emphasis in original)

These insights provide a possible explanation for the absence of the users of financial statements that would otherwise be difficult to explain. At the same time, they point to the complexity of accounting and the importance of having accepted sources of expertise at one's disposal. This renders experience in the field of accounting a crucial qualification for working on the Board. The preponderance of individuals of Anglo-American background ensures that their pragmatic orientation and appreciation for private sector self-regulation is accepted as the common ground reflecting shared basic values, which Board members from other countries are committed to as well. Therefore, following a liberal tradition and applying evidence-based deliberation favors decisions catering to international capital markets. The absence of users of financial statements, however, to some degree remains an open question and needs more empirical analysis. This also includes investigating to what extent analysts and investors, particularly those specialized in administering the allocation of capital, use the information provided in financial statements. It would be worth considering whether they have additional and perhaps even more precise information at their disposal and want to enjoy this advantage over competitors.

This possibility does not contradict the dominance of the Big Four, which have not only played an active part in standard setting but also a crucial role in standards interpretation in particular. In providing their expertise, they influence the direction of the IASB. This enhances the prospects of maintaining their worldwide monopoly on the provision of auditing services since they have an edge over their competitors and their involvement in the IASB yields additional benefits in terms of reputation. The Big Four have even gained greater significance in recent years, as the result of market concentration (Suddaby et al., 2007), on one hand, while they have been successful in displacing the professional associations, both nationally and internationally, as the *locus* of defining relevant expertise in the field of accounting, on the other (see Greenwood et al., 2002; Botzem, 2008; Mennicken, 2008).

In terms of the influence the members of the IASB decision-making body exert on transnational standard setting, it can be maintained that their professional knowledge plays a significant role. With regard to the IASB network, we may conclude that the four globally operating account-ing firms are the key actors. Both aspects are closely related: As long as a situation persists where the majority of the Board members owe their qualifications for employment with the IASB to the time spent working for one of the Big Four, they can hardly be expected to take a critical view of the latter's predominance. That dominant position is further reinforced by the fact that the four major accounting firms not only provide significant expertise but also a substantial share of the necessary financial resources to the Board. Finally, the ambiguity of the concept of decision usefulness and the absence of user interests guarantee that there will continue to be sufficient demand for the services that they have to offer.

## NOTES

1.  The trend is essentially the same even if we only take into consideration IASB member-ship since 2001. Mean membership for the time span from 2001 to 2007 is 6.4 years. In my view, however, the similarity of tasks between the IASC and the IASB underscores the continuity and justifies the simple addition of the period of service on the board of the earlier organization. The recent reappointments do not significantly affect the mean value for 2008 either, since the three members that left the Board in summer 2007 had not been on the former IASC Board. This is an additional indication of the high stability in the core membership of the IASB Board.
2.  The Monitoring Board has been omitted from this analysis because its composition is fixed and its role so far unclear. The following account uses the official names of IASB bodies before the relabeling in March 2010.
3.  Freeman's approach to measuring degree centrality is a way of assessing power positions in social networks. It identifies power positions based on connections between actors. The calculations show that in each year analyzed accounting firms are the most powerful actors in the network. The calculation of Bonacich's power measure, which additionally takes into account the power positions of the actors one is connected to, yields similar results (for both measures, see Hanneman and Riddle, 2005, Chapter 10). Both meas-ures, however, are premised on the equivalence of ties between organizations, which in our case is a problematic assumption since it conflicts with the IASB constitution that assigns its committees different tasks and sizes. For this reason, analyses of both the Freeman and Bonacich measures cannot be expected to render meaningful results in relation to the IASB network.

# 7. The politics of transnational accounting regulation

Recent financial, economic, and political crises have put the cross-border regulation of economic affairs into the limelight. Vibrant discussions are taking place about how rules and regulation might be shaped to address the flaws of global financialized capitalism. However, three years after the collapse of Lehman Brothers, when everyone briefly paused for breath because the very survival of the global financial system seemed at stake, the picture is rather mixed: Serious change in financial regulation appears to be slow, cumbersome, and incremental at best. This is equally true for accounting where, for a short while, the content of International Financial Reporting Standards and the organizational configuration of the IASB made it into business press headlines and the G20 summit documents. Transnational accounting standardization was discussed far beyond the small circles of experts that usually debate business combinations, operating segments, or fair value measurement. Most important, public deliberations revealed the political nature not only of accounting standards but also of the procedures of standard setting.

After a brief period of public discourse, outrage appears to have calmed down. However, empirical scrutiny of transnational accounting standardization shows that paying close attention is merited now more than ever. Organizational aspects of accounting regulation are particularly instructive and help us to understand the emergence of the IASB and the dominant position it enjoys today. In this book, I have analyzed the interrelated changes in norms, organizational procedures, and actor constellations to explain developments in accounting standardization over the past four decades. The reconstruction of the IASB not only traces significant events; it also allows an institutionalist explanation to be given for the standard setter's unique position in financial market regulation. I will return to the conceptual conclusions at the end of this chapter after giving a brief summary of the book's findings.

## 7.1 CHANGING CONFLICTS OVER TIME: DYNAMICS OF TRANSNATIONAL STANDARD SETTING

Continuous change is a key characteristic of the IASB's development and also explains how the organization managed to become the leading standard setter in accounting. Initially, accounting standardization was dominated by a loosely coupled network of accounting practitioners delegated by national professional associations. The IASB's predecessor was above all an arena in which actors got together to exchange ideas and coordinate their standard setting activities. During its first 25 years, the prospects were far from certain: The International Accounting Standards Committee was only a marginal player, hardly able to deliver a coherent set of precise standards for financial reporting. Nevertheless, the backing received from some international organizations, such as the OECD, and a coalition supported by the International Chamber of Commerce and other business advocates bolstered the organization in rivaling European and UN attempts to harmonize accounting standards.

Up to today, transnational accounting regulation has remained contested terrain—in terms of both the content of standards and the general rules of the game. However, the scope of today's conflicts has reduced significantly. While incompatible principles and cultural and economic singularities initially stood in open contrast to each other, now friction largely occurs within the widely accepted Anglo-American, anti-statist, pro-market paradigm. In addition, the IASB has itself become a viable actor, shaping international accounting standards and thus the regulatory requirements for thousands of companies all over the world. A key explanation for the establishment of a transnational regulatory path in accountancy is the organization's power to manage and control standard setting and define the required expertise through and for these procedures. Thus, the emergence of the private transnational regulator can be traced back to three analytically distinct, yet empirically interwoven aspects of accounting standardization: The content of rules, organizational procedures, and the actors involved.

First, the content of IAS/IFRS clearly caters to the needs of capital markets. Initially, the integrative approach led to opening the organization up to a variety of diverse interests and to collecting a set of imprecise, sometimes even contradicting normative prescriptions. For many years this hampered the adoption of standards by firms and impeded recognition by national regulators. However, widening the spectrum of parties interested in the issue never endangered the market-oriented majority but rather consolidated the dominance of private firms, mainly preparers and auditors, and led to market-oriented standards: After a number of revisions, IAS/IFRS clearly privileged actors eager to address the information needs of capital market actors. Limiting the scope of standards mostly to shareholders and other capital providers was accompanied by an orientation towards fair value accounting. Identifying market values and privileging them over other information further spurred dynamics to narrow IAS/IFRS by marginalizing many elements of historical cost accounting. A cyclical relationship between narrowing the addressees of IAS/IFRS and the expansion of fair value accounting can be identified.

The dispute between assumptions of what constitutes shareholder value and stewardship principles documented in Chapter 4 is particularly instructive with regard to this shift in conflicts. On one hand, it highlights differences between a British–continental European understanding of the purpose of management accounting on the one hand and a US conception of reporting purposes on the other. It also shows that solely considering logics of capital allocation, which US actors frequently argue for, is not a universally shared goal in financial reporting. Nevertheless, these differences must not be overestimated. They point to nuances within the camp of rationalist, Anglo-American, market orientation. While the role of management in presenting financial reports is debated, the dominant logic is left intact: The information needs of all economic and societal actors are subsumed under the assumed information needs of capital providers. The ambiguous term "decision usefulness" indicates that not only do standard setters not always agree on what is meant in detail, but also the term's imprecision allows them to pursue a market-oriented paradigm without needing to agree on all details. The ambiguity gives the actors involved in standard setting, and those applying the rules, some freedom to define and interpret IAS/IFRS according to their own needs.

This also enables the IASB to work on rules and regulations that extend the application of IAS/IFRS beyond listed corporations. The organization's intention to issue standards applicable to small and medium-sized enterprises (SMEs) and even to not-for-profit entities, such as foundations, charities, and housing cooperatives, underlines its wide-ranging ambitions. The endeavor to issue standards for entities not seeking investment capital makes it clear that the dominant actors deem IAS/IFRS to be a suitable accounting framework, not just for publicly listed corporations but for the economy as a whole. Capital market orientation, as defined in IAS/IFRS, is becoming a basic guiding principle of modern globalized capitalism.

Criticism that the procyclical nature of IAS/IFRS has spurred the financial crisis has revealed the political nature of IASB standards and the distributive effects they entail. Framing the crisis as a "very rare circumstance," the IASB and the FASB departed from their basic principles and allowed banks to circumvent fair value accounting by reclassifying assets from the trading book to the bank book. In public debates, the market orientation of certain standards was criticized, but the underlying logic was rarely questioned. This corresponds to the debates within the IASB: Rather than arguing over the pros and cons of fair value accounting in general, arguments are exchanged over the depth and range of market values. In short, fair value accounting remains largely unchallenged while the debate is instead about the limits and limitations of "full fair value".

Second, the IASB's organizational configuration epitomizes the principles of Anglo-American self-regulation: The Board is assigned sole authority in all matters of "technical" decision-making in standard setting. It is kept free of what practitioners consider illegitimate, political interference. Trustees exercise oversight (recently joined in this by the Monitoring Board), determine the overall policy of the organization, and ensure adequate funding. Formally, rules and procedures measure up to the frequently invoked principles of transparency, accessibility, responsiveness, and accountability. In practice, the organizational configuration and the formalized process attract criticism because of hurdles for participation and a biased organizational structure favoring selected groups of actors. Initially, the Board guaranteed the representation of certain status groups and reserved seats for seven national standard setters. These requirements were eased, but in 2010 a geographic quota for Board membership was introduced. This can be interpreted as an attempt at enhancing the IASB's credibility in emerging markets while securing the supremacy of Anglo-American actors.

For the composition of the board of trustees, quotas were relaxed when requirements for certain professional backgrounds were abolished. Instead, requirements to include trustees from Africa and South America are welcome signals to peripheral economies, but there remain serious weaknesses in accountability regarding trustee recruitment. Non-transparent procedures of cooptation were overcome by setting up a trustee appointments advisory group aimed at assisting the recruitment process, a task now exercised by the newly installed Monitoring Board. Given severe criticism from the ranks of the G20, the European Parliament, and also some academics, the changes undertaken by the IASB are minimal, however. Lack of accountability remains the weak point of the IASB structure. In particular, the Board's full independence remains irreconcilable with democratic decision making and input legitimacy based on inclusion and participation. Instead, standard setters refer to the high quality of their work, pointing to practical relevance and acceptance in the field, thereby emphasizing output legitimacy instead.

An additional means of legitimizing IASB activities is formalized consultation. The due process clearly outlines the successive steps to be applied in developing a standard, an interpretation, or parts of the new conceptual framework. A more thorough analysis, however, reveals that the process does not allow for much long-lasting influence. The Board is mostly interested in gathering new information on which to base its decisions. The process is limited to complementing the Board's work; it is a channel for information, not a mode of participation or codetermination. Inclusiveness is more of a legitimation strategy than an operational practice (cf. Quack, 2010, pp. 11ff.). Regarding the process, most academics and accounting practitioners perceive the consultation procedures as intended to organize the bottom-upward flow of information. However, this tends to underestimate the opposite effect of spreading the IASB's perspective via these processes. In issuing a discussion paper or an exposure draft, the IASB puts forth carefully presented arguments that usually demand intensive consideration and require substantial material and intellectual resources to adequately deal with. The multiplication of IASB processes by national and European standard-setting bodies leads to the Board's positions on "technical" issues being further disseminated. Thus, the process is becoming more than a mode of consulting the interested public. It is also turning into a means of informing the general debate and framing how accounting issues are to be perceived. Board members can use the process to put forward their views on how accounting solutions should be adequately treated, thus making it a powerful tool for communicating their views top-downward.

Both the organizational configuration and the consultation procedures are contested. The most obvious sticking point has been the considerable accountability deficit criticized by political actors but also by industry, most often from continental Europe. While the IASB carefully reacted to the discomfort voiced openly, other issues remain untouched, such as the complete independence of the Board and the formalistic and resource-intensive consultation procedures. So far, the IASB has proven successful in fending off most outside claims. Even the Monitoring Board does not seem to usher in substantial change, largely due to the fact that its decisions require consensus and it can only try to influence trustee selection. It explicitly lacks any influence over "technical" decisions. The introduction of the Monitoring Board could even have the adverse effect of binding national and international regulators and committing them to the IASB's cause without granting any substantial influence.

Disputes over organizational configuration are not likely to disappear, but recent changes make it more difficult for critics to tease out the political nature of the IFRS Foundation and its consultation procedures. It is precisely the formalistic, seemingly transparent nature of the organizational structure and procedures that, at first sight, paints an impressive picture of state-of-the-art transnational governance. Classifying the IASB as a private standard setter issuing voluntary rules would indeed lead to a positive assessment. But the fact that IAS/IFRS are de facto binding for many thousands of corporations and potentially many other organizations leads to a more pessimistic view: The IASB should not only live up to the accountability requirements of a private club but must be regarded as a powerful, transnational rule setter affecting both private and public third parties. In view of its substantial impact, the IASB's self-regulatory governance provisions remain highly problematic.

Third, the composition of the organization's Board and the wider network underline the uncontested dominance of Anglo-American accountants, of auditing firms, and of some national and international regulatory agencies. Recently, the IASB has increased Board size to accommodate a wider spectrum of individuals, predominately to include representatives of emerging economies without displacing experts from industrialized countries. Representation in the wider IASB network via three selected bodies also shows incremental change over time. Nevertheless, the inner core continues to be dominated by auditing firms, some international organizations, a few preparers, and recently a small number of national standard setters.

National and professional backgrounds are important because they shape standardization practices. Shared norms and beliefs are crucial in reaching consensus but also constitute the normative foundation of the transnational community of accounting policy bureaucrats (cf. Power, 2009, p. 329). Empirical analysis indicates that a common background in auditing experience, namely as partners of globally active accounting firms, has been an essential element in constituting the IASB during its first years. The coexistence of the G4+1, the network of Anglo-American standard setters, is particularly revealing because it indicates the firm determination of Anglo-American interest groups to accept no other solution than the one advocated and enforced by them, which is essentially today's IASB. The European Commission and some other actors mainly from continental Europe tried to push for a different, more participatory, bottom-up model of transnational standardization but lost out to the expertise-based structure advanced by the well-connected elite network of Anglo-American standard setters.

Despite the recent introduction of geographic background as a criterion for Board recruitment, national backgrounds are becoming increasingly insignificant as an indicator of material interests (cf. Djelic and Quack, 2010). As the case of the India-born member of the Board shows, national background is increasingly less meaningful as a category for measuring representation: He acquired much of his practical experience in North America, India, and Europe, received his PhD in the USA, and is a chartered accountant in India as well as a US Certified Public Accountant. There is reason to believe national origin and positions on selected issues are only loosely coupled. Shared cultural knowledge might ease decision making, but individuals should not be mistaken for national representatives as they are not delegated by any country or jurisdiction. In fact, the IASB is very explicit in granting individual Board membership exclusively on the basis of "technical" expertise. The simultaneous adoption of a geographic quota indicates that the IASB is trying to square the circle by pacifying a number of potentially conflicting interests without giving up real power.

This becomes clear when observing discussions on the Board. "Technical" issues are deliberated at an extremely sophisticated level. Arguments are exchanged with a high degree of abstraction, requiring profound knowledge and superb skill in the English language. The quasi-academic discourse during Board meetings allows IASB staff to play a major role, as they are often the ones most knowledgeable about specific accountancy issues. In 2009 more than 50 full-time staff members were tasked with working exclusively on the content of standards. They constitute an important pool of knowledge which gives the IASB considerable independence and allows coordination with other relevant players at eye level, such as the US FASB.

In contrast, national professional associations no longer play a prominent role in standard setting. At the national level they have often been replaced by regulators, standard setters, and professional services firms. The global oligopoly of the Big Four auditing firms has moved to a central position in standard setting, not merely in their capacity as services firms; they are also central *loci* of expertise. Moreover, they strive to establish their practical knowledge as authoritative expertise by using their position to define issues and frame practical accounting problems. These attempts have been evidenced through network analysis covering the last nine years. It shows that the Big Four not only supply 20 percent of all delegated individuals and secure about a third of the IASB's funding, but also represent the only type of organization positioned at the heart of the organizational network throughout the entire period, no matter what the constellation. Furthermore, the Big Four by themselves roughly match the total number of "users of financial statements" represented on the IASB bodies when applying the most inclusive definition for the term. Opting for a narrow understanding of "users" (which includes only funds, financial analysts, and their respective associations) each of the Big Four firms individually matches the weight of all of these users taken together.

In light of the striking underrepresentation of the users of financial statements, the official rhetoric of "decision usefulness" as the prime criterion for all IASB activities needs explanation. This is a finding that was not initially expected, and I can only make three tentative suggestions to explain the absence of users in transnational standard setting. First, my interviews with IASB standard setters suggest that the organization is aware of this absence but is simply unable to motivate these actors to engage in standard setting activities. Second, despite constant pledges to integrate users, standard setting practitioners, above all auditors and big firms, are content with this absence and take advantage of this circumstance. They manage to hold on to their positions by defining those problems to be considered relevant and the corresponding "technical" answers. As they benefit from user absence, they are not overly interested in seriously engaging users. Third, the users of financial statements, in particular big funds and specialized analysts, have at their disposal, on which to base their investment decisions, information that is more detailed and timelier than that provided by preparers in their financial statements. Users therefore might not care too much about the IASB's standards so long as these are principally in line with capital market orientation and a financialized global economy.

The absence of the users merits further research. Here it can only be speculated why users are not engaged and perhaps do not think anything is really at stake for them. For now, the representation of user interests is mainly left to investment banks, which are at the same time users and preparers of financial statements. The dominance of accountants and auditing firms is not seriously challenged, and they continue to play the main part in framing accounting issues, thus ensuring that the firms' interpretation of relevant expertise remains uncontested. This is unproblematic for resourceful users as they are able to access additional, perhaps even more valuable information than is presented in financial reports. They might even want to keep the information most relevant to their investment decisions from being disclosed in standardized form in order to stay ahead of competition.

## 7.2   POLITICAL DIMENSIONS OF ACCOUNTING REGULATION

Among accounting scholars with an interest in social science there is no doubt that the content of standards defined in IAS/IFRS is eminently political (cf. Hopwood, 1983, 1990; Ordelheide, 2004). This book complements these insights by showing that the modes of standard setting also have far reaching social and political effects. Organizational procedures and the inclusion—and exclusion—of interested parties are political aspects of transnational accounting regulation. So far, this political dimension has been underrated in analyzing standard setting and the particular distribution of corporate profits following from those standards. Open public criticism during the financial crisis highlights the unease shared by many practitioners and politicians as the political nature of the IASB has begun to become more clearly discernible. The quick disappearance of transnational accounting standardization from financial press headlines does not mean that this has changed substantially.

Even in the light of recent organizational changes, specifically the establishment of the Monitoring Board, the stability and continuity of the self-regulatory governance arrangements are remarkable. And despite recent interpretations by international political economists that consider these changes to be a restoration of public authority over private standard setting (cf. Posner, 2010; Leblond, 2011), the findings presented here support an alternative assessment. As I have shown in my analysis, there is little evidence to justify such hopes. Instead, the IASB has managed to emerge from the financial crisis largely unchanged (Nölke, 2009); it is still exercising private, expertise-based standard setting.

Increasing activity at the European level does not stand in contrast to these findings. Quite the opposite: continued differentiation of standard setting procedures under the auspices of EFRAG, increasing coordination amongst national standard setters within Europe (for example PAAinE), and above all a more demanding approach by the European Parliament are encouraging signs that the economic and social impact of IAS/IFRS are given more weight. Heightened European demands for accountability and a more comprehensive inclusion of societal stakeholders have the potential to counter the expertise-based Anglo-American dominance still characterizing the IASB and its standards. Interpreting the IASB simply as an agent of the European Commission, as some advocates of principal–agent theory would suggest, is misleading, however (cf. Leblond, 2011), because it underestimates the dynamics within Europe and suggests that the EC would be able and willing to distill a coherent European position out of divergent interests. As with the national background of Board members, geographic jurisdictions are becoming less and less indicative of influence on transnational standard setting. While some interests still might be successfully aggregated at the national level, large and resourceful actors are able to dig their own channels for promoting their interests and shaping their environment. That notwithstanding, politics, even partisan politics, may surge every once in a while, but sustained influence is unlikely to be exercised in this way unless internal structures and the procedures of the IASB are well understood and openly discussed, so that they can be adapted accordingly.

This leads to the problematic dominance of accountants and the big auditing firms as standard setters. The latter were able to displace professional associations in at least two ways: First, big firms have become the *locus* of relevant expertise and have managed to secure their oligopoly by becoming an indispensable source of reputation for preparers of financial statements. Not only has this allowed them to acquire the practical expertise that they bring to the IASB but also it has provided the opportunity to secure their leading position in service provision. Second, working for a big firm has become an essential career step for auditors aspiring to play in the global league of auditing and standard setting. The big firms' personal networks enable their professional staff to acquire unique professional skills when doing cutting-edge work for the firm concerned and its clients. The global concentration in the auditing industry has led to the first tier of globally operating firms clearly drawing further and further ahead of the overwhelming majority of the industry and fortifying their central position in standard setting. The recent inclusion in the IASB network of a second tier of firms, such as BDO and Grant Thornton, has so far been largely symbolic.

The most significant inclusion of new constituents is the coopting of national regulators. When the IASB opened up to include board members who had previously been employed by the Chinese state bureaucracy or gained practical experience in India and Brazil, this gave a clear indication of its intention to diffuse standards to all corners of the globe. The prominent position granted the US Securities and Exchange Commission can also be interpreted as an attempt to finally bring the USA under the IASB umbrella and make IAS/IFRS the only relevant set of standards for listed companies worldwide.

Care in assembling the core gatekeepers of IAS/IFRS is also an explanation for the IASB's late but final success in diffusing its rules. This underlines the differences between the transnational standardization project under the auspices of the IASB and other private initiatives, for example, in setting industry standards (cf. Botzem and Dobusch, 2009). Mainstream standardization literature often identifies the effective diffusion of rules as a prerequisite for organizational development. In accounting, the IASB and its predecessor had worked on voluntary standards for 30 years before they enjoyed significant recognition. It was the European Union that opted for IAS/IFRS and recognized them for fear that listed corporations would otherwise submit to US standards. The EU endowed the IASB indirectly with desperately needed public authority to set standards. Without the EU's support, the IASB would quite likely have failed. The organization's confrontational stance towards the EC and the European Parliament gives evidence of the experts' independence and their determination to fend off public influence. It also suggests that the explanatory potential of principal–agent approaches is low at best when studying the IASB as these only permit an inadequate account of the organization's leeway and underrate the importance of expertise, which is concentrated with the IASB to a greater extent than with public bodies.

Struggles with the European Union and over the carve-out of single provisions in IAS 39 show that the global diffusion of IAS/IFRS involves maintaining a delicate balance between developing rules that are universally applicable to corporations wherever they do business, on one hand, and allowing sufficient discretion in interpreting and applying those rules to account for local specificities, on the other. One possible way to reconcile this tension is to issue abstract standards that deliberately leave room for local adaption, even though this poses the risk of complicating the comparability of financial reports. While such a fragmentation cannot entirely be ruled out, it would be premature to insist on overly strict homogeneity in financial reporting. The ambiguity inherent in many basic concepts, such as fair value accounting and decision usefulness, reserves a considerable degree of discretion for actors; it is, however, important to note that the Board members themselves interpret and legitimize such ambiguity. Given regional and cultural specificities and different corporate needs, abstract characterizations of recognition and measurement are instrumental in leaving room to accommodate vast economic variety. Underneath the surface of one set of standards, we are likely to find wide-ranging differences in accounting practice.

Widespread adoption of standards is the central source of legitimacy for the IASB. However, output legitimacy is ensured only if IAS/IFRS manage to strike a balance between optimal "technical" solutions and general acceptance among accounting practitioners. The harsh criticism experienced during the financial crisis indicates the fragility of relying too greatly on output legitimacy—particularly since input legitimacy is of little significance to the IASB. The strong reliance on output legitimacy is accompanied by transparent procedures invoking generally accepted norms such as neutrality of consultation and responsiveness to special needs. However, while the IASB's procedural legitimacy might harmonize with the dominant discourse of transparent and efficient global self-regulation (cf. Quack, 2010), my analysis reveals that it is much more fragile than it appears at first sight. Increasing discontent with the process might quickly lead to an erosion of the claims for legitimacy attached to the standard setting procedures.

## 7.3   CONCLUSION: TRANSNATIONAL INSTITUTION BUILDING THROUGH EXPERTISE

As the theoretical overview in Chapter 2 has shown, an interdisciplinary perspective is insightful in explaining the transformation and firm establishment of the International Accounting Standards Board (IASB) in the course of four decades. The emergence of this successful, private, transnational, regulatory body can be explained by drawing on different conceptual building blocks from the neighboring disciplines of accounting studies, sociology, and political economy. The findings of my book draw on this type of integrative approach and also contribute to theory building in the respective subdisciplines.

The main theoretical contributions can be characterized as follows: The core insight of accounting studies lies in profound knowledge about standards, their content, and how the rules are applied in practice. In particular, critical approaches sensitive to organizational and societal aspects help to understand the contested and political nature of accounting standardization. With regard to standard setting, the focus of these perspectives has predominantly been on national developments. The results presented here can contribute to strengthening a transnational perspective that overcomes national stereotypes that are often taken for granted without denying the relevance of specific conditions for agency.

Equally, the sociology of professions provides key insights that highlight shared beliefs and organizational aspects of social closure. The dominant, Anglo-American, self-regulatory paradigm shared by standard setters can only be understood against the background of self-confident, independent experts united by skepticism toward the state and the conviction of being the guardians of an ambitious global harmonization project. However, as the book shows, professional associations are no longer the main *loci* of expertise. Status and knowledge are primarily provided by big auditing firms and by the IASB as the single most important organization in standard setting. These findings enrich the sociology of professions by providing proof that big firms and global bureaucracies such as the IASB are new and perhaps even more important *loci* for shaping the normative foundations upon which experts rely and determining new criteria for social closure. The analysis has also unearthed insights valuable to organizational studies interested in transnational standard setting: Formalized procedures provide a controlled way of opening an organization by determining the rules of access for individuals and the flow of information. Consultation procedures constitute a semipermeable boundary used by the core organization to extend its influence by structuring its interorganizational environment.

Approaches in international political economy point to the important distributive effects of seemingly "technical" standards. The clear-cut orientation toward the needs of financial market actors is a key explanation for financialization, a process which shifts attention to the logics of profit accumulation and away from corporate production and old fashioned value generation. Political economists have pointed to the dynamics that increasingly turn firms into bundles of assets instead of socially embedded economic entities. However, the general claim of financialization needs to be contextualized and deconstructed in order to become verifiable. The empirical findings of this book have shown how these dynamics are implemented, usually as a compromise in the wake of intensive power games. A second stream of literature in comparative political economy has discussed the nature of private authority at play and taken note of the increasing interest of some public authorities in accountancy issues, mainly in Europe. Discussing this theme is helpful in countering an overly simplistic view that regulatory capacity simply moves from the public to the private realm. However, most public authority perspectives have the tendency to overestimate the significance of the mandate, competences, and intentions of public actors. The results presented here do not confirm the functional and apolitical notion of technical authority applied in some works (cf. Porter, 2005), while they do testify to the relevance attributed to the expertise-based modes of rule setting. As has become clear in the empirical chapters, the official rhetoric of "technical" expertise constitutes a domination strategy and is not to be mistaken for evidence of "technical" authority as a source of regulation bridging private and public rule making. At the heart of this book lies the key insight that expertise is used to depoliticize standard setting—one of the central power strategies in accounting standardization. This depoliticization is supported even by public actors when they accept the IASB and its rules of the game. A mere increase in competences should not be mistaken for democratically legitimized authority. Instead, the analysis has shown that accounting standardization is characterized by a hybrid structure of private–public actors and has repercussions for public authority; publicly mandated actors have to adapt to the rules of the private standard setter. This challenges the very nature of public authority, which has to cope with a newly emergent landscape of closely intertwined national and international institutions.

In addition to the theoretical contributions to existing theories, the case of the IASB also provides empirical insights into the dynamics of transnational institution building. First of all, it confirms the general observation that institutional density is increasing (Pierson, 2000). Transnational

accounting standardization serves as an example of complex social inter-
dependence characterized by new institutions effectively formulating new
policies. In accounting this is evidenced by a reduction in heterogeneity
working toward pro-market rules and procedures. At the heart of these
dynamics lie institutional mechanisms such as financialization, formalization, and domination. Their reinforcing nature makes these mechanisms
key to understanding how transnational institutions emerge, stabilize, and
remain adaptive.

First, regarding the content of standards, the successive exclusion
of alternative principles has led to an orientation toward fueling and
safeguarding the distributive logics of capital markets. Establishing and
reformulating fair value accounting reaffirms the financialized modes of
economic decision making. Second, with respect to continuous organizational adjustment and formalized procedures of rule making, the emphasis
on the transparent and responsive steps in standard setting indicates that
procedural logics are a core building block in transnational institutionalization. Formalized procedures are an important resource for actors
striving to issue de facto binding rules spanning the globe. Third, the
domination of core actors, individuals and organizations alike, involves
the strategic inclusion of gatekeepers while at the same time marginalizing and excluding weak societal stakeholders. The construction of absent
third parties, such as users of financial statements, is an additional indication of how the mechanism of domination works in practice. The mutually
reinforcing nature of all three mechanisms, however, must not be mistaken
for a linear, teleological development.

In institutional terms, the central element in explaining the IASB's
viability is the complementary nature of three aspects: Normative content,
procedures, and actor constellations. Over time, they have moved closer
together, exhibiting spillover effects and creating mutual linkages. The
three elements do more than complement each other along the lines of
expertise-based self-regulation: They also compensate for potential weaknesses in the others. For instance, successfully diffused standards might
make up for procedural shortcomings while the positional power of key
actors enables them to overcome a lack of precision in the authoritative pronouncements. Complementarity of transnational institutions in
accounting standardization is further enhanced by homogeneity of pro-
market, self-regulatory norms spanning the three aspects identified above.

The IASB and the wider institutional network it is embedded in can
be considered a transnational regulatory path characterized by reinforcing dynamics that are created and shaped by actors. The transnational
institutional arrangement has gained momentum but is not fixed. Under
conditions of dispersed authority and distributed agency, the regulatory

path exhibits elements of stability and reinforcement in which resourceful and knowledgeable actors embed their interests, making use of existing biases in their favor. In contrast to concepts of path dependence, the transnational regulatory path analyzed here is one shaped, maintained, and constantly reconfigured by powerful actors. Power is not expressed only in their capacity to dominate procedures and co-opt interested parties. In addition to *power over* others, they are also exercising *power to* establish and sustain the transnational standardization regime as the rules of the game, thus expanding their influence and the reach of IAS/IFRS.

The IASB's role as a "forum of collective sense making" (Garud and Karnøe, 2003) is one expression of the power to shape transnational regulatory institutions. More precisely, it is a "very particular field of relations [. . .] between certain institutions, economic and administrative processes, bodies of knowledge, systems of norms and measurement and classification techniques" (Burchell et al., 1985, p. 400). Drawing on Burchell and others, we can speak of the IASB and the environment in which the organization is embedded as representing a transnational regulatory constellation. A core element is the power to define relevant expertise. Accordingly, experts and practitioners play a key role in exercising their power to define expertise to exclude societal stakeholders unable to frame their interests in abstract, "technical" language. Expertise is the core building block of transnational institution building.

To sum up, the analysis presented here underscores the IASB's central role in regulating global financial markets. The increasing diffusion of its standards is proof of the organization's importance in structuring the environment of thousands of firms and countless individuals engaged in bookkeeping, accounting, and auditing for listed corporations. Soon, many more organizations will have to cope with the normative prescriptions initially developed for allocating financial capital but now claiming to represent the general logic of globalized capitalism. The expansion of IAS/IFRS underlines the political dimension of accounting regulation as codifying rationales in line with markets and their valuation principles.

There is little doubt that the IASB is here to stay. Even the most profound financial crisis in decades has not seriously unsettled the expertise-based mode of private rule setting. Instead, it has underscored the importance of the work undertaken by the organization and the individuals responsible for setting standards. It has also revealed some serious flaws in the governance structure of standard setting, not least concerning the practice of only selectively including certain interest groups. Weaknesses in accountability will remain on the agenda and could provide an avenue for societal actors to step up their claims against the IASB. Developments at the European level are instructive in this regard. National standard setters team up to coordinate their interests and civil-society actors start to cooperate with parliamentarians with the goal of weaving an institutional fabric that will allow previously excluded actors to participate even though this might not draw applause from "technical" experts, who would prefer to keep their own company. A comprehensive socioeconomic perspective clearly situates accounting standardization at the heart of socioeconomic decision making and suggests that the IASB should be opened up further. The organization could take some steps proactively and establish arenas for exchange as it has done in order to approach users. Should no such initiatives be taken, stakeholders and civil-society actors will have to find other ways to make themselves heard. The financial crisis has made it clear that too much is at stake to leave the rules that determine the definition and distribution of profits to insiders alone.

# Appendix:   Network data

| Abbreviation | Employing organization | Year | Body |
|---|---|---|---|
| AA | Arthur Andersen | 2001 | I, S, S |
| AAOIFI | Accounting and Auditing Organization for Islamic Financial Institutions | 2001 | S |
| | | 2002 | S |
| | | 2003 | S |
| | | 2009 | T |
| ABN | ABN Amro Bank | 2008 | T |
| | | 2009 | T |
| Acteo | ACTEO (Association pour la participation des entreprises françaises à l'harmonisation comptable internationale) | 2006 | S |
| | | 2007 | S |
| | | 2008 | S |
| | | 2009 | S |
| Aegon | Aegon Group NV | 2005 | S |
| | | 2007 | S |
| AMCOR | Amcor | 2001 | S |
| | | 2002 | S |
| | | 2003 | S |
| | | 2004 | S |
| AMF | Autorité des Marchés Financiers | 2001 | S |
| | | 2002 | S |
| | | 2003 | S |
| | | 2004 | S |
| | | 2005 | S |
| AssBankSG | Association of Banks in Singapore | 2009 | S |
| ASSBritI | Association of British Insurers | 2009 | S |
| AssIMR | Association for Investment Management and Research | 2001 | I |
| | | 2002 | I |
| | | 2003 | I |
| AUASB | Australian Accounting Standards Board | 2001 | T |
| | | 2002 | T |
| | | 2003 | T |
| AUEX | Australian Stock Exchange | 2004 | T |
| AUFRC | Australian Financial Reporting Council | 2008 | T |
| | | 2009 | T, S |

| Abbreviation | Employing organization | Year | Body |
|---|---|---|---|
| AUNZBank | Australian & New Zealand Banking Group Ltd | 2005 | S |
| | | 2006 | S |
| | | 2007 | S |
| | | 2008 | S |
| BanSant | Banco Santander | 2005 | S |
| | | 2006 | S |
| | | 2007 | S |
| | | 2008 | S |
| BASF | BASF AG | 2003 | T |
| | | 2004 | T |
| | | 2005 | T |
| | | 2006 | T |
| | | 2007 | T |
| | | 2008 | T |
| BDO | BDO International | 2009 | S |
| Bear | Bear, Stearns & Co. Inc. | 2001 | S |
| | | 2002 | S |
| | | 2003 | S |
| | | 2005 | S |
| | | 2006 | S |
| | | 2007 | S |
| Billimoria | S. B. Billimoria & Co. | 2001 | S |
| | | 2002 | S |
| | | 2003 | S |
| BIS | Bank for International Settlements | 2001 | S, T |
| | | 2002 | S, T |
| | | 2003 | S, T, T |
| | | 2004 | S, T |
| | | 2005 | S, T |
| | | 2006 | S, T |
| | | 2007 | S, T |
| | | 2008 | S |
| | | 2009 | S |
| Bombardier | Bombardier Inc. | 2007 | T |
| | | 2008 | I, T |
| | | 2009 | I, T |
| BRAssInd | Brazilian Association of Listed Companies | 2009 | S |
| BRSEx | Brazilian Securities and Exchange Commission (CVM) | 2001 | T |
| | | 2002 | T |
| | | 2003 | T |
| | | 2004 | T |
| | | 2005 | T |
| | | 2006 | T |
| | | 2007 | T |

| Abbreviation | Employing organization | Year | Body |
|---|---|---|---|
| CAASB | Canadian Accounting Standards Board | 2009 | S |
| CamCPA | Institute of Chartered Public Accountants of Cameroon | 2005 | S |
| | | 2006 | S |
| | | 2007 | S |
| | | 2008 | S |
| | | 2009 | S |
| CapInt | Capital International | 2005 | T |
| | | 2006 | T |
| | | 2007 | T |
| | | 2008 | T |
| | | 2009 | T |
| Cemex | Cemex SA de CV | 2005 | S |
| | | 2006 | S |
| | | 2007 | S |
| | | 2008 | S |
| CenCapMark | Centre for Capital Markets Development | 2001 | S |
| | | 2002 | S |
| | | 2003 | S |
| CFA | CFA Institute | 2004 | I, S |
| | | 2009 | S |
| CII | Council of Institutional Investors | 2009 | S |
| CNASC | China Accounting Standards Committee | 2001 | S |
| | | 2002 | S |
| | | 2003 | S |
| | | 2005 | S |
| | | 2009 | S |
| CNBudget | China Budget Authority | 2004 | S |
| CNCPA | Chinese Institute of Certified Public Accountants | 2006 | T |
| | | 2007 | T |
| | | 2008 | T |
| | | 2009 | T |
| CNFinMin | Ministry of Finance, People's Republic of China | 2006 | S |
| | | 2007 | S |
| | | 2008 | S |
| Consob | Commissione Nazionale per le Società e la Borsa (Italy) | 2008 | T |
| | | 2009 | T |
| CRUF | Corporate Reporting Users' Forum | 2009 | S |
| DBank | Deutsche Bank AG | 2001 | T |
| | | 2002 | T |
| | | 2003 | T |
| | | 2004 | T |
| | | 2005 | T |
| | | 2009 | T |

| Abbreviation | Employing organization | Year | Body |
|---|---|---|---|
| DisAna | Disclosure Analytics, Inc. | 2005 | I |
| Dow | Dow Chemical | 2005 | S |
| DRSC | Deutsches Rechnungslegungs Standards Comittee eV | 2005 | S |
| | | 2006 | S |
| | | 2007 | S |
| | | 2008 | S |
| DTT | Deloitte Touche Tohmatsu International | 2001 | I, S, S, S, S, T |
| | | 2002 | I, S, S, S, S, T |
| | | 2003 | I, S, S, S, T |
| | | 2004 | I, S, S, S, T |
| | | 2005 | I, S, S |
| | | 2006 | I, S, S |
| | | 2007 | I, S, S |
| | | 2008 | I, S, S |
| | | 2009 | I, S |
| ECB | European Central Bank | 2005 | S |
| | | 2006 | S |
| | | 2007 | S |
| | | 2008 | S |
| | | 2009 | S |
| Eckler | Eckler Partners | 2001 | S |
| | | 2002 | S |
| | | 2003 | S |
| | | 2004 | S |
| ECSAFA | Eastern Central and Southern African Federation of Accountants | 2001 | S |
| | | 2002 | S |
| | | 2003 | S |
| | | 2004 | S |
| EFRAG | European Financial Reporting Advisory Group | 2003 | S |
| | | 2004 | S |
| | | 2009 | S |
| EIRF | European Insurance and Reinsurance Federation | 2009 | S |
| Eni | Eni SpA | 2008 | I |
| | | 2009 | Î |

| Abbreviation | Employing organization | Year | Body |
|---|---|---|---|
| EU | European Commission | 2001 | I, S |
| | | 2002 | I, S |
| | | 2003 | I, S |
| | | 2004 | I, S |
| | | 2005 | I, S |
| | | 2006 | I |
| | | 2007 | I, S |
| | | 2008 | I, S |
| | | 2009 | I, S |
| EuroNatStan | Group of European national standard setters (France, Germany, Italy, and the UK) | 2009 | S |
| EuroRT | European Round Table of Industrialists | 2009 | S |
| EY | Ernst & Young | 2001 | I, S, T |
| | | 2002 | I, S, S, T |
| | | 2003 | I, S, S, S, T |
| | | 2004 | I, S, S, S, T |
| | | 2005 | I, S, S, T |
| | | 2006 | I, S, S, T |
| | | 2007 | I, S, S, T |
| | | 2008 | I, S, S, T |
| | | 2009 | I, S, T |
| Fed | US Federal Reserve Board | 2001 | S, T |
| | | 2002 | S, T |
| | | 2003 | S, T |
| | | 2004 | S, T |
| | | 2005 | T |
| FEI | Financial Executives International | 2001 | S |
| | | 2002 | S |
| | | 2003 | S |
| | | 2004 | S |
| | | 2005 | S |
| | | 2006 | S |
| | | 2007 | S |
| | | 2008 | S |
| | | 2009 | S, S |

| Abbreviation | Employing organization | Year | Body |
|---|---|---|---|
| FirstBank | FirstRand Bank Ltd | 2005 | S |
| | | 2006 | S |
| | | 2007 | I |
| | | 2008 | I |
| | | 2009 | I |
| GE | General Electric Company | 2001 | I, S |
| | | 2002 | I, S |
| | | 2003 | I, S |
| | | 2004 | I, S |
| | | 2005 | I |
| | | 2006 | I |
| | | 2007 | I |
| Generali | Assicurazioni Generali SpA | 2001 | S |
| | | 2002 | S |
| | | 2003 | S |
| | | 2004 | S |
| GNAIE | Group of North American Insurance Enterprises | 2009 | S |
| Goldman | The Goldman Sachs Group, Inc. | 2001 | S |
| | | 2002 | S |
| GrantThorn | Grant Thornton | 2009 | S |
| Group100 | Group of 100 (Australia) | 2009 | S |
| Haribhakti | Haribhakti & Co. | 2005 | S |
| | | 2006 | S |
| | | 2007 | S |
| | | 2008 | S |
| Hitachi | Hitachi Ltd | 2001 | S |
| | | 2002 | S |
| | | 2003 | S |
| | | 2004 | S |
| | | 2006 | S |
| | | 2007 | S |
| | | 2008 | S |
| HKEx | Hong Kong Exchanges & Clearing Ltd | 2001 | T |
| | | 2002 | T |
| | | 2003 | T |
| | | 2004 | T, S |
| | | 2005 | T |
| HKHotel | Hong Kong and Shanghai Hotels Ltd | 2001 | I |
| | | 2002 | I |
| | | 2003 | I |
| HSBC | Hongkong and Shanghai Banking Corporation Holdings plc | 2001 | S |
| | | 2002 | S |

| Abbreviation | Employing organization | Year | Body |
|---|---|---|---|
| | | 2003 | S |
| | | 2004 | S |
| | | 2005 | T |
| | | 2006 | T |
| | | 2007 | T |
| IAA | International Actuarial Association | 2007 | S |
| | | 2009 | S |
| IAAER | International Association for Accounting Education and Research | 2009 | S |
| IAIS | International Association of Insurance Supervisors | 2002 | S |
| | | 2003 | S |
| | | 2004 | S |
| | | 2005 | S |
| | | 2006 | S |
| | | 2007 | S |
| | | 2008 | S |
| | | 2009 | S |
| IASB | International Accounting Standards Board | 2001 | I |
| | | 2002 | I |
| | | 2003 | I |
| | | 2004 | I |
| | | 2005 | I |
| | | 2006 | I |
| | | 2007 | I |
| | | 2008 | I |
| | | 2009 | I |
| ICGN | International Corporate Governance Network | 2009 | S |
| IFAC | International Federation of Accountants | 2001 | S |
| | | 2002 | S, S |
| | | 2003 | S, S |
| | | 2004 | S, S |
| | | 2005 | S |
| | | 2006 | S |
| | | 2007 | S |
| | | 2008 | S |
| | | 2009 | S |
| IIF | Institute of International Finance | 2009 | S |
| IMF | International Monetary Fund | 2001 | S |
| | | 2002 | S |
| | | 2003 | S |
| | | 2004 | S |
| | | 2005 | S |

| Abbreviation | Employing organization | Year | Body |
|---|---|---|---|
| | | 2006 | S |
| | | 2007 | S |
| | | 2008 | S |
| | | 2009 | S |
| Infosys | Infosys | 2006 | T |
| | | 2007 | T |
| | | 2008 | T |
| | | 2009 | T |
| INNAdCAS | National Advisory Committee on Accounting Standards, India | 2004 | S |
| InvestCom | Investment Company Institute | 2009 | S |
| IOSCO | International Organization of Securities Commissions | 2001 | I, S, S |
| | | 2002 | I, S, S |
| | | 2003 | I, S, S |
| | | 2004 | I, S, S |
| | | 2005 | I, S, S |
| | | 2006 | I, S, S |
| | | 2007 | I, S, S |
| | | 2008 | I, S, S |
| | | 2009 | I, S, S, S |
| IslFSB | Islamic Financial Services Board | 2004 | S |
| | | 2005 | S |
| | | 2006 | S |
| | | 2007 | S |
| | | 2008 | S |
| JardMath | Jardine Matheson Ltd | 2005 | S |
| | | 2006 | S |
| | | 2007 | S |
| | | 2008 | S |
| | | 2009 | S |
| JPASB | Accounting Standards Board of Japan | 2001 | S |
| | | 2002 | S |
| | | 2003 | S |
| | | 2004 | S |
| | | 2005 | S |
| JPCPA | Japanese Institute of Certified Public Accountants | 2005 | T |
| | | 2006 | T |
| | | 2007 | T |
| | | 2008 | T |
| | | 2009 | T |

| Abbreviation | Employing organization | Year | Body |
|---|---|---|---|
| JPFSA | Japanese Financial Service Agency | 2001 | S |
| | | 2002 | S |
| | | 2003 | S |
| | | 2004 | S |
| | | 2005 | S |
| | | 2007 | S |
| | | 2008 | S |
| | | 2009 | S |
| JPMor | JP Morgan | 2001 | S |
| | | 2002 | S |
| | | 2003 | S, T |
| | | 2004 | T |
| | | 2005 | S, T |
| | | 2006 | S |
| | | 2007 | S |
| | | 2008 | S, S |
| JPSAA | Securities Analysts Association of Japan | 2009 | S |
| Keidanren | Nippon Keidanren | 2005 | S |
| | | 2009 | S |
| KPMG | KPMG (Klynveld, Peat, Marwick and Goerdeler) | 2001 | I, S, S, S, S |
| | | 2002 | I, S, S, S, S |
| | | 2003 | I, S, S, S, S |
| | | 2004 | I, S, S; S; S |
| | | 2005 | I, S |
| | | 2006 | I, S, T |
| | | 2007 | I, S, T |
| | | 2008 | I, T |
| | | 2009 | I, S, T |
| KRASB | Korea Accounting Standards Board | 2001 | S |
| | | 2002 | S |
| | | 2003 | S |
| | | 2004 | S |
| | | 2009 | S |
| Lafarge | Lafarge SA | 2001 | S |
| | | 2002 | S |
| | | 2003 | S |
| | | 2004 | S, T |
| | | 2005 | T |
| | | 2006 | T |
| | | 2007 | T |

| Abbreviation | Employing organization | Year | Body |
|---|---|---|---|
| | | 2008 | T |
| | | 2009 | T |
| Liberty | The Liberty Group Ltd | 2001 | T |
| | | 2002 | T |
| Lonergan | Lonergan Edwards & Associates Ltd | 2001 | I |
| | | 2002 | I |
| | | 2003 | I |
| Marchese | Marchese, Grandi, Mesón & Asoc. | 2001 | I |
| | | 2002 | I |
| | | 2003 | I |
| | | 2004 | I |
| | | 2005 | I |
| | | 2006 | I |
| Mazars | Mazars | 2004 | I |
| | | 2005 | I |
| | | 2006 | I |
| | | 2007 | I |
| | | 2008 | I |
| | | 2009 | I |
| Merrill | Merrill Lynch & Co., Inc. | 2006 | T |
| | | 2007 | T |
| Microsoft | Microsoft Corp | 2006 | S |
| | | 2007 | S |
| Mitsui | Mitsui & Co. Ltd | 2001 | T |
| MorStan | Morgan Stanley | 2001 | S |
| | | 2002 | I, S |
| | | 2003 | I, S, S |
| | | 2004 | I, S |
| | | 2005 | I, S |
| | | 2006 | I, S |
| | | 2007 | S, T |
| | | 2008 | S, T |
| | | 2009 | T |
| MumEx | Mumbai Stock Exchange | 2009 | S |
| MurrayRob | Murray and Roberts Holdings | 2003 | T |
| NAInsure | Group of North American Insurance Enterprises | 2009 | S |
| NASD | National Association of Securities Dealers | 2008 | T |
| | | 2009 | T |
| NEC | NEC Corporation (previously: Nippon Electric Company) | 2005 | I |
| Nokia | Nokia | 2001 | S |
| | | 2002 | S |
| | | 2003 | S |
| | | 2004 | S |

| Abbreviation | Employing organization | Year | Body |
|---|---|---|---|
| Nomura | Nomura Holdings Inc. | 2006 | T |
| | | 2007 | T |
| | | 2008 | T |
| NZFRSB | New Zealand Financial Reporting Standards Board | 2008 | I |
| | | 2009 | I |
| Ogilvy | Ogilvy Renault, Barristers and Solicitors | 2001 | T |
| | | 2002 | T |
| | | 2003 | T |
| | | 2004 | T |
| | | 2005 | T |
| | | 2006 | T |
| Omega | Omega Capital | 2005 | T |
| | | 2006 | T |
| | | 2007 | T |
| | | 2008 | T |
| | | 2009 | T |
| Pfizer | Pfizer Inc. | 2001 | S, T |
| | | 2002 | S |
| | | 2003 | S |
| | | 2004 | S |
| | | 2006 | T |
| | | 2007 | T |
| | | 2008 | T |
| Philips | Royal Philips Electronics NV | 2001 | S |
| | | 2002 | S |
| | | 2003 | S |
| | | 2004 | S |
| Pirelli | Pirelli SpA | 2001 | I |
| | | 2002 | I |
| | | 2003 | I |
| | | 2004 | I |
| | | 2005 | I |
| | | 2006 | I |
| | | 2007 | I |
| Polus | Polus Goldmining Company | 2004 | S |
| PPR | PPR (Pinault-Printemps-Redoute) | 2005 | S |
| PWC | PricewaterhouseCoopers | 2001 | I, S, S, S, S, T |
| | | 2002 | I, S, S, S, S, T |
| | | 2003 | I, S, S, S, S, T |

| Abbreviation | Employing organization | Year | Body |
|---|---|---|---|
| | | 2004 | I, S, S, S, S, T |
| | | 2005 | I, S, S, T |
| | | 2006 | I, S, S, T |
| | | 2007 | I, S, S, T |
| | | 2008 | I, S, S, T |
| | | 2009 | I, S, T |
| Repsol | Repsol – YPF | 2001 | S |
| | | 2002 | S |
| | | 2003 | S |
| | | 2004 | S |
| SAFA | South Asian Federation of Accountants | 2009 | S |
| Samsung | Samsung Electronics Co. Ltd | 2005 | S |
| | | 2006 | S |
| | | 2007 | S |
| | | 2008 | S |
| SandP | Standard & Poor's, Inc. | 2009 | S |
| Sanlam | Sanlam Ltd | 2004 | T |
| | | 2005 | T |
| | | 2006 | T |
| Sasol | Sasol Ltd | 2007 | S |
| | | 2008 | S |
| Schneider | Schneider Electric | 2001 | T |
| | | 2002 | T |
| | | 2003 | T |
| SEC | Securities and Exchange Commission | 2001 | S |
| | | 2002 | S |
| | | 2003 | S |
| | | 2004 | S |
| | | 2005 | S |
| | | 2007 | S |
| | | 2008 | S, I |
| | | 2009 | S, I |
| Shell | Shell International Ltd | 2001 | T |
| | | 2002 | T |
| | | 2003 | T |
| | | 2004 | T |
| | | 2005 | T |
| | | 2006 | T |
| SibCoal | Siberian Coal Energy Company | 2005 | S |

| Abbreviation | Employing organization | Year | Body |
|---|---|---|---|
| | | 2006 | S |
| | | 2007 | S |
| | | 2008 | S |
| Siemens | Siemens AG | 2007 | I |
| | | 2008 | I |
| | | 2009 | I |
| Sumitomo | Sumitomo Corp | 2006 | I |
| | | 2007 | I |
| | | 2008 | I |
| | | 2009 | I, T |
| Sword | Sword Management Ltd | 2001 | S |
| TIAA | TIAA–CREF (Teachers Insurance and Annuity Association – College Retirement Equities Fund) | 2001 | T |
| | | 2002 | T |
| | | 2003 | T |
| | | 2004 | T |
| | | 2009 | T |
| UBS | UBS AG | 2005 | S, S |
| | | 2006 | S, S |
| | | 2007 | S, S |
| | | 2008 | S, S, S |
| UKFRC | UK Financial Reporting Council | 2001 | T |
| | | 2002 | T |
| | | 2003 | T |
| | | 2004 | T |
| | | 2005 | T |
| | | 2006 | T |
| | | 2007 | T |
| | | 2008 | T |
| | | 2009 | T |
| UKFSA | UK Financial Services Authority | 2006 | S |
| | | 2007 | S |
| | | 2008 | S |
| | | 2009 | S |
| UKSIP | United Kingdom Society of Investment Professionals | 2002 | S |
| | | 2003 | S |
| UNCTAD | United Nations Conference on Trade and Development | 2003 | S |
| | | 2004 | S |
| | | 2005 | S |
| | | 2006 | S |
| | | 2007 | S |

| Abbreviation | Employing organization | Year | Body |
|---|---|---|---|
| | | 2008 | S |
| Unibanco | Itaú Unibanco Banco Múltiplo SA (Brazil) | 2008 | T |
| | | 2009 | T |
| Unicredit | UniCredit SpA | 2006 | T |
| | | 2007 | T |
| | | 2008 | T |
| | | 2009 | T |
| UniGenoa | University of Genoa | 2001 | T |
| | | 2002 | T |
| | | 2003 | T |
| | | 2004 | T |
| UniMassey | Massey College, Toronto | 2007 | I |
| UniNW | Northwestern University, Evanston and Chicago | 2001 | T |
| | | 2002 | T |
| | | 2003 | T |
| | | 2004 | T |
| | | 2005 | T |
| UniSP | Universidade de São Paulo | 2001 | S |
| | | 2002 | S |
| | | 2003 | S |
| | | 2004 | S |
| | | 2005 | S |
| | | 2006 | S |
| | | 2007 | S |
| | | 2008 | S |
| UniTama | Tama University, Tokyo | 2001 | I |
| | | 2002 | I |
| | | 2003 | I |
| | | 2004 | I |
| Unitec | Unitec Institute of Technology (New Zealand) | 2004 | I |
| | | 2005 | I |
| | | 2006 | I |
| | | 2008 | I |
| | | 2009 | I |
| UniWaseda | Waseda University, Tokyo | 2006 | S |
| | | 2007 | S |
| | | 2008 | S |
| UniWell | University of Wellington, New Zealand | 2001 | S |
| Uranus | Uranus Investment Holdings | 2007 | T |

| Abbreviation | Employing organization | Year | Body |
|---|---|---|---|
| | | 2008 | T |
| | | 2009 | T |
| WB | International Bank for Reconstruction and Development | 2001 | S |
| | | 2002 | S |
| | | 2003 | S |
| | | 2004 | S |
| | | 2005 | S |
| | | 2006 | S, I |
| | | 2007 | S, I |
| | | 2008 | S, I |
| | | 2009 | S, I |
| ZAABP | South Africa Accounting Practices Board | 2009 | S |

*Source:* Author's composition based on IASCF-AR, 2002–10.

# References

Abbott, Andrew (1988), *The System of Professions: An Essay on the Division of Expert Labor*, Chicago: University of Chicago Press.

Abbott, Kenneth W. and Duncan Snidal (2001), "International 'standards' and international governance," *Journal of European Public Policy*, **8** (3), 345–70.

AICPA (2011), "IFRS FAQs," available at http://www.ifrs.com/ifrs_faqs.html#q3 (accessed January 10, 2011).

Allen, Abigail and Karthik Ramanna (2010), "Towards an understanding of the role of standard setters in standard setting," Harvard Business School Accounting & Management Unit Working Paper No. 10–105, Boston, MA: Harvard Business School.

Ansell, Christopher K. and Steven Weber (1999), "Organizing international politics: Sovereignty and open systems," *International Political Science Review*, **20** (1), 73–93.

Armstrong, Christopher, Mary E. Barth, Alan Jagolinzer, and Edward J. Rieds (2006), "Market reaction to events surrounding the adoption of IFRS in Europe," No. 1937, Palo Alto, CA: Stanford Graduate School of Business.

Arnold, Patricia J. (2005), "Disciplining domestic regulation: The World Trade Organization and the market for professional services," *Accounting, Organizations and Society*, **30**, 299–330.

Arthur, W. Brian (1989), "Competing technologies, increasing returns and lock-in by historical events," *Economic Journal*, **99**, 116–31.

Arthur, W. Brian (1994), *Increasing Returns and Path Dependence in the Economy*, Ann Arbor: University of Michigan Press.

Bachrach, Peter and Morton S. Baratz (1970), *Power and Poverty: Theory and Practices,* New York: Oxford University Press.

Baker, C. Richard and Elena M. Barbu (2007), "Evolution of research on international accounting harmonization: A historical and institutional perspective," *Socio-Economic Review*, **5**, 603–32.

Biondi, Yuri and Tomo Suzuki (2007), "Socio-economic impacts of international accounting standards: An introduction," *Socio-Economic Review*, **5**, 585–602.

Blaufus, Kay (2005), *Fair Value Accounting: Zweckmäßigkeitsanalyse und konzeptioneller Rahmen*, Wiesbaden: Gabler.

Borgatti, Stephen Peter, Martin G. Everett, and Linton C. Freeman (2002), *Ucinet for Windows: Software for Social Network Analysis*, Cambridge, MA: Analytic Technologies.

Botzem, Sebastian (2008), "Transnational expert-driven standardisation—accountancy governance from a professional point of view," in Jean-Christophe Graz and Andreas Nölke (eds), *Transnational Private Governance and its Limits*, London: Routledge, pp. 44–57.

Botzem, Sebastian and Sigrid Quack (2006), "Contested rules and shifting boundaries: International standard setting in accounting," in Marie-Laure Djelic and Kerstin Sahlin-Andersson (eds), *Transnational Governance: Institutional Dynamics of Regulation*, Cambridge: Cambridge University Press, pp. 266–86.

Botzem, Sebastian and Sigrid Quack (2009), "(No) limits to Anglo-American accounting? Reconstructing the history of the International Accounting Standards Committee: A review article," *Accounting, Organizations and Society*, **34** (8), 988–98.

Botzem, Sebastian and Leonhard Dobusch (2009), "The rule of standards: Codifying power in the transnational arena," paper presented at the EGOS Colloquium, Barcelona, July 2–4, 2009.

Boyer, Robert (2007), "Assessing the impact of fair value upon financial crisis," *Socio-Economic Review*, **5**, 779–807.

Braithwaite, John and Peter Drahos (2000), *Global Business Regulation*, Cambridge: Cambridge University Press.

Bromwich, Michael (2007), "Fair values; imaginary prices and mystical markets," in Peter J. Walton (ed.), *The Routledge Companion to Fair Value and Financial Reporting*, London: Routledge, pp. 46–68.

Brunsson, Nils and Bengt Jacobsson (2000), *A World of Standards*, Oxford: Oxford University Press.

Burchell, Stuart, Colin Clubb, and Anthony G. Hopwood (1985), "Accounting in its social context: Towards a history of value added in the United Kingdom," *Accounting Organizations and Society*, **10** (4), 381–413.

Bush, Tim (2005), *"Divided by Common Language". Where Economics Meets the Law: US versus Non-US financial Reporting Models*, The Institute of Chartered Accountants in England and Wales (ICAEW).

Büthe, Tim (2010), "Global private politics: A research agenda," *Business and Politics*, **12** (3), Art. 12.

Büthe, Tim and Walter Mattli (2011), *The New Global Rulers: The Privatization of Regulation in the World Economy*, Princeton, NJ: Princeton University Press.

Cairns, David (2001), "The conceptual framework—the international experience," Working Paper, June 22, 2001, Henley-on-Thames: International Financial Reporting.

Camfferman, Kees and Stephen A. Zeff (2007), *Financial Reporting and Global Capital Markets: A History of the International Accounting Standards Committee 1973–2000*, Oxford: Oxford University Press.

Campbell, John L. (2005), "Where do we stand? Common mechanisms in organizations and social movements research," in Gerald F. Davis, Doug McAdam, W. Richard Scott, and Mayer N. Zald (eds), *Social Movements and Organization Theory*, Cambridge: Cambridge University Press, pp. 41–68.

Chahed, Yasmine (2011), "Words and numbers: The reconfiguring of financial reporting as a form of economic narrative," paper presented at the EGOS Colloquium, Gothenburg, July 6–9, 2011.

Chapman, Christopher S., David J. Cooper, and Peter B. Miller (2009), "Linking accounting, organizations, and institutions," in Christopher S. Chapman, David J. Cooper and Peter B. Miller (eds), *Accounting, Organizations & Institutions: Essays in Honour of Anthony Hopwood*, Oxford: Oxford University Press, pp. 1–29.

Chiapello, Eve and Karim Medjad (2007), *Unprecedented Privatisation of Standard-setting: The Case of European Accounting Policy*, Communication at the European Accounting Association Congress, April 25–27, 2007, Lisbon.

Cooper, David J. and Keith Robson (2006), "Accounting, professions and regulation: Locating the sites of professionalization," *Accounting, Organizations and Society*, **31**, 415–44.

Covaleski, Mark A., Mark W. Dirsmith, and Larry Rittenberg (2003), "Jurisdictional disputes over professional work: The institutionalization of the global knowledge expert," *Accounting, Organizations and Society*, **28**, 323–55.

Crouch, Colin (2005), "Three meanings of complementarity," *Socio-Economic Review*, **3**, 359–63.

Crouch, Colin and Henry Farrell (2004), "Breaking the path of institutional development? Alternatives to the new determinism," *Rationality and Society*, **16** (1), 5–44.

Cuijpers, Rick and Willem Buijink (2005), "Voluntary adoption of non-local GAAP in the European Union: A study of determinants and consequences," *European Accounting Review*, **14** (3), 487–524.

Cutler, A. Claire, Virginia Haufler, and Tony Porter (eds) (1999), *Private Authority and International Affairs*, Albany, NY: State University of New York Press.

Czarniawska, Barbara and Bernward Joerges (1996), "Travels of ideas," in

Barbara Czarniawska and Guje Sevón (eds), *Translating Organizational Change*, Berlin: Walter de Gruyter, pp. 13–48.

Czarniawska, Barbara and Guje Sevón (eds) (1996), *Translating Organizational Change*, Berlin and New York: Walter de Gruyter.

Dahl, Robert A. (1957), "The concept of power," *Behavioural Sciences*, 2 (July), 201–15.

Daniels, Peter W., Nigel J. Thrift, and Andrew Leyshon (1989), "Internationalisation of professional producer services: Accountancy conglomerates," in Peter Enderwick (ed.), *Multinational Service Firms*, London and New York: Routledge, pp. 79–106.

D'Arcy, Anne (2001), "Accounting classification and the international harmonisation debate—An empirical investigation," *Accounting, Organizations and Society*, **26** (4–5), 327–49.

David, Paul A. (1985), "Clio and the economics of QWERTY," *American Economic Review*, **75**, 332–37.

David, Paul A. and Shane Greenstein (1990), "The economics of compatibility standards: An introduction to recent research," *Economics of Innovation and New Technologies*, **1**, 3–41.

Davis, Gerald F. and Christopher Marquis (2005), "Prospects for organization theory in the early twenty-first century: Institutional fields and mechanisms," *Organization Science*, **16** (14), 332–43.

Davis, James H., F. David Schoorman, and Lex Donaldson (1997), "Toward a stewardship theory of management," *The Academy of Management Review*, **22** (1), 20–47.

De Lange, Paul and Brian Howieson (2006), "International accounting standards setting and US exceptionalism," *Critical Perspectives on Accounting*, **17**, 1007–32.

Deeg, Richard (2001), "Institutional change and the uses and limits of path dependency: The case of German finance," Discussion Paper 01/6 Max Planck Institute for the Study of Societies (MPIfG), Cologne.

Deeg, Richard (2010), "Institutional change in financial systems," in Glenn Morgan, John L. Campbell, Colin Crouch, and Ove K. Pedersen (eds), *The Oxford Handbook of Comparative Institutional Analysis*, Oxford: Oxford University Press, pp. 309–34.

DiMaggio, Paul J. and Walter W. Powell (1983), "The Iron Cage revisited: Institutional isomorphism and collective rationality in organizational fields," *American Sociological Review*, **48** (2), 147–60.

Djelic, Marie-Laure and Kerstin Sahlin-Andersson (2006), "Institutional dynamics in a reordering world," in Marie-Laure Djelic and Kerstin Sahlin-Andersson (eds), *Transnational Governance: Institutional Dynamics of Regulation*, Cambridge: Cambridge University Press, pp. 375–97.

Djelic, Marie-Laure and Sigrid Quack (2003), *Globalization and Institutions: Redefining the Rules of the Economic Game*, Cheltenham, UK and Northampton, MA, USA: Edward Elgar.

Djelic, Marie-Laure and Sigrid Quack (2007), "Overcoming path dependencies—path generation in open systems," *Theory and Society*, **36**, 161–86.

Djelic, Marie-Laure and Sigrid Quack (eds) (2010), *Transnational Communities: Shaping Global Economic Governance*, Cambridge: Cambridge University Press.

Donaldson, Lex and James H. Davis (1991), "Stewardship theory or agency theory: CEO governance and shareholder returns," *Australian Journal of Management*, **16** (1), 49–64.

Drori, Gili S., Yong Suk Jang, and John W. Meyer (2004), *Sources of Rationalized Governance: Cross-National Longitudinal Analyses, 1985–2002*, Stanford, CA: Centre on Democracy, Development, and the Rule of Law, Stanford Institute for International Studies.

DRSC (2005), *Jahresbericht* [Annual Report] *2005*, Berlin: Deutsches Rechnungslegungs Standards Committee eV [Accounting Standards Committee of Germany].

DRSC (2008), *Jahresbericht* [Annual Report] *2008*, Berlin: Deutsches Rechnungslegungs Standards Committee eV.

Eaton, Sarah B. (2005), "Crisis and the consolidation of International Accounting Standards: Enron, The IASB, and America," *Business and Politics*, **7** (3), Art. 4.

ECB (2004), "Monthly Bulletin, February," Frankfurt: European Central Bank.

ECOFIN (2006), "Economic and financial affairs," press release, 2741st Council Meeting, July 11, 2006, 11370/06 (Presse 209), Brussels: Council of the European Union.

EFRAG (2005), *Annual Review 2004*, Brussels.

Eisenhardt, Kathleen M. (1989), "Building theories from case study research," *The Academy of Management Review*, **14** (4), 532–50.

Epstein, Gerald A. (2005), "Introduction: Financialization and the world economy," in Gerald A. Epstein (ed.), *Financialization and the World Economy*, Cheltenham, UK and Northampton, MA, USA: Edward Elgar, pp. 3–16.

EU (2002), "Financial reporting: Commission welcomes IASB/FASB convergence agreement," Press release: IP/02/1576, available at http://europa.eu/rapid/pressReleasesAction.do?reference=IP/02/1576&format=HTML&aged=1&language=EN&guiLanguage=en (accessed June 1, 2011).

EU (2003), "Comments concerning certain Articles of the Regulation (EC) No 1606/2002 of the European Parliament and of the Council of

19 July 2002 on the application of international accounting standards and the Fourth Council Directive 78/660/EEC of 25 July 1978 and the Seventh Council Directive 83/349/EEC of 13 June 1983 on accounting," Brussels: Commission of the European Communities, available at http://ec.europa.eu/internal_market/accounting/docs/ias/200311-comments/ias-200311-comments_en.pdf (accessed April 30, 2010).

European Commission (1995), *Accounting Harmonisation: A New Strategy vis-à-vis International Harmonisation*, COM 95 (508), EN.

European Commission (1999), "Comment letter 46," Comment to the IASC, April 28, 1999, pp. 1–16.

European Commission (2008), "Accounting standards: Commission adopts changes to mitigate consequences of financial turmoil," available at http://europa.eu/rapid/pressReleasesAction.do?reference=IP/08/1513& (accessed June 8, 2011).

Evans, Lisa and Kersten Honold (2007), "The division of expert labour in the European audit market: The case of Germany," *Critical Perspectives on Accounting*, **18**, 61–88.

Falleti, Tulia G. and Julia F. Lynch (2009), "Context and causal mechanisms in political analysis," *Comparative Political Studies*, **42** (9), 1143–66.

Ferree, Myra Marx, William A. Gamson, Jürgen Gerhards, and Dieter Rucht (2002), *Shaping Abortion Discourse: Democracy and the Public Sphere in Germany and the United States*, Cambridge: Cambridge University Press.

Flower, John (1997), "The future shape of harmonization: The EU versus the IASC versus the SEC," *The European Accounting Review*, **6** (2), 281–303.

Forrester, David A. R. (1984), *An Invitation to Accounting History*, Glasgow: Strathclyde Convergencies.

Fransen, Luc W. and Ans Kolk (2007), "Global rule-setting for business: A critical analysis of multi-stakeholder standards," *Organization*, **14** (5), 667–84.

Froud, Julie, Colin Haslam, Sukhdev Johal, and Karel Williams (2000), "Shareholder value and financialization: Consultancy promises, management moves," *Economy and Society*, 29 (1), 80–110.

Froud, Julie, Sukhdev Johal, Viken Papazian, and Karel Williams (2004), "The temptation of Houston: A case study of financialisation," *Critical Perspectives on Accounting*, **15**, 885–909.

Froud, Julie, Sukhdev Johal, Adam Leaver, and Karel Williams (2006), *Financialization and Strategy: Narrative and Numbers*, London: Routledge.

FSB (2011), "Key standards for sound financial systems," available

at     http://www.financialstabilityboard.org/cos/key_standards.htm
(accessed May 13, 2011).

G20 (2008), "Declaration summit of financial markets and the world
economy," November 15, 2008, available at http://www.g20.org/
Documents/g20_summit_declaration.pdf (accessed April 1, 2011).

Gallhofer, Sonja and Jim Haslam (2006), "The accounting–globalisation
interrelation: An overview with some reflections on the neglected dimension of emancipatory potentiality," *Critical Perspectives on Accounting*,
**17**, 903–34.

Gallhofer, Sonja and Jim Haslam (2007), "Exploring social, political
and economic dimensions of accounting in the global context: The
International Accounting Standards Board and accounting disaggrega-
tion," *Socio-Economic Review*, **5**, 633–64.

Gamson, William A. (1992), *Talking Politics*, Cambridge: Cambridge
University Press.

Gamson, William A. and Andre Modigliani (1989), "Media discourse
and public opinion on nuclear power: A constructionist approach,"
*American Journal of Sociology*, **95** (1), 1–37.

Garud, Raghu and Peter Karnøe (2001), "Path creation as a process of
mindful deviation," in Raghu Garud and Peter Karnøe (eds), *Path
Dependence and Creation*, Mahwah, NJ: Lawrence Erlbaum Associates,
pp. 1–38.

Garud, Raghu and Peter Karnøe (2003), "*Bricolage* versus breakthrough:
Distributed and embedded agency in technology entrepreneurship,"
*Research Policy*, **32**, 277–300.

Garud, Raghu, Cynthia Hardy, and Steve Maguire (2007), "Institutional
entrepreneurship as embedded agency: An introduction to the Special
Issue," *Organization Studies*, **28**, 957–69.

Glaum, Martin (2000), "Bridging the GAAP: The changing attitude of
German managers towards Anglo-American accounting and account-
ing harmonization," *Journal of International Financial Management and
Accounting*, **11** (1), 23–47.

Greenwood, Royston and Laura Empson (2003), "The professional
partnership: Relic or exemplary form of governance?," *Organization
Studies*, **24** (6), 909–33.

Greenwood, Royston, Roy Suddaby, and C. R. Hinings (2002),
"Theorizing change: The role of professional associations in the transformation of institutionalized fields," *Academy of Management Journal*,
**45** (1), 58–80.

Greenwood, Royston, David L. Deephouse, and Stan Xiao Li (2007),
"Ownership and performance of professional service firms,"
*Organization Studies* **28** (2), 219–38.

Haas, Peter M. (1992), "Introduction: Epistemic communities and international policy coordination," *International Organization*, **46** (1), 1–37.

Hall, Peter A. and David Soskice (2001), *Varieties of Capitalism: The Institutional Foundations of Comparative Advantage*, Oxford: Oxford University Press.

Haller, Axel (2002), "Financial accounting developments in the European Union: Past events and future prospects," *The European Accounting Review*, **11** (1), 153–90.

Halliday, Terence C. and Bruce G. Carruthers (2007), "The recursivity of law: Global norm making and national law-making in the globalization of corporate insolvency regimes," *American Journal of Sociology*, **112** (4), 1135–202.

Hanneman, Robert A. and Mark Riddle (2005), "Introduction to social network methods," Riverside: University of California, available at http://faculty.ucr.edu/~hanneman/ (accessed March 16, 2008).

Hegarty, John, Frédéric Gielen, and Ana Cristina Hirata Barros (2005), "Implementation of International Accounting and Auditing Standards. Lessons learned from the World Bank's Accounting and Auditing ROSC Program," in UNCTAD, *2004 Review, Reporting Issues*, New York and Geneva: United Nations, pp. 50–73.

Herz, Robert H. (2007), "Towards a global reporting system: Where are we and where are we going?," AICPA National Conference on SEC and PCAOB Reporting Developments, Robert H. Herz, Chairman, FASB, December 10, 2007, available at http://www.iasplus.com/usa/fasb/0712herz.pdf (accessed March 15, 2008).

Hoffman, Andrew J. (1999), "Institutional evolution and change: Environmentalism and the US chemical industry," *Academy of Management Journal*, **42** (4), 351–71.

Höpner, Martin (2005), "Epilogue to 'Explaining institutional complementarity': What have we learnt? Complementarity, coherence and institutional change," *Socio-Economic Review*, **3**, 383–87.

Hopwood, Anthony G. (1983), "On trying to study accounting in the contexts in which it operates," *Accounting, Organizations and Society*, **8** (2–3), 287–305.

Hopwood, Anthony G. (1987), "The archaeology of accounting systems," *Accounting Organizations and Society*, **12** (3), 207–34.

Hopwood, Anthony G. (1990), "Harmonization of accounting standards within the EC: A perspective for the future," in Commission of the European Communities (eds), *The Future of Harmonisation of Accounting Standards within the European Communities*, Brussels, pp. 46–90.

Hopwood, Anthony G. (1994), "Some reflections on the harmonization of accounting in the EU," *European Accounting Review*, **3** (2), 241–53.

Hopwood, Anthony G. (1996), "Looking across rather than up and down: On the need to explore the lateral processing of information," *Accounting, Organizations and Society*, 589–90.

Hopwood, Anthony G. (1997), "Internationalising international accounting research," *Accounting, Organizations and Society*, **22** (8), iii–iv.

Hopwood, Anthony G. and Peter Miller (1994), *Accounting as Social and Institutional Practice*, Cambridge: Cambridge University Press.

IASB (2006), "Preliminary views on an improved conceptual framework for financial reporting: The objective of financial reporting and qualitative characteristics of decision-useful financial reporting information," Discussion Paper, July, London: International Accounting Standards Board (IASB).

IASB (2007), "Phase A: Objective of financial reporting and qualitative characteristics—comment letter summary (agenda paper 3A)," London: IASB.

IASB (2008), Press release of February 11, 2008, London: IASB, available at http://www.iasb.org/News/Press+Releases/Update+on+Funding+for+2008.htm (accessed March 11, 2008).

IASB (2010), "Agenda Paper 6B, Information for Observers," IASCF Trustees' Meeting, London March 29 to April 1, 2010, available at http://www.iasb.org/NR/rdonlyres/11C76B10-4406-4E86-8B9C-EAB8680ABD3C/0/Agendapaper6BEUFundingMechanism.pdf (accessed June 5, 2011).

IASC (1987), *Annual Report 1987*, London: International Accounting Standards Committee (IASC).

IASC (1988), *Annual Report 1988*, London: IASC.

IASC (1989), *Annual Report 1989*, London: IASC.

IASC (1990), *Annual Report 1990*, London: IASC.

IASC (1991), *Annual Report 1991*, London: IASC.

IASC (1992), *Annual Report 1992*, London: IASC.

IASC (1993), *Annual Report 1993*, London: IASC.

IASC (1994), *Annual Report 1994*, London: IASC.

IASC (1995), *Annual Report 1995*, London: IASC.

IASC (1997), *Annual Report 1997*, London: IASC.

IASC (1998), *Annual Report 1998*, London: IASC.

IASC (1999), *Annual Report 1999*, London: IASC.

IASC (2000), *Annual Report 2000*, London: IASC.

IASCF (2002), *Constitution*, London: IASCF.

IASCF (2004), *Review of the Constitution. Proposals for Change*, London: IASCF.

IASCF (2005), *Constitution*, London: IASCF.

IASCF (2006), *Due Process Handbook for the IASB*, London: IASCF.

IASCF (2007), *Annual Report 2006*, London: IASCF.

IASCF (2009), *Constitution*, London: IASCF.

IASCF (2010), *Constitution*, London: IASCF.

IASCF–AR (2002), *Annual Report 2001*, London: IASCF.

IASCF–AR (2003), *Annual Report 2002*, London: IASCF.

IASCF–AR (2004), *Annual Report 2003*, London: IASCF.

IASCF–AR (2005), *Annual Report 2004*, London: IASCF.

IASCF–AR (2006), *Annual Report 2005*, London: IASCF.

IASCF–AR (2007), *Annual Report 2006*, London: IASCF.

IASCF–AR (2008), *Annual Report 2007*, London: IASCF.

IASCF–AR (2009), *Annual Report 2008*, London: IASCF.

IASCF–AR (2010), *Annual Report 2009*, London: IASCF.

IASplus (2008), "Agenda and decisions at past IASB meetings. IASB Board Meeting 13–17 October 2008 and Joint Meeting of IASB and FASB 20–21 October 2008," available at http://www.iasplus.com/agenda/0810.htm (accessed May 23, 2011).

IASplus (2010), "Chronology of the IASC and the IASB," available at http://www.iasplus.com/restruct/chrono.htm (accessed January 20, 2011).

IASplus (2011a), "Use of IFRSs by jurisdiction," available at http://www.iasplus.com/country/useias.htm# (accessed March 19, 2011).

IASplus (2011b), "Summaries of International Financial Reporting Standards. IAS 39 Financial Instruments: Recognition and Measurement," available at http://www.iasplus.com/standard/ias39.htm (accessed June 5, 2011).

IASplus (2011c), "Summaries of International Financial Reporting Standards. IFRS 9 Financial Instruments," available at http://www.iasplus.com/standard/ifrs09.htm (accessed April 4, 2011).

ICAEW (2007), *EU Implementation of IFRS and the Fair Value Directive. A Report for the European Commission*, London.

IOSCO (2000), *A Resolution on IASC Standards. Passed by the President's Committee, May 2000*.

Janis, Irving L. (1972), *Victims of Groupthink: A Psychological Study of Foreign Policy Decisions and Fiascos*, Boston, MA: Houghton Mifflin.

Kerwer, Dieter (2005), "Rules that many use: Standards and global regulation," *Governance*, **18** (4), 611–32.

Kindleberger, Charles P. (2000), *Manias, Panics, and Crashes: A History of Financial Crises*, New York: John Wiley & Sons, Inc.

Kirsch, Robert J. (2007), *The International Accounting Standards Committee: A Political History*, London: Wolters Kluwer.

Krippner, Greta R. (2005), "The financialization of the American economy," *Socio-Economic Review*, 3, 173–208.

Larson, Robert K. (1997), "Corporate lobbying of the International Accounting Standards Committee," *Journal of International Financial Management and Accounting*, **8** (3), 175–203.

Lazonick, William and Mary O'Sullivan (2000), "Maximizing shareholder value: A new ideology for corporate governance," *Economy and Society*, **29** (1), 13–35.

Leblond, Patrick (2011), "EU, US and international accounting standards: A delicate balancing act in governing global finance," *Journal of European Public Policy*, **18** (3), 443–61.

Llewellyn, Sue (2007), "Introducing the agents. . .," *Organization Studies*, **28** (2), 133–53.

Lukes, Steven (1974), *Power—A Radical View*, London: Macmillan.

Lütz, Susanne and Dagmar Eberle (2008), "Varieties of change in German capitalism: Transforming the rules of corporate control," *New Political Economy*, **13** (4), 377–95.

MacArthur, John B. (1996), "An investigation into the influence of cultural factors in the international lobbying of the International Accounting Standards Committee: The case of E32, *Comparability of Financial Statements*," *The International Journal of Accounting*, **31** (2), 213–37.

Macdonald, Keith M. (1995), *The Sociology of the Professions*, London: Sage Publications.

Macdonald, Keith M. (2000), "A professional project—The case of accountancy," in John Richard Edwards (ed.), *The History of Accounting: Critical Perspectives on Business and Management*, volume IV—*Professionalisation of Accounting*, London: Routledge, pp. 36–59.

MacKenzie, Donald and Yuval Millo (2003), "Constructing a market, performing theory: The historical sociology of a financial derivatives exchange," *The American Journal of Sociology*, 109 (1), 107–45.

Mahoney, James (2000), "Path dependence in historical sociology," *Theory and Society*, **29** (4), 507–48.

Mahoney, James (2001), "Beyond correlational analysis: Recent innovations in theory and method," *Sociological Forum*, **16** (3), 575–93.

Mallin, Christine A. (2004), *Corporate Governance*, Oxford and New York: Oxford University Press.

Markus, Hugh Brian (1996), *Der Wirtschaftsprüfer: Entstehung und Entwicklung des Berufes im nationalen und internationalen Bereich*, Munich: C. H. Beck.

Martinez-Diaz, Leonardo (2005), "Strategic experts and improvising regulators: Explaining the IASC's rise to global influence, 1973–2001," *Business and Politics*, **7** (3), Art. 3.

Mattli, Walter (2003), "Public and private governance in setting international standards," in Miles Kahler and David Lake (eds), *Governance in a Global Economy: Political Authority in Transition*, Princeton, NJ: Princeton University Press, pp. 199–225.

Mattli, Walter and Tim Büthe (2003), "Setting international standards: Technological rationality or primacy of power?," *World Politics*, **56** (1), 1–42.

Mattli, Walter and Tim Büthe (2005), "Accountability in accounting? The politics of private rule-making in the public interest," *Governance*, **18** (3), 399–429.

Mayntz, Renate (2004), "Mechanisms in the analysis of social macrophenomena," *Philosophy of the Social Sciences*, **34** (2), June, 237–59.

Mayntz, Renate (2010), "Legitimacy and compliance in transnational governance," MPIFG Working Paper 10/5, Max Planck Institute for the Study of Societies (MPIfG), Cologne.

McLeay, Stuart, Dieter Ordelheide, and Steven Young (2000), "Constituent lobbying and its impact on the development of financial reporting regulations: Evidence from Germany," *Accounting, Organizations and Society*, **25** (1), 79–98.

Mennicken, Andrea (2008), "Connecting worlds: The translation of international auditing standards into post-Soviet audit practice," *Accounting, Organizations and Society*, **33** (4–5), 384–414.

Mennicken, Andrea and Alexandra Heßling (2007), "Welt(en) regulierter Zahlenproduktion zwischen Globalität und Lokalität: Reflexionen zu globalen Standards in Rechnungslegung und Wirtschaftsprüfung," in Andrea Mennicken and Hendrik Vollmer (eds), *Zahlenwerk. Kalkulation, Organisation und Gesellschaft*, Wiesbaden: VS Verlag für Sozialwissenschaften, pp. 207–27.

Meyer, Uli and Cornelius Schubert (2005), *Die Konstitution technologischer Pfade. Überlegungen jenseits der Dichotomie von Pfadabhängigkeit und Pfadkreation*, TUTS-WP-6-2005, Berlin: TU Berlin.

Miller, Paul B. W., Rodney J. Redding, and Paul R. Bahnson (1998), *The FASB: The People, the Process and the Politics*, Boston, MA and Burr Ridge, IL: Irwin McGraw-Hill.

Miller, Peter (1986), "Accounting for progress: National accounting and planning in France: A review essay," *Accounting, Organizations and Society*, **11** (1), 83–104.

Miller, Peter (2002), "Sociology and accounting," in Hans-Ulruch Küpper and Alfred Wagenhofer (eds), *Handwörterbuch Unternehmensrechnung und Controlling*, Stuttgart: Schaeffer-Poeschel Verlag, pp. 1772–84.

Morgan, Glenn and Sigrid Quack (2005), "Internationalization and capability development in professional service firms," in Glenn

Morgan, Richard Whitley, and Eli Moen (eds), *Changing Capitalisms? Internationalization, Institutional Change and Systems of Economic Organization*, Oxford: Oxford University Press, pp. 277–311.

Müller, Matthias (2001), "EU setzt auf weltweite Vergleichbarkeit," *Magazin Mitbestimmung—international edition*, **5**, available at: http://www.boeckler.de/92462_29242.html (accessed June 6, 2011).

Neu, Dean and Elizabeth Ocampo (2007), "Doing missionary work: The World Bank and the diffusion of financial practices," *Critical Perspectives on Accounting*, **18**, 363–89.

Nobes, Christopher (1985), "Harmonisation of financial reporting," in Christopher Nobes and Robert Parker (eds), *Comparative International Accounting*, New York: St. Martin's Press, pp. 331–52.

Nobes, Christopher (2004a), "International classification of financial reporting," in Christopher Nobes and Robert Parker (eds), *Comparative International Accounting*, 8th edn, Essex: Pearson Education, pp. 53–75.

Nobes, Christopher (2004b), "On accounting classification and the international harmonisation debate," *Accounting, Organizations and Society*, **29**, 189–200.

Nobes, Christopher and Robert Parker (eds) (1985), *Comparative International Accounting*, New York: St. Martin's Press.

Nobes, Christopher and Robert Parker (eds) (2004), *Comparative International Accounting*, Essex: Pearson Education.

Nölke, Andreas (2009), "The politics of accounting regulation. Responses to the subprime crisis," in Eric Helleiner, Stefano Pagliari, and Hubert Zimmermann (eds), *Global Finance in Crisis: The Politics of International Regulatory Change*, London and New York: Routledge, pp. 37–55.

Nölke, Andreas and James Perry (2007), "The power of transnational private governance: Financialization and the IASB," *Business and Politics*, **9** (3), Art. 4.

North, Douglass C. (1990), *Institutions, Institutional Change and Economic Performance*, Cambridge: Cambridge University Press.

Ordelheide, Dieter (2004), "The politics of accounting: A framework," in Christian Leuz, Dieter Pfaff, and Anthony G. Hopwood (eds), *The Economics and Politics of Accounting: International Perspectives on Research Trends, Policy, and Practice*, Oxford: Oxford University Press, pp. 269–84.

Orenstein, M. A. and H. P. Schmitz (2006), "The new transnationalism and comparative politics," paper presented at the annual meeting of the American Political Science Association, Philadelphia, August 31, 2006.

Oxera Consulting Limited (2006), *Competition and Choice in the UK Audit Market*, a Report for the Department of Trade and Industry, 12 April.

PAAinE (2007), "Stewardship/accountability as an objective of financial reporting: A comment on the IASB/FASB conceptual framework project," available at http://www.efrag.org/files/ProjectDocuments/Other%20projects/070823%20%20PAAinE%20Stewardship%20paper%20final%20version.pdf (accessed June 7, 2011).

Padoa-Schioppa, Tommaso (2006), "Statement and comments," at conference "Future of IASB Funding," Frankfurt am Main, available at http://www.ifrs.org/NR/rdonlyres/F9AA7025-226A-4FD9-8A6B-0896B93FDF8C/0/SchioppaMarch2006.pdf (accessed June 9, 2011).

Pattberg, Philipp (2005), "The institutionalization of private governance: How business and nonprofit organizations agree on transnational rules," *Governance: An International Journal of Policy, Administration, and Institutions*, **18** (4), 589–610.

Pellens, Bernhard, Rolf Uwe Fülbier, and Joachim Gassen (2004), *Internationale Rechnungslegung*, Stuttgart: Schäffer Poeschel.

Perry, James and Andreas Nölke (2005), "International Accounting Standard setting: A network approach," *Business and Politics*, **7** (3), Art. 5.

Perry, James and Andreas Nölke (2006), "The political economy of International Accounting Standards," *Review of International Political Economy*, **13** (4), 559–86.

Pettigrew, Andrew M. (1990), "Longitudinal field research on change: Theory and practice," *Organization Science*, **1** (3), 267–92.

Pierson, Paul (2000), "Increasing returns, path dependence, and the study of politics," *American Political Science Review*, 94, S. 251–68.

Pierson, Paul (2004), *Politics in Time: History, Institutions, and Social Analysis*, Princeton, NJ: Princeton University Press.

Porter, Theodore M. (1995), *Trust in Numbers: The Pursuit of Objectivity in Science and Public Life*, Princeton, NJ: Princeton University Press.

Porter, Tony (2005), "Private authority, technical authority, and the globalization of accounting standards," *Business and Politics*, **7** (3), Art. 2.

Posner, Elliot (2009), "Making rules for global finance: Transatlantic regulatory cooperation at the turn of the millennium," *International Organization*, 63, 665–99.

Posner, Elliot (2010), "Sequence as explanation: The international politics of accounting standards," *Review of International Political Economy*, **17** (4), 639–64.

Power, Michael (1994), "The audit society," in Anthony G. Hopwood and Peter Miller (eds), *Accounting as Social and Institutional Practice*, Cambridge: Cambridge University Press, pp. 299–316.

Power, Michael (1997), *The Audit Society: Rituals of Verification*, Oxford: Oxford University Press.

Power, Michael (2009), "Financial accounting without a state," in

Christopher S. Chapman, David Cooper, and Peter Miller (eds), *Accounting, Organizations, and Institutions: Essays in Honour of Anthony Hopwood*, Oxford: Oxford University Press, pp. 325–40.

Power, Michael (2010), "Fair value accounting, financial economics and the transformation of reliability," *Accounting and Business Research, International Accounting Policy Forum*, **40** (3), 197–210.

Quack, Sigrid (2007), "Legal professionals and transnational law-making: A case of distributed agency," *Organization*, **14** (5), 643–66.

Quack, Sigrid (2010), "Law, expertise and legitimacy in transnational economic governance: An introduction," *Socio-Economic Review*, **8** (1), 3–16.

Radwan, Alexander (2008), *Report on International Financial Reporting Standards (IFRS) and the Governance of the International Accounting Standards Board (IASB) (2006/2248(INI))*, *A6–0032/2008*, Brussels: European Parliament.

Rahman, Sheikh F. (1998), "International accounting regulation by the United Nations: A power perspective," *Accounting, Auditing and Accountability Journal*, **11** (5), 593–623.

Ramirez, Carlos (2001), "Understanding social closure in its cultural context: Accounting practitioners in France (1920–1939)," *Accounting, Organizations and Society*, **26** (4–5), 391–418.

Ramirez, Carlos (2007), *Exporting Professional Models: The Expansion of the Multinational Audit Firm and the Transformation of the French Accountancy Profession since 1970*, Paris: Département Comptabilité-Contrôle, HEC School of Management, Paris.

Ramirez, Carlos (2010), "Promoting transnational professionalism: Forays of the 'Big Firm' accounting community into France," in Marie-Laure Djelic and Sigrid Quack (eds), *Transnational Communities: Shaping Global Economic Governance*, Cambridge: Cambridge University Press, pp. 174–95.

Reed, Michael I. (1996), "Expert power and control in late modernity: An empirical review and theoretical synthesis," *Organization Studies*, **17** (4), 573–98.

Roadmap IASB–FASB (2006), *A Roadmap for Convergence between IFRSs and US GAAP—2006–2008*, Memorandum of Understanding between the FASB and the IASB, available at http://www.fasb.org/cs/ContentServer?c=Document_C&pagename=FASB%2FDocument_C%2FDocumentPage&cid=1176156245558 (accessed June 4, 2011).

Rose, Nikolas and Peter Miller (1992), "Political power beyond the state: Problematics of government," *British Journal of Sociology*, **43** (2), 172–205.

Ruhnke, Klaus (2005), *Rechnungslegung nach IFRS und HGB. Lehrbuch zur Theorie und Praxis der Unternehmenspublizität mit Beispielen und Übungen*, Stuttgart: Schäffer-Poeschel Verlag.

Sahlin-Andersson, Kerstin (1996), "Imitating by editing success: The construction of organizational fields," in Barbara Czarniawska and Guje Sevón (eds), *Translating Organizational Change*, Berlin/New York: Walter de Gruyter, pp. 69–92.

Sal. Oppenheim (2007), "IFRS changes increase and distort earnings trends of many German companies," press release of January 11, 2007, available at http://www.oppenheim.lu/internet/presseportal/10_pressemitteilungen/2007/2007-01-11_accounting-does-matter/2007-01-11_pr_accounting-does-matter.pdf (accessed June 6, 2011).

Samuels, John M. and Andrew G. Piper (1985), *International Accounting: A Survey*, London: Croom Helm.

Scharpf, Fritz W. (2004), "Legitimationskonzepte jenseits des Nationalstaats," MPIfG Working Paper 04/6, Cologne: Max Planck Institute for the Study of Societies (MPIfG).

Schmidt, Susanne K. and Raymund Werle (1998), *Coordinating Technology: Studies in the International Standardization of Telecommunications*, Cambridge, MA: MIT Press.

Schneiberg, Marc (2007), "What's on the path? Path dependence, organizational diversity and the problem of institutional change in the US economy, 1900–1950," *Socio-Economic Review*, **5**, 47–80.

Scott, W. Richard (2001), *Institutions and Organizations*, 2nd edn, Thousand Oaks, CA: Sage Publications.

SEC (1999), "Comment letter 62," Comment to the IASC, May 15, 1999, pp. 1–7.

SEC (2007), "Concept release on allowing US issuers to prepare financial statements in accordance with International Financial Reporting Standards," available at http://www.sec.gov/rules/concept/2007/33-8831.pdf (accessed April 20, 2010).

Simmons, Beth A. (2001), "The international politics of harmonization: The case of capital market regulation," *International Organization*, **55** (3), 589–620.

SpencerStuart (2010), *2010 UK Board Index. Current board trends and practices at major UK companies*, available at http://content.spencerstuart.com/sswebsite/pdf/lib/UKBI_2010_web.pdf (accessed June 7, 2011).

Stolowy, Hervé and Yuan Ding (2003), "Regulatory flexibility and management opportunism in the choice of alternative accounting standards: An illustration based on large French groups," *The International Journal of Accounting*, **38** (2), 195–213.

Storz, Cornelia (2007), "Compliance with international standards: The EDIFACT and ISO 9000 standards in Japan," *Social Science Japan Journal*, **10** (2), 217–41.

Streeck, Wolfgang (1994), "Staat und Verbände: Neue Fragen. Neue

Antworten?" in Wolfgang Streeck (ed.), *Politische Vierteljahresschrift*, Opladen: Westdeutscher Verlag, pp. 7–34.

Streeck, Wolfgang and Kathleen Thelen (2005), *Beyond Continuity— Institutional Change in Advanced Political Economies*, Oxford: Oxford University Press.

Street, Donna L. (2006), "The G4's role in the evolution of the International Accounting Standard setting process and partnership with the IASB," *Journal of International Accounting, Auditing and Taxation*, **15**, 109–26.

Suddaby, Roy, David J. Cooper, and Royston Greenwood (2007), "Transnational regulation of professional services: Governance dynamics of field level organizational change," *Accounting, Organizations and Society*, **32**, 333–62.

Sugarman, David (1995), "Who colonized whom? Historical reflections on the intersection between law, lawyers and accountants in England," in Yves Dezalay and David Sugarman (eds), *Professional Competition and Professional Power: Lawyers, Accountants and the Social Construction of Markets*, London: Routledge, pp. 226–37.

Sunder, Shyam (2002), "Regulatory competition among accounting standards within and across international boundaries," *Journal of Accounting and Public Policy*, **21**, 219–34.

Suzuki, Tomo (2003), "The accounting figuration of business statistics as a foundation for the spread of economic ideas," *Accounting, Organizations and Society*, **28**, 65–95.

Suzuki, Tomo, Yan Yan, and Bingyi Chen (2007), "Accounting for the growth and transformation of Chinese businesses and the Chinese economy: Implications for transitional and development economics," *Socio-Economic Review*, **5**, 665–94.

SWP (1998), "Shaping IASC for the future," a discussion paper issued for comment by the Strategy Working Party of the International Accounting Standards Committee, London: IASC.

Sydow, Jörg, Georg Schreyögg, and Jochen Koch (2009), "Organizational path dependence: Opening the black box," *Academy of Management Review*, **34** (4), 689–709.

Tamm Hallström, Kristina (2004), *Organizing International Standardization: ISO and the IASC in Quest of Authority*, Cheltenham, UK and Northampton, MA, USA: Edward Elgar.

Tamm Hallström, Kristina and Magnus Boström (eds) (2010), *Transnational Multi-stakeholder Standardization: Organizing Fragile Non-state Authority*, Cheltenham, UK and Northampton, MA, USA: Edward Elgar.

Thomas, R. Douglas (1970), "The Accountants International Study Group— The first three years," *International Journal of Accounting*, Fall, 59–65.

Thorell, Per and Geoffrey Whittington (1994), "The harmonization of accounting within the EU. Problems, perspectives and strategies," *The European Accounting Review*, **3** (2), 215–39.

Timmermans, Stefan and Steven Epstein (2010), "A world of standards but not a standard world: Toward a sociology of standards and standardization," *The Annual Review of Sociology*, **36**, 69–89.

Tsingou, Elini (2008), "Transnational private governance and the Basel process: Banking regulation and supervision, private interests and Basel II," in Jean-Christophe Graz and Andreas Nölke (eds), *Transnational Private Governance and its Limits*, London: Routledge, pp. 58–68.

UNCTAD (1982), "ISAR—corporate transparency—Accounting Division on investment and enterprise," available at http://www.unctad.org/Templates/Startpage.asp?intItemID=2531 (accessed July 12, 2011).

UNCTAD (2006), *World Investment Report 2006. FDI from Developing and Transition Economies: Implications for Development*, Geneva: UNCTAD.

van Hulle, Karel (2004), "From accounting directives to International Accounting Standards," in Christian Leuz, Dieter Pfaff, and Anthony G. Hopwood (eds), *The Economics and Politics of Accounting: International Perspectives on Research Trends, Policy, and Practice*, Oxford: Oxford University Press, pp. 349–75.

Véron, Nicolas (2007), *The Global Accounting Experiment*, Brussels: Bruegel.

Vollmer, Hendrik (2007), "How to do more with numbers. Elementary stakes, framing, keying, and the three-dimensional character of numerical signs," *Accounting, Organizations and Society*, **32**, 577–600.

Volmer, Philipp B., Jörg Richard Werner, and Jochen Zimmerman (2007), "New governance modes for Germany's financial reporting system: Another retreat of the nation state?" *Socio-Economic Review*, **5**, 437–65.

von Eitzen, Bernd (1996), *Der Wirtschaftsprüfer im internationalen Umfeld*, Freiburg im Breisgau: Albert-Ludwig-Universität.

Walton, Peter (2003), "International Accounting Standards: The new regime," in UNCTAD, *2004 Review, Reporting Issues*, Geneva: United Nations, pp. 59–64.

Walton, Peter (2004a), "The International Accounting Standards Board and its proceedings," in UNCTAD, *2004 Review, Reporting Issues*, New York and Geneva: United Nations, pp. 117–21.

Walton, Peter (2004b), "IAS 39: Where different accounting models collide," *Accounting in Europe*, **1**, 5–16.

Walton, Peter (2007) (ed.), *The Routledge Companion to Fair Value and Financial Reporting*, London: Routledge.

Williamson, Oliver E. (1975), *Markets and Hierarchies: Analysis and Antitrust Implications*, New York: The Free Press.

Williamson, Oliver E. (1985), *The Economic Institutions of Capitalism: Firms, Markets, Relational Contracting*, New York: The Free Press.

Willmott, Hugh (2000), "Organising the profession: A theoretical and historical examination of the development of the major accountancy bodies in the UK," in John Richard Edwards (ed.), *The History of Accounting: Critical Perspectives on Business and Management*, volume IV – *Professionalisation of Accounting*, London: Routledge, pp. 233–69.

Willmott, Hugh and Prem Sikka (1997), "On the commercialization of accountancy thesis: A review essay," *Accounting, Organizations and Society*, **22** (8), 831–42.

Willmott, Hugh, David J. Cooper and Tony Puxty (2000), "Maintaining self-regulation: Making 'interests' coincide in discourses on the governance of the ICAEW," in John Richard Edwards (ed.), *The History of Accounting: Critical Perspectives on Business and Management*, volume IV – *Professionalisation of Accounting*, London: Routledge, pp. 344–74.

Wüstemann, Jens and Sonja Kierzek (2007a), "Transnational legalization of accounting: The case of International Financial Reporting Standards," in Christian Brütsch and Dirk Lehmkuhl (eds), *Law and Legalization in Transnational Relations*, Oxford: Routledge, pp. 33–57.

Wüstemann, Jens and Sonja Kierzek (2007b), "Normative Bilanztheorie und Grundsätze ordnungsmäßiger Gewinnrealisierung für Mehrkomponentenverträge," working paper, Mannheim.

Yin, Robert K. (2009), *Case Study Research: Design and Methods*, Thousand Oaks, CA: Sage Publications.

York Kenny, Sara and Robert K. Larson (1993), "Lobbying behaviour and the development of international accounting standards," *European Accounting Review*, **3**, 531–54.

Young, Joni J. (1994), "Outlining regulatory space: Agenda issues and the FASB," *Accounting, Organizations and Society*, **19** (1), 83–109.

Young, Joni J. (2006), "Making up users," *Accounting, Organizations and Society*, **31**, 579–600.

Zimmermann, Jochen, Jörg Richard Werner, and Philipp B. Volmer (2008), *Global Governance in Accounting: Rebalancing Public Power and Private Commitment*, Houndmills, Basingstoke: Palgrave Macmillan.

# Index

Abbott, A. 23, 36
Abbott, K. W. 17, 19
accountability deficit 107–10, 169,
    179–80
Accountants International Study
    Group (AISG) 48–9
Accounting Advisory Forum 42
accounting constellation 22–3, 31
accounting for financial instruments
    see IAS 39
accounting globalization see
    globalization of accounting
accounting norms, diffusion of 11–16
accounting regulation
    comparison of initiatives 55–60
    harmonization initiatives 38–54
    historical overview 32–3
    multinational corporations 45–8
    national traditions 33–8
    politics
        institution building through
            expertise 176–80
        overview 165
        political dimensions 172–5
        standard setting dynamics 166–72
    politics of 7–11
Accounting Regulatory Committee
    (ARC), EC 77
accounting standardization see
    international accounting
    standards; standard setting;
    standardization
accounting standards boards
    Australia/New Zealand (AASB) 53
    Canada (AcSB) 53, 134
    Germany see Deutsches
        Rechnungslegungs Standards
        Committee (DRSC)
    UK (ASB) 53, 89, 123
accounting studies 20–23
accounting treatments, alternative 65–6

addressees of reporting information
    83–90
AICPA 16, 88
Allen, A. 138
American Institute of Certified Public
    Accountants (AICPA) 16, 88
Analyst Representative Group (ARG)
    161, 162
Ansell, C. K. 25
Argentina 16
Armstrong, C. 78
Arnold, P. J. 13
Arthur Andersen 25, 145, 147, 150, 151
Arthur, W. B. 29, 30
Asian financial crisis 1997–1998 12–13,
    43, 66
assets, reclassification of 81
associations, professional 36–7, 47,
    101, 124, 128, 166, 176
auditing services 37
Australia 15–16, 49, 88, 130, 132, 133
    see also Group of Four
Australian Financial Reporting
    Council 147, 150, 152
Autorité des Marchés Financiers
    (AMF) 132

Bachrach, P. 28
Baker, C. R. 20
Bank for International Settlements 88,
    145, 147, 150, 154
Baratz, M. S. 28
Barbu, E. M. 20
Barth, M. 130, 131, 135, 137
BDO International 174
Belgium 34, 50, 78, 93
Benson, Sir Henry 48–9
Big Four 37–8, 88, 101, 111, 112, 115,
    124, 127, 135, 147, 150, 153,
    154–5, 157, 163–4, 171
Biondi, Y. 11, 22

Blaufus, K. 68, 71
Bombardier 147, 150, 152
Borgatti, S. P. 140, 144, 145
Boström, M. 24, 28
Botzem, S. 21, 25, 27, 39, 60, 74, 100, 155, 164, 174
Boyer, R. 10, 26, 70, 72
Braithwaite, J. 6, 25, 30, 46, 50, 58
Brazil 15–16, 135–6, 139, 174
Bromwich, M. 70
Brunsson, N. 18
Buijink, W. 13–14
Burchell, S. 21, 22, 23, 179
Bush, T. 35, 90, 96
Büthe, T. 19, 26, 28, 36, 95

Cairns, D. 47, 65, 84, 92, 120, 159
Camfferman, K. 21, 42, 48, 49–50, 51, 52, 53, 60, 63, 64–5, 66, 74, 76, 93, 97, 98, 111, 128, 129, 132, 134, 137, 153
Campbell, J. L. 30
Canada 16, 23, 38, 42, 49
    *see also* Group of Four
Canadian Institute of Chartered Accountants (CICA) 76, 134
capital
    availability of investment 35, 59–60
    markets 89, 92, 179–80
    mobility 35, 39, 40
capital market-oriented standards 4, 19, 90–93, 166–7
Carruthers, B. G. 18
Chahed, Y. 5
Chapman, C. S. 9, 21
Chartered Financial Analyst Institute (CFA) 88, 145, 150, 152, 160
Chiapello, E. 44, 77
China 14, 52, 132, 133, 135, 139
comparability
    of national rules 40, 49, 55
    project 65–6, 92
competitiveness 36
comprehensive income 70, 71–3
Conseil National de al Comptabilité (CNC) 89
consultation 115–24
Cooper, D. J. 9, 12, 20, 22, 23, 25, 36, 38, 39, 46
Cooper, S. 130, 131, 135, 137

Covaleski, M. A. 23, 36
Crouch, C. 28, 29
Cuijpers, R. 13–14
Cutler, A. C. 19
Czarniawska, B. 19, 63

Dahl, R. A. 21, 28
Daimler-Benz 9, 43
Daniels, P. W. 13, 48
Danjou, P. 131, 132, 136, 137
D'Arcy, A. 59
David, P. A. 19, 29, 30
Davis, G. F. 30
Davis, J. H. 86, 87
De Lange, P. 26
decision usefulness 88, 159–60, 172
    ambiguity 85, 91, 164, 167
    of IAS/IFRS 15
Deeg, R. 10, 26, 29
Deloitte Touche Tohmatsu (DTT) 37, 145, 147, 151, 157
    *see also* Big Four
Denmark 41
derivatives 74–5, 78–9, 92–3
Deutsches Rechnungslegungs Standards Committee (DRSC) 10
DiMaggio, P. J. 22
Ding, Y. 14, 34, 64
directives
    Fourth EC Directive 39, 40, 44, 60
    Seventh EC Directive 39, 40, 60
disclosure requirements 45–8
discounted cash flow (DCF) method 70–71
Djelic, M.-L. 19, 25, 27, 28–9, 170
Dobusch, L. 174
Dodd–Frank Act 15
dominance 130–36, 150–55, 162–4, 174
Donaldson, L. 86
Drahos, P. 30, 46, 50, 58
Drori, G.S. 23
"due process," formalized 117–20

earnings per period 62, 70, 72
Eaton, S. B. 26
Eberle, D. 10, 26
EC *see* European Commission
Economic and Social Council (ECOSOC) 45, 46
Empson, L. 24

Engström, J. 130, 131, 133, 136, 137
Epstein, G. A. 11
Epstein, S. 18, 19
Ernst & Young 145, 147, 150, 151
    *see also* Big Four
EU *see* European Union
European Association of Co-operative
    Banks (EACB) 93
European Association of Craft, Small-
    and Medium-sized Enterprises
    (UEAPME) 93
European Banking Federation (FBE)
    77, 93
European Central Bank (ECB) 69, 78
European Commission 12, 52
    Accounting Advisory Forum 42
    board appointments 134
    and harmonization in accounting
        55, 57–8
    IAS 39 79, 81–2
    IAS in Europe 66, 77
    observer status 129
    role in standardization 91, 97, 145,
        147, 150, 151, 170
    support for IASB 42–3, 44, 115,
        173
    support for IASC 55, 56
European Council of Economic and
    Finance Ministers (ECOFIN)
    81–2, 112
European Federation of Accountants
    and Auditors (EFAA) 93
European Federation of Financial
    Analysts Societies (EFFAS) 93
European Financial Reporting
    Advisory Group (EFRAG) 44, 77,
    78, 89, 93, 122–3, 173
European Insurance Association
    (CEA) 93
European Parliament 107–8, 110, 168,
    173, 175
European Round Table (ERT) 93
European Savings Banks Group
    (ESBG) 93
European Union (EU) 67, 80, 85
    adoption of regulations 76–7, 78
    support for IASC 59, 66, 91, 93,
        174–5
Evans, L. 37
expert-based self-regulation 123–5

expertise
    and institution building 176–80
    as recruitment criteria 104–6,
        109–10, 129–30, 171
    "technical" 103–4, 106–10, 171, 177

fair value accounting (FVA) 11, 15, 61,
    68–75, 71, 78, 83, 167–8
Falleti, T. G. 30
Farrell, H. 29
FASB *see* Financial Accounting
    Standards Board
Fédération des Experts Comptables
    Européens (FEE) 13, 41
Federation of European Securities
    Exchanges (FESE) 93
Federation of Swiss Industrial Holding
    Companies 52, 128
Ferree, M. M. 31
Financial Accounting Standards
    Board, USA (FASB)
    agreement with IASB 52, 66, 67, 89,
        95, 125, 134–5
    Group of Four 52–3
    harmonization of standards 66–8
    historical development 95–6, 97
    IAS 39 76
    members' tenure 138
    observer status 129
    reclassification of assets 81, 168
    review of framework 83, 85–6, 89, 93
    and SEC 95–6, 123–4
financial crisis 2007–2009 1, 15, 81, 165
    and fair value accounting 73, 75, 83,
        167–8
    relaxation of accounting rules 92–3
    and standard setting 179–80
Financial Executives International
    (FEI) 88
financial instruments, accounting for
    *see* IAS 39
financial reporting
    defining addressees 83–90
    relevance of 7–11
Financial Services Authority (FSA),
    UK 38
Financial Stability Board (FSB) 2
financial statements
    absence of users 153, 155–61, 172
    users by type of organization 159

Finnegan, P. 135, 161
Flower, J. 42–3
Forrester, D. A. R. 48
France 14, 34, 38, 49, 77, 78, 93, 129
Fransen, L. W. 24
Froud, J. 11, 15, 84

G4+1 (Group of Four plus One) 53,
    133–4, 138–9, 162, 170
    *see also* Group of Four
G20 1, 82
Gallhofer, S. 22, 39, 60, 74, 125, 155
Gamson, W. A. 31
Garnett, R. 130, 131, 137
Garud, R. 29, 179
Gélard, G. 130, 131, 133, 137, 138
General Agreement on Trade in
    Services (GATS) 13
General Electric Company (GE) 147,
    150, 152, 156
Germany 9–10, 34, 37, 38, 40, 49, 72,
    78, 88, 96, 112
Glaum, M. 9, 35
globalization of accounting 1–7
    diffusion of accounting norms 11–16
    relevance of reporting 7–11
Goldman Sachs Group, Inc. 88
Grant Thornton 60, 174
Greenstein, S. 19
Greenwood, R. 23, 24, 37, 164
Group of Four 42, 44, 52–3, 101, 130,
    134
    *see also* G4+1 (Group of Four plus
    One)

Hall, P. A. 9, 34
Haller, A. 40, 49
Halliday, T. C. 18
Hanneman, R. A. 144, 164
harmonization of accounting
    regulation 38–9, 57–8
    comparison of initiatives 55–60
    multinational corporations 45–8
    professional self-regulation 48–54
    single European market project
    39–45
Haslam, J. 22, 39, 60, 74, 125, 155
hedge accounting 74–5, 77–8, 79, 80
Hegarty, J. 47
Herz, R. H. 68, 136

Heßling, A. 63, 92
historical costs accounting 68–9, 75
Hoffman, A. J. 22
Honold, K. 37
Höpner, M. 28
Hopwood, A. G. 9, 20, 21, 22, 36, 40,
    42, 43, 44, 172
Howieson, B. 26

IAS *see* International Accounting
    Standards
IAS 39 (Accounting for Financial
    Instruments) 44, 62, 70, 74–83, 93,
    153, 175
IAS/IFRC *see* International
    Accounting Standards;
    International Financial Reporting
    Standards
IASB *see* International Accounting
    Standards Board
IASC *see* International Accounting
    Standards Committee
improvements project 50, 92
India 50, 132–3, 135, 139, 170–71, 174
Institute of Chartered Accountants
    in England and Wales (ICAEW)
    78, 123
institution building 27–9, 176–80
institutional complementarity 28
institutional density 29
international accounting norms 11–16
international accounting standards
    capital market-oriented standards
        90–93
    development of IAS 62–73
    international standardization
        controversies 73–90
    overview 61–2
    *see also* standardization
International Accounting Standards
    Board (IASB)
    autonomy 26, 27
    the Board 127–30
        Anglo-American dominance
            130–36
        composition over time 136–9,
            168–70
        length of service on 137, 138, 164
    broadening financial base 111–15
    change of name 16, 59

conceptual framework 83–90, 93
consultation 115–17
    formalized "due process" 117–20
    legitimizing through 120–24, 169
development of standardization
        62–93, 166
and diffusion of standards 11–16
and European Commission 42–3, 44
expert-based self-regulation 123–5
foundations of 3–6
and harmonization in accounting
        55, 57–8
membership by interest group 158
organizational configuration 95–6
    abolishing recruitment
            requirements 101–7, 102
    accountability deficit 107–10, 169,
            179–80
    organizational structure 94,
            98–101
    US blueprint 96–8
origins and early history 48–54, 59
and politics of accounting regulation
        165–80
standard setting network 140–42,
        146, 148, 149, 151–2
    absence of financial statements
            users 153, 155–61, 172
    composition over time 142–4
    domination 150–55, 162–4
    number of representatives 143
    properties 144–9
    representation by interest group
            156
    rules of bodies 141
standards production 63
and United Nations 46, 47
International Accounting Standards
        Committee Foundation annual
        reports (IASCF-AR) 95, 111, 112,
        113, 114, 128, 137, 143, 195
International Accounting Standards
        Committee Foundation (IASCF)
        66, 83, 84, 95, 98, 99, 100, 102,
        103, 104, 107, 112, 115, 116, 117,
        119, 128, 129, 132, 135, 140, 141,
        142
International Accounting Standards
        Committee (IASC) 13, 16, 42, 59
Board 127–32, 136–8, 164

Consultative Group 51–2, 129
    establishment 13, 46, 49, 95
    historical development of 50–54,
            97–8, 104
    recognition 47
    as standard setter 56, 58–9
    support from EC 55, 56
    support from EU 59, 66, 91, 93,
            174–5
    transformation to IASB 98,
            100–101, 103
International Accounting Standards
        (IAS)
    development 62–3
    elimination of alternatives 64–6
    fair value accounting 68–73
    role of USA 66–8
    *see also* International Financial
            Reporting Standards (IFRS)
International Association of Financial
        Executives Institutes (IAFEI) 52,
        128
International Chamber of Commerce
        46, 51, 166
International Confederation of Free
        Trade Unions (ICFTU) 51
International Corporate Governance
        Network (ICGN) 125
International Federation of
        Accountants (IFAC) 2, 13, 50–51,
        98, 100
International Financial Reporting
        Interpretations Committee
        (IFRIC)
    in relation to IASB 99, 104, 143, 144,
            145–7, 154, 156
    role 63, 92, 118, 141, 142
International Financial Reporting
        Standards (IFRS) 4, 61, 165
    convergence with GAAP 62, 66–8
    criticism of 167–8
    dissemination 6, 10, 12–16, 139,
            167
    in Europe 34, 41, 43, 44, 66, 76–7,
            79–80, 174–5
    fair value orientation 68, 69, 91
    IFRS 9 82–3
    support from associations 47–8, 142,
            153
    use and recognition 94, 97, 107, 109

*see also* International Accounting
    Standards (IAS)
International Monetary Fund (IMF)
    2, 12
International Organization of
    Securities Commissions (IOSCO)
    cooperation with IASC 52
    as drafter of rules 2
    observer status 129
    as part of standard setting network
        145–7, 150, 154
    recognition of IAS 64–6, 76, 96
    as "reference organization" 24
    revision of standards 49–50
    and SEC 54, 64–5, 66
    on stewardship 88
international political economy 25–7,
    177
International Standards in Accounting
    and Reporting (ISAR) 47
International Standards on Auditing
    (ISA) 51
investment capital, availability 35,
    59–60
IOSCO *see* International Organization
    of Securities Commissions
Ireland 41
Italy 38, 93, 115, 129

Jacobsson, B. 18
Janis, I. L. 119
Japan 16, 34, 38, 49, 60, 112–13, 129
Joerges, B. 63
Jones, T. E. 130, 131, 135, 137, 138
JP Morgan 145, 150, 151

Kalavacherla, P. 130, 131, 132–3, 137
Karnøe, P. 29, 179
Kerwer, D. 19
Kierzek, S. 20, 43, 77, 122
Kindleberger, C. P. 15
Kirsch, R. J. 20, 60, 63, 64, 74, 75, 93,
    96, 97, 98, 111, 127, 134
Kolk, A. 24
Korea 16
KPMG (Klynveld, Peat, Marwick and
    Goerdeler) 37–8, 130, 145, 147,
    151, 157
    *see also* Big Four
Krippner, G. R. 11

Larson, R. K. 21
Lazonick, W. 10
Leblond, P. 27, 83, 173
legal systems 35–6
Leisenring, J. 130, 131, 137
Llewellyn, S. 29
Lukes, S. 9, 28
Lütz, S. 10, 26
Luxembourg 78
Lynch, J. F. 30

MacArthur, J. B. 21
Macdonald, K. M. 24, 36, 109
MacKenzie, D. 71, 74
Mahoney, J. 29, 30
Mallin, C. A. 86–7
management accountability 89–90
Markus, H. B. 37
Marquis, C. 30
Martinez-Diaz, L. 12, 13, 26, 43, 53,
    66, 76, 97
Mattli, W. 19, 26, 33, 36, 95
Mayntz, R. 28, 29–30
McConnell, P. 135, 161
McGregor, W. J. 132, 137, 138
McLeay, S. 21
Medjad, K. 44, 77
Mennicken, A. 63, 92, 164
methodology 29–31
Mexico 16, 49, 129
Miller, P. B. 9, 11, 21, 22, 23, 31, 36
Miller, P. B. W. 95
Millo, Y. 71, 74
Modigliani, A. 31
Monitoring Board 99, 101, 104, 109,
    124, 141, 164, 169
Morgan, G. 37
Morgan Stanley 145–6, 147, 150, 151
Müller, M. 51
multinational corporations regulation
    45–8

Netherlands 34, 35, 38, 49, 50, 115
Neu, D. 13
New Zealand 42, 44, 50, 88
Nigeria 48, 50, 129
Nobes, C. 2, 20, 34–5, 40, 41, 59–60
Nölke, A. 3, 11, 26, 27, 72, 73, 93,
    107, 110, 124, 140, 144–5, 153,
    173

North, D. C. 17
Norwalk Agreement 66–7

Ocampo, E. 13
Ordelheide, D. 8, 11, 172
Orenstein, M. A. 28
Organisation for Economic Co-
    operation and Development
    (OECD) 46, 166
organization studies 23–5, 176
O'Sullivan, M. 10
Oxera Consulting Limited 25, 38

Padoa-Schioppa, T. 111
Pakistan 50
Parker, R. 2, 20
Pattberg, P. 19
Pellens, B. 72, 120
Perry, J. 3, 11, 26, 27, 72, 73, 107, 124,
    140, 144–5, 153
Pettigrew, A. M. 74
Pfizer Inc. 145, 150, 152
Pierson, P. 29, 30, 177
Piper, A. G. 13, 41, 46, 48, 51
political economy, international 25–7
politics of accounting regulation 7–11,
    165–80
Porter, T. 3, 26, 79, 109, 177
Porter, T. M. 11
positive accounting theory 8, 20
Posner, E. 2, 26, 27, 30, 173
Powell, W. W. 22
power 28, 164, 179
Power, M. 11, 15, 19, 22, 25, 61, 135,
    170
PricewaterhouseCoopers (PwC) 37, 60,
    130, 145, 147, 151, 157
    *see also* Big Four
Pro-active Accounting Activities in
    Europe (PAAinE) 89, 90, 173
professional associations *see*
    associations, professional
professions, sociology of 23–5, 109,
    176

Quack, S. 18, 21, 25, 28–9, 37, 39, 60,
    169, 170, 175

Radwan, A. 107–8, 110
Rahman, S. F. 45–6

Ramanna, K. 138
Ramirez, C. 23, 25, 36, 37, 133, 155
raw materials exploitation 45
recruitment requirements, abolition of
    101–7
Reed, M. I. 36, 110
regulation *see* accounting regulation
regulations
    EU Regulation (EC) No. 1606/2002
        43, 77
    EU Regulation (EC) No. 1864/2005
        78
    EU Regulation (EC) No. 2086/2004
        78
reporting *see* financial reporting
research on transnational
        standardization
    accounting studies 20–23
    institution building 27–9
    international political economy 25–7
    methodology 29–31
    research overview 17–19
    sociology of professions and
        organization studies 23–5
Riddle, M. 144, 164
Roadmap IASB–FASB 67
Robson, K. 9, 12, 20, 22, 23, 25, 36, 38,
    39, 46
Rose, N. 11, 23
Ruhnke, K. 75
Russia 38

Sahlin-Andersson, K. 19, 27, 61
Sal. Oppenheim 10
Samuels, J. M. 13, 41, 46, 48, 51
Sarbanes–Oxley Act 15, 90
Scharpf, F. W. 109
Schmid, H. 136, 137, 138
Schmidt, S. K. 19
Schmitz, H. P. 28
Schneiberg, M. 29
Scott, W. R. 30
Securities and Exchange Commission
        (SEC)
    and FASB 95–6, 123–4
    and IASC 50
    influence 67, 68, 91
    and IOSCO 54, 64–5, 66
    as part of standard setting network
        152

and SWP 96–7
views on standard setting 97–8,
    123–4
self-regulation 168
    expert-based 123–5, 178
    private sector 154, 163
    professional 23–4, 48–54, 56, 59, 80,
        109
Sevón, G. 19
shareholder value 84, 87, 167
Sikka, P. 22
Simmons, B. A. 2, 25–6, 54
Single European Market project 39–45
small and medium-sized companies
    (SMEs) 15, 106–7, 167
Smith, J. T. 130, 132, 137
Snidal, D. 17, 19
sociology of professions 23–5
Soskice, D. 9, 34
South Africa 48, 50, 88, 129, 132
Spain 34, 93
SpencerStuart 138
standard setting
    consultation as element of 115–24
    domination of individuals and
        organizations 162–4
    dynamics of transnational 166–72
    IASB Board 127–39
    IASB network characteristics 140–61
standardization
    development of standards 49–54
    research on transnational 17–31
    *see also* international accounting
        standards
Standards Advisory Council (SAC) 99,
    140–45, 150, 156
Standing Interpretations Committee
    (SIC) 92
stewardship 86–90, 91, 167
Stolowy, H. 14, 34, 64
Storz, C. 19
Strategic Working Party (SWP) 14–15,
    96–7, 98, 129
Streeck, W. 29, 36
Street, D. L. 53, 134
Suddaby, R. 22, 37, 164
Sugarman, D. 23, 36, 109
Sumitomo Corp. 147, 150, 152
Sunder, S. 2
Suzuki, T. 11, 22, 33, 46

Sweden 34, 78, 133
Switzerland 12
SWP *see* Strategic Working Party
Sydow, J. 29

Tamm Hallström, K. 19, 24, 28, 52, 53,
    60, 65, 74, 94, 127
Tanzania 12
"technical" expertise 103–4, 106–10,
    171, 177
Thelen, K. 29
Thomas, R. D. 48, 49
Thorell, P. 38, 49, 64, 65
Timmermans, S. 18, 19
transaction cost accounting theory 8,
    20
"true and fair view" 39, 40, 41, 55, 60
Tsingou, E. 150
Tweedie, Sir David 67, 75, 80, 86, 89,
    98, 108, 119, 121, 130, 131, 135,
    137, 138, 139, 160

UCINET software 140, 144, 145
UN Conference on Trade and
    Development (UNCTAD) 45,
    46–8
Union Européenne des Experts
    Comptables, Economiques et
    Financiers (UEC) 41
Union of Industrial and Employers'
    Confederations of Europe
    (UNICE) 93
United Kingdom (UK)
    dominance of IASB Board 130–36,
        162
    establishment of IASC 49, 50
    fair value accounting (FVA) 68–9
    fear of political influence 109
    funding IASB 112, 115
    legal framework 96
    as liberal economy 34
    opposition to directives 40, 42
    as part of Big Four 38
    privatizing standardization 44
    self-regulation 23–4, 168
    on stewardship 87–9
    true and fair view 40
    *see also* Group of Four
United Nations (UN)
    cross-border harmonization 57–8

and disclosure 55–6
regulation of multinationals 45–8
United States of America (USA)
    blueprint relating to IASB 96–8
    dominance of IASB Board 130–36,
        162, 174
    establishment of IASC 50
    fair value accounting (FVA) 68–9
    funding IASB 112, 115
    generally accepted accounting
        principles (US GAAP) 9, 13–14,
        43, 62, 66–8, 98
    legal framework 96
    as liberal economy 34
    self-regulation 23–4, 168
    special role in international
        accounting 66–8
    on stewardship 87–8
    *see also* Group of Four

van Hulle, K. 39, 40, 41, 42, 43–4, 153
Véron, N. 108, 110, 125
Vollmer, H. 21, 23
Volmer, P. B. 10, 36
von Eitzen, B. 37

Walton, P. 25, 38, 53, 69, 79, 93
Weber, S. 25
Werle, R. 19
Whittington, G. 38, 49, 64, 65, 79,
    86, 88–9, 120, 121, 136, 137,
    160
Williamson, O. E. 17, 20
Willmott, H. 13, 22, 24, 36
World Bank 12–13, 15, 147, 151, 154
World Trade Organization (WTO) 12,
    13
Wüstemann, J. 20, 43, 77, 122

Yamada, T. 130, 132, 137, 138
Yin, R. K. 30
York Kenny, S. 21
Young, J. J. 22, 36, 84, 163

Zeff, S. A. 21, 42, 48, 49–50, 51, 52,
    53, 60, 63, 64–5, 66, 74, 76, 93, 97,
    98, 111, 128, 129, 132, 134, 137,
    153
Zhang, W. G. 132, 133, 137
Zimbabwe 50
Zimmermann, J. 20

Printed and bound by CPI Group (UK) Ltd, Croydon, CR0 4YY

16/04/2025

14658492-0003